BREAKING POINTS

"Gripping and affecting."   —*Publishers Weekly*

"An engrossing confessional."   —*Parade*

"BREAKING POINTS is convincing."   —*Newsweek*

"A harrowing account . . ."   —*The New York Times*

"A terrifying account of the unpredictability with which serious mental illnesses strike individuals and their families. If out of the Hinckleys' tragedy a better public awareness of the reality of serious mental illnesses results, then their suffering and struggling will not have been in vain." —John A. Talbott, M.D.

President, *American Psychiatric Association*

"That they write about this with as little bitterness as they do is further evidence of the decency that permeates this book."   —*The Washington Post*

"I expected not to like them . . . But I found them a very recognizable pair." —Joyce Maynard, *Mademoiselle*

Royalties of this book in part will be donated to the American Mental Health Fund, a nonprofit organization established by the Hinckleys to raise public awareness and subsidize research on mental illness.

Jack and Jo Ann Hinckley founded the American Mental Health Fund in 1983 to support research and public education in mental illness. Elizabeth Sherrill has coauthored such bestsellers as THE HIDING PLACE, THE CROSS AND THE SWITCHBLADE, and GOD'S SMUGGLER. Her books, frequently written in collaboration with her husband, have more than 30 million copies in print and have been translated into over 20 languages.

BREAKING POINTS

JACK & JO ANN HINCKLEY

with Elizabeth Sherrill

BERKLEY BOOKS, NEW YORK

BREAKING POINTS

A Berkley Book/published by arrangement with
Chosen Books

PRINTING HISTORY
Chosen Books edition published in 1985
Berkley edition/June 1986

ACKNOWLEDGMENTS

It is impossible to name everyone who deserves our thanks and who played an important role in our story. In addition to those named in the book there have been many, both friends and strangers, who have encouraged us through their letters, prayers and expressions of love. Of these we mention only a few:

Anne Atwood, John and Mary Bazemore, Vic Beeby, Sheriff Harold Bray, Jim Colisanto, Tom and Pat Carlson, Mary Caton, Neil Cleaver family, Doug Coe, Leslie deVeau, Jim Early, Jim Ellis, Ray Elder, Ted Engstrom, Leigh Fitz, Randy and Janet Gradishar, Alec Greaves family, David George, Wayne Harding, Fred Heyn, Marvin Kirsten, Harvey L. Moore family, David C. Morris family, Jacque Morris, Jim and Bea Munn, Clarence Netherland, Mary Noonan, Larry and Nancy O'Neill, Rev. Richard Parke, Capt. Darrell Penner, David and Lois Rice, Paul and Anne Riley, Jim and Nancy Roberts, Jim Robinson, Don Sall, Pete and Erla Slaybaugh, Ed and Dee Spinzig, Gil and Barbara Willcox, Tom and Edie Williams, Al and Marion Whittaker, Rike Wootten.

To our children
Scott, Diane and John

and to our parents
Harvey and Ardis
Percy, Kib and Katherine

BREAKING POINTS

1

JO ANN:

Noon. March 30, 1981. I got out a suitcase and laid it on the bed. It felt odd to be packing cottons when the thermometer outside the bedroom window hovered right at freezing. Here it was, almost April, and there were still patches of snow in our yard beneath the Ponderosa pines that give our town of Evergreen, Colorado, its name.

From the laundry basket I took some clean shirts for my husband. Jack and I were leaving for Guatemala first thing tomorrow morning—my second trip, his fourth or fifth, helping develop systems to provide clean drinking water for Indian villages. Jack was a petroleum engineer, but it had been a long time since I'd seen him as excited about the oil business as he was over this volunteer water project. Of course I wanted to go along, help any way I could. It was just that—well, I worried about going so far when our youngest was so obviously at loose ends.

"Stop treating him like a child," Jack would say. "John is 25 years old, for crying out loud!"

We could seldom agree on what was best for John, though it helped to know that many of our friends were going through something similar—the father wanting a son to show more responsibility, the mother urging patience. It was probably fortunate for all families, I thought, that young men don't spend a lot of time at home after high school. John had attended a college in Texas, off-again, on-again, without ever getting a degree; he'd spent some time in California; he'd

1

visited his girlfriend Lynn in New York; he'd held a number of short-term jobs in Dallas.

John seemed to prefer his sister's home, nowadays, to Jack's and mine. Diane and her husband still lived in Dallas where all three of our children had grown up. Jack and I had moved to Colorado the summer John had graduated from high school, and he had never really felt that Colorado was home. How well I understood, recalling my own lonely first year in Denver. Eventually, of course, we'd built our home here in Evergreen, 30 miles west of Denver in the Front Range of the Rockies. I'd found a church, made some golfing friends, joined a Bible study group.

But John, I thought, gazing out at the snow-covered mountain peaks, had never really found himself since that summer nearly seven years ago. Nothing seemed to work out for John after high school. Not the college courses he took, not the jobs he tried, not the music world he dreamed of breaking into. It didn't make it any easier that his older brother and sister were doing so well—Scott working for Jack here in Denver, Diane's husband, Steve, rising in the insurance field—while John couldn't seem to make a success of anything. And health problems, too, from dizzy spells to pains in his legs—and that awful overweight. He'd been to doctor after doctor without being helped. These last few months, in fact, after the writing school at Yale turned into another disappointment, he seemed increasingly depressed and confused, till Jack and I insisted that he see a psychiatrist.

And here I was, about to spend another day fretting over John when there were a million things to do before Jack and I got away in the morning. The psychiatrist had assured us that John was simply an immature young person who would never grow up as long as he had this home to retreat to. Push him out of the nest, he advised. And so, five days ago, I'd put John on a plane for Los Angeles. He'd made some music contacts out there a few years back. Maybe in California, without my "smother love" to spoil him, he would begin to find himself.

But oh, I thought as I set up the ironing board beside the bed, it was one thing to remove a child physically from the house, another to take away the ache in the heart. I plugged in the iron. How many shirts had I pressed in 34 years of marriage, I wondered . . . and every one with pride. To me my husband was as handsome today as the first time I caught sight of him, a big-man-on-campus at the University of Oklahoma where I was an impressionable freshman.

Waiting for the iron to heat I switched on the bedroom TV. The bedside clock read 12:40—maybe I could catch a game show while I ironed. But the picture coming into focus on the screen was not a TV studio. It was outside somewhere—a street, men running, ". . . do not believe the President was hit."

The scene switched to a newsroom, an announcer reading from a slip of paper. "It is confirmed that there has been an attempt on the life of the President. Mr. Reagan and members of his staff were leaving the Washington Hilton when an assailant opened fire. The videotape you are about to see is of the actual shooting."

I stood with my hand on the iron. Onto the screen came a picture of the President in a dark blue suit, waving and smiling as he crossed a sidewalk. Then there were popping sounds, like firecrackers, and people were crouching and shouting.

Oh no! Not again! the silent cry rose in my throat. I stared transfixed with horror. We'd been living in Dallas at the time President Kennedy was killed. Jack had actually watched the motorcade go by, downtown, moments before the shooting. I remembered the children arriving home early from school, eight-year-old John asking what "assassin" meant.

". . . gunman arrested at the scene," the newscaster was saying. "The assailant has not been identified, but witnesses describe him as a light-haired white male in his twenties."

I thought of our own blond young son and my heart went out to that young man's family. Thank God that, whatever our worries over John, there'd never been any violence or law-breaking.

While the TV screen replayed the shooting, I went to the bedside phone to be sure Jack had heard the news. He was out to lunch, the receptionist told me. Was Scott there, then? No, he was out too. I left word that I'd called, and turned back to the set, ironing forgotten. What was our country coming to? Martin Luther King and Robert Kennedy and Governor Wallace—and just recently John Lennon. Though Jack and I couldn't understand the appeal of that music, Lennon had been our John's idol; his death had devastated him.

3

I was glad no one in our family used guns. Though hunting was popular here in Colorado, Jack would never go—and Scott and John felt the same. None of the three could bear the idea of shooting an animal. Especially John. He'd sleep without a pillow rather than move Titter, our old orange housecat, off his.

The TV was showing scenes of the confused milling in front of that Washington hotel. Although the President had apparently escaped, three people *had* been hit. One of them was the White House press secretary, James Brady.

I unplugged the iron and telephoned my next-door neighbor, Sue Sells. "Is your TV on, Sue? Isn't it awful!"

"I just turned it on, Jo Ann! Bill called from work."

Sue and I talked for a minute, then hung up to go on watching. I had barely set down the phone when it rang again. Probably Jack back from lunch. But the man's voice on the line was not Jack's.

"Is this Mrs. John W. Hinckley, Sr.?"

"Yes, this is Mrs. Hinckley."

"Mrs. Hinckley, this is *The Washington Post*. Is your television set on?"

"Why . . . yes." One of these ridiculous polls, no doubt, to find out how "the public" was reacting, as if anyone could react any way except—

"Do you know that your son John has been identified as the man who fired at the President?"

I lowered the receiver and stared at it. What kind of tasteless, terrible . . . "Is this your idea of a joke?" I demanded as I slammed down the phone.

My legs were trembling. Who would be cruel enough—inhuman enough—to make up such a thing? John of all people! The gentlest, most harmless—Jack's worry was always that John wasn't aggressive *enough*.

How I wished Jack were here right now. Jack would shrug away this ugly call. I grabbed the phone to try him at his office again. I wanted to hear him say, "Don't let some crank upset you."

There was no dial tone.

Fear squeezed my heart. I jiggled the cradle: the line was dead.

I ran down the stairs and out the door, not stopping to put on

4

a coat or lock the house behind me, not even sure what I was frightened of. Dashing across the side yard to Sue's house I slipped in the snow, fell to my knees, scrambled up again. Sue opened the front door before I could ring the bell. Beneath her short-bobbed gray hair her face was ashen.

"Oh, Jo Ann," she whispered.

But . . . I hadn't said a word about the phone call. Sue led me into her living room, supporting me. How did she know? Did this mean that on the TV too they were saying . . . my legs buckled again and I went down in a heap on her oriental rug. Sue tried to get me up onto the sofa. "Call Jack," I begged. "Our telephone's dead."

Sue went to the phone in the kitchen. In a minute she was back: "Ours is dead too." I heard her footsteps running upstairs. The Sells' TV was showing a man sprawled on the sidewalk, face down. There was a lot of blood. "Please, God," I prayed, "I want to wake up now."

Sue came back downstairs: "The bedroom phone's out, too! It was all right a minute ago when you and I were talking."

Sue alternated between kneeling beside me on the floor and going out to the kitchen to try the phone. Suddenly she called, "I'm getting a tone!" Then: "I'm dialing Jack."

I don't remember getting to the kitchen and I don't remember falling. I only knew I was sitting on Sue Sells' linoleum floor, and Jack's voice on the phone was saying he would get to Evergreen as fast as he could. I tried to warn him about people with guns. I wasn't sure what I meant, but Jack kept saying he would be careful.

Sue hung up the phone and I realized there were other people in the kitchen—friends and neighbors—bending over me: "Jo Ann, you've got to get up! You don't want Jack to find you like this!" Several of them got me into the Sells' den, right off the kitchen and made me lie down on the extra-long couch.

There were people in this room too, people all over the house, with more arriving all the time. Neighbors were there, and members of my prayer group, but it was all so disconnected that I'm sure I was drifting in and out of consciousness, seeing Mr. Brady lying on the sidewalk.

Emerson Harvey, our friend and family doctor, was sitting beside me on the big sofa. "Em," I kept saying, "I don't understand what's happening." And he'd say, "I know, I know. I don't either."

Everyone was very kind but they kept trying to make me stay on the sofa when where I wanted to be was on the floor, curled up small, waiting to wake up. . . .

2

JACK:

What the devil was taking the waitress so long with our bill. I had to get back to the office. *Calm down*, I told myself. Jo Ann was always after me about my impatience.

But look at all I had to do before getting off to Guatemala in the morning! Naturally there'd been a crisis just as I got ready to leave. Our exploration manager had resigned and I was having lunch with a possible replacement. I had a couple of other men coming for interviews this afternoon, a lot of correspondence. That's why I'd chosen this little seafood place near our office in downtown Denver, where the service was usually speedy. Today there didn't even seem to be a busboy around.

At last the girl showed up. The whole staff, she said, was gathered around the TV set in the bar area. "Someone shot at the President."

"No! Was he hurt?"

"I don't think so. No one seems to know."

As I paid our bill out front, the TV was reporting that the President had not been hit. Some people standing near had been wounded, but Reagan was unharmed. "Terrorists, do you think?" my guest asked as we reached the sidewalk.

I shook my head. "Probably just some nut." Well, there

was nothing we could do by worrying. "Do you mind if I run in here and get some film?" I asked. I wanted to get some pictures of the Water Projects in Guatemala. Pretty ironic, really: taking U.S. "know how" to Central American Indians. How much did we really know, with violence like this thing in Washington on the rise?

From the film store my lunch guest came back with me to Vanderbilt Energy Corporation on the seventeenth floor of the Colorado National building. We were talking in my office when our company accountant, Arnie Bjork, appeared in the doorway. I looked up in surprise. It wasn't like Arnie to burst in on a private conversation this way.

"Jack, there's something you need to hear!"

Mystified, I excused myself and followed Arnie down the hall. On Arnie's desk a portable radio was playing. They were saying now that the President *had* been hit; he had been rushed to George Washington University Hospital where he was about to undergo emergency surgery. The assailant was in custody.

Next moment I thought I heard my own name coming from that tabletop radio: " . . . John W. Hinckley," the announcer was saying, impossibly, incomprehensibly, " . . . son of a Denver oil man."

John? John junior? Our son John? John was in Los Angeles, thousands of miles from the Hilton Hotel in Washington!

Somehow I got from Arnie's office back to my own. I suppose I must have said goodbye to the man I'd been interviewing. I only remember standing at my desk, trying to reach Jo Ann, listening to our home telephone ring and ring, wondering where she was.

I had just hung up when my desk phone rang and it was Jo Ann herself. She wasn't making sense—seemed to have the idea someone was going to shoot *me*.

"I'll be home right away," I told her.

In the hallway by the elevators I met our son Scott coming back from lunch. His offhand "Hi!" told me he knew nothing. I blurted out what I'd heard; Scott turned around and went down in the elevator with me.

"I'll get my car, Dad. Meet you in Evergreen!"

I ran the block and a half to the Theater Center parking garage, backed my Omega from its space, sped down the ramp and thrust my monthly parking permit at the attendant. As I gunned the car out onto Arapahoe Street, every station on the

7

car radio was carrying the same story: "Authorities have confirmed that the gunman who opened fire on the Presidential party as it left the Hilton Hotel was John Hinckley of Evergreen, Colorado. At this hour no other arrests have been made, but police and FBI agents are pursuing the search for possible accomplices."

John . . . the *gunman?* Impossible! John had his problems, God knew. Jo Ann and I had lost more sleep over this third child, had more arguments, prayed more prayers, than over the older two combined. But his difficulties were just the opposite of aggressiveness—getting John to assert himself was the problem.

Getting him to do anything, I thought, as I fumed at a traffic light. Not since he and Lynn broke up had he showed any enthusiasm about life. That wasn't quite true; there'd been that brief flurry of interest in a writing course at Yale the past fall. Otherwise he simply moped around in his room down on the ground floor, listening to old Beatles records and playing with the cat. He didn't want to meet people his own age in Evergreen, didn't want to play tennis, wouldn't even go for a walk with me.

"You know how his legs hurt," Jo Ann would excuse him. Or his throat. Or his head. Or wherever the current aches and pains were. I was convinced it was nothing but laziness and overweight; whatever the reason, John just got more listless and inactive all the time. Was this a person who could buy a gun, travel clear across the country, and shoot the President of the United States?

And Reagan, at that. I swung around a truck and back into my lane. John, typically, hadn't shown much interest in the campaign. But he liked Reagan. I remembered election night, less than five months before. John hadn't made the effort to get out and vote, of course. But as the returns started rolling in, he'd seemed as pleased as Jo Ann and I. "Maybe there's hope for this country yet," he'd said.

And now Reagan was shot, and the voice on the car radio was saying that John Hinckley Jr., had pulled the trigger.

I had reached the outskirts of Denver where Interstate 70 begins its long climb from the plains up into the Front Range. I pressed the accelerator of the Omega flat to the floor, willing the 30 miles behind me. It was the drive I took every evening home from work, my mind so occupied with the never-ending problems of oil and gas that I'd stopped seeing the majestic wall of mountains stretching left and right out of sight. It loomed before me now without warning: impenetrable, impassable. My car was standing still, a painted car on a painted road—and I was a man who was used to action.

All my life I'd believed that the way to handle a problem was to attack it head on. Go all out. Give it all you've got. In college, in the Navy, in business, this approach had worked for me. Now, March 30, 1981, I had encountered a situation that would not respond to effort, no matter how determined. I think I knew even then, driving home to Evergreen, before I really believed any of it was happening, that a new kind of problem had come into our lives—a problem of which these motionless mountains were the symbol.

Several of the radio stations I flipped to were identifying *me* as the attacker. "The police have charged John W. Hinckley, head of a Denver oil firm, with the shooting, and are currently questioning him about others involved in the assassination attempt."

Of course they were questioning someone who'd shot the President! An hour ago I would have wanted them to use whatever tactics were necessary. I was sick to death of violence, sick of seeing criminals treated with kid gloves. But . . . this suspect was our John. At the thought of him surrounded by lawmen firing angry challenges, I half wished it *could* be me. John had always been tongue-tied with strangers. Even with Jo Ann and me he found it easier to write his thoughts than express them face to face. How would he fare in a police grilling?

It seemed hours and hours before I drove at last into Evergreen. By then most of the news commentators had been apprised that there were two people named John W. Hinckley and were adding the "Jr." to John's name. Evergreen . . . quiet, residential. How our neighbors were going to hate having our family-centered community linked with this ugly event!

I swung into Brookline Road—and found our winding mountain street jammed with automobiles, TV trucks, police cars. A highway patrolman blocked our driveway. I rolled down my window and identified myself. The patrolman pulled up a few feet and I plunged down our steep driveway.

In the garage I sat still for a moment; Jo Ann mustn't see me

9

upset. I had to be the calm one, in control—she counted on me for that. To my left in the three-car garage was her little brown Dodge Omni, to my right, John's old white Plymouth Volare. My heart twisted at the sight of that rust-speckled heap.

Not that John had used the car a lot—that was just it. It had sat there, like it did now, most of the time. Jo Ann even had to chauffeur him to his doctors' appointments. I climbed out of the Omega. Stacked against the back wall of the garage were cartons and cartons of God-knows-what that John had shipped home over the years from Texas Tech. That was another thing about John; he was like a squirrel—never threw out anything.

I let myself into the house through the garage entrance. Standing three feet inside the door was a total stranger, a broad-shouldered young man in a gray business suit.

"FBI," he said, flashing a badge.

I blinked at him. "Where's my wife?"

"Mr. Hinckley? Your wife is next door."

I stared at him for a moment longer, then dove out the front door. Cameras whirred up on the street as I ran across the side yard. As I rapped at the Sells' door I saw Scott climb from his car up on the street. Sue Sells opened the door on its chain, then unfastened it. "Jo Ann's in the den, Jack." She kept the door open for Scott, then bolted and chained it again.

A sliding partition had been drawn shut between the front hall and the den. Jo Ann was inside alone, curled up small on the braided rug. I lifted her to her feet and eased her down onto the couch, holding her tight. It was a long time before either of us could speak. Scott sat down on her other side. "It's all right, Mom," he kept saying, "it's all right," although nothing was right.

The rest of the house was full of people, many of them law officers. The state troopers and the sheriff's deputies I recognized by their uniforms, but the Secret Service men and the FBI agents wore ordinary business suits. "The telephone's free now, Mrs. Hinckley," one of them said from the kitchen doorway. Jo Ann's head was pressed against my chest so I looked to Sue for an explanation.

"Jo Ann wanted to call Diane and her parents, but the phone's been out of order." Apparently, the minute the words "Evergreen, Colorado" went out over the wire services, the local telephone system had been swamped. So many calls came in that phone service to the whole town had been disrupted—and whenever there *was* a dial tone, the line had been monopolized by the various government men.

Jo Ann straightened up, her face deathly pale. "I've got to talk to Mother and Daddy."

"You better not try to do anything for a while," I said.

"But I've got to, Jack! They love John so—the shock could kill them both! You know how ill Mother's been."

The image I always associated with Grandma Moore flashed across my mind: she was in her kitchen in Oklahoma City, custom making BLT sandwiches for the kids. Scott's bacon extra crisp, no mayonnaise. Untoasted bread, lots of mayonnaise on Diane's. The bread toasted dark for John's. Each child's preference noted and remembered. Each child certain that with Grandma he was a very very special person. Eighty-two years old now, Grandma Moore was not well: the news about John could be life-threatening indeed. . . .

3

JO ANN:

My legs were still unsteady as I walked to the telephone, but now that Jack was here I felt capable of functioning. Sue handed me the kitchen phone through the pass-through into the den. The phone rang only once in my childhood home in Oklahoma City; my brother's voice answered.

"Harvey! Oh thank God you're with them!"

Harvey and his wife Shirley lived across town from the little white house where the two of us had grown up and where Mother and Daddy still lived. Harvey said he'd heard the news first, been able to break it to the folks himself.

"How are they handling it, Harvey? How's Mother?"

"Holding up. We're going to stay right with them." On the extension phone Shirley, from her own deep faith, tried to assure me of God's love.

Daddy's voice came on next, perplexed as much as sorrowing. "They're sure it's our John? I can't believe that boy would do a thing like that."

"Neither can we, Daddy!" But my heart broke especially for my beloved parents. How utterly strange to their modest, hardworking lives this tragedy was. Until his retirement Daddy had been a plumber; he'd built that little white frame house with his own hands sixty years ago, to bring his bride to. Their lives centered around their children, grandchildren and great-grandchildren, and the Disciples of Christ church down the street. Social life was a church supper, or a game of Canasta, or a meal at the local cafeteria. Other people's needs came first with my parents, and it was so in this emergency. *They* were fine, Daddy kept assuring me; their concern was for John—and Jack and me.

I spoke to Mother then, her steady voice reassuring me more than any words. Like Daddy, once she knew *I* was all right, her chief reaction was bewilderment. "John was such a gentle child," she said. "The gentlest of all the grandchildren."

It was the thought that had been haunting me. Why, I'd never even seen John lose his temper. As youngsters Scott and Diane would shout sometimes, slam doors. John never did.

"I know, Mother," I said. "The quietest, gentlest child that ever was."

Talking to our daughter, Diane, was in some ways hardest of all. Her house in Dallas had been a second home to John—especially since our grandson Chris was born. John had a special relationship with small children, as he did with animals. I'd seen him rock Chris to sleep, push him on his tricycle, play toy cars with him by the hour.

Chris was nearly four now, old enough to know that something terrible was happening. His brand new sister, two-month-old Stephanie, was too small for that, of course, but even she must be picking up her mother's distress. How I yearned to say something wise and comforting to Diane! Instead, when I heard her voice over the phone, I burst into tears.

And it was this 28-year-old daughter who comforted me.

There's only one thing we can give each other at such a moment, and Diane gave it.

"I love you, Mother," she said.

That was all. Again and again: "I love you, Mother."

Jack and Scott talked with Diane too. Then Diane's husband, Steve, came on the line—he'd rushed straight home from work—and the family circle was complete. Except of course for the one on whom all our thoughts were centered. Where was John at this moment?

Jack and I couldn't bring ourselves to watch the TV reports, but neighbors who had gathered at the Sells' monitored television and radio sets for us in other parts of the house. John was "being interrogated" was all they could discover. As the endless afternoon wore on, medical bulletins on the President, they told us, were guardedly hopeful. Although the bullet had come to rest inches from his heart, he was said to have remained conscious throughout the pre-surgical procedures. By late afternoon it was reported that he had come through the two-hour ordeal on the operating table and the loss of several quarts of blood with the stamina of a much younger man. At six p.m., Denver time, the hospital announced that he was in the recovery room, "breathing well" with the help of a respirator.

Timothy McCarthy, the young Secret Service agent who had received a bullet in the chest when he stepped heroically into the line of fire to shield the President, had also undergone emergency surgery at George Washington University Hospital. Police Officer Thomas Delahanty, hit in the neck, had been rushed to the critical-care tower of the Washington Hospital Center where surgeons were debating whether to risk removing the bullet, so close to the spinal column.

The worst news of all, however, was about the President's 40-year-old press secretary, Jim Brady. Most of the commentators appeared to know him personally: he seemed tremendously well-liked. Shot in the head, Mr. Brady was not expected to live.

And still there was no word as to John's whereabouts. FBI and Secret Service men had congregated in the Sells' kitchen; from the family room we could hear the endless placing of phone calls to Washington. Jack went out and asked if they could find out where John was being held and help us get a call through to him. They assured us they would try.

13

4

JACK:

Waiting.

Inaction. It went against everything I knew. Sitting on the sofa in the Sells' family room, a long-ago memory came to mind. . . .

I was six years old, setting out for my very first day of school in a white shirt and pants, and long blond curls. My widowed mother, who came from an old Connecticut family, doubtless considered this proper attire. But in Okmulgee, Oklahoma, in the depths of the Depression, it was a disaster. Every boy on the playground, it seemed, wanted to be the first to rub dirt on the snow-white outfit. I knew nothing about fighting—my father had died when I was two—but in some unformulated way I grasped that the bigger the problem, the faster and more determined the response had to be. I closed my eyes and started swinging. When it was over I ran home in tears, my nose broken, my white clothes covered with blood. But I never again had to defend myself on that playground.

Give it all you've got. From that day to this, it had been my watchword. And now, in the biggest crisis of my life, I could only sit. . . .

Bill Sells had come home from his job at Johns-Manville and taken charge of the mob scene his home had become. He ruled on who could come in the house, decided which phone calls to pass on to us, kept people away from the room where Scott and Jo Ann and I were holed up. Sue had drawn the window drapes in here as soon as Jo Ann arrived. The den faced the street where from the sound of it the traffic jam was continuing to grow.

Bill said reporters were demanding a "statement" from Jo Ann and me. What could we tell them that they didn't know? That our hearts were broken, our lives destroyed? Bill also told us that the FBI men were waiting the arrival of a federal search warrant for our house next door.

A warrant . . . so whatever they came up with could be introduced in court. For the very first time my mind inched beyond this unspeakable day. "John's going to need a lawyer," I told Jo Ann.

I looked at my watch. In Dallas, where our company attorney lived, it would be 6:30 in the evening. I'd have to call Joe Bates at his home. The agents in the kitchen seemed to be on a non-stop telephone marathon. Next time I heard the receiver go down I got Sue to hand the phone through the pass-through and dialed Dallas.

"Joe? Jack. Sorry to bother you at home. I guess you know what this is about."

"Yes. We're as stunned as you are, Jack."

"Joe, do you know any lawyers in Washington?"

"In D.C.?" Joe considered for only a minute. "Vince Fuller," he said. "He was at Georgetown with me. Graduated at the top of the class and went with Williams & Connolly."

It was eight p.m. on the east coast when I finally reached Mr. Fuller at his home. He was noncommittal: there were partners to consult. I hung up with his promise to call back in the morning—aware what an ugly, distasteful case this would be for any law firm.

Sue slipped through the door from the kitchen and asked again if we didn't want to eat something. Heaven knows there was plenty of food. Every time the doorbell rang Bill Sells would carry another casserole out to the kitchen. It was like a house where someone had died. Neighbors wanted to do something, so they brought food. It was welcome, I knew, with all the people around, but neither Jo Ann nor I could swallow a bite.

I went to the front window and drew back the drapes half an inch. Now that it was getting dark I expected the various newspaper photographers and TV camera crews to go home. All afternoon they'd taken photos of the Sells' home and anyone going in or out—they must have a thousand pictures by now.

Friends following the TV coverage told us the Sells' place was being identified on some programs as "John Hinckley's childhood home." They were wrong on both counts. John hadn't grown up here, but in Dallas, and our cedar and moss rock home next door—"mountain modern" our builder had called it—couldn't be more different from this brick and stucco Tudor-style place of the Sells.

Our generous neighbors . . . sucked into the bottomless pit of John's tragedy, their home stared at in fifty million living rooms as though it were some hall of horrors. . . .

I peered through the drapes again. If anything the crowd up on the street was getting larger. Some of the trucks had floodlights mounted on them throwing a surreal glow over the tangle of cables and sound equipment. People were walking about, slapping their arms against the cold. Bill said one of the neighborhood kids had set up a little business selling coffee.

A row of television cameras mounted on tripods lined the near side of the road, all aimed at the front door of the Sells. As I let the drapes drop back into place I had the eerie impression that they were machine guns.

5

JO ANN:

An FBI man came into the den, showed us a badge and pulled up a chair to face us. For the first time I was aware of how disheveled I must look. I'd dashed out of the house in the blue jeans and old plaid shirt I'd been ironing in. No makeup—I hadn't combed my hair since early morning.

"I'm sorry, Mr. and Mrs. Hinckley," the man said courteously, "but we need some information from you." He was interested, specifically, in knowing who John's friends were in the neighborhood.

"They think the shooting might have been part of a conspiracy," Jack explained to me.

I would have laughed, except that I was so close to crying. I'd tried a dozen different ways to introduce John to other young people in Evergreen. "John doesn't have any friends around here," I said.

The investigator gave me a disbelieving stare. What about at work? Had he held jobs in the area?

One, four years ago, Jack told him. After he came back from California he'd worked for five months at a nightclub down in Denver. "A nightclub?" The agent's pen flew across his notepad. "As a singer?"

Jack and I exchanged glances. John must be telling them, in Washington, about his ambition to become a rock star. "No," I said, "not as a singer."

I felt like a traitor to John even as I said it. In his mind, I knew, the appeal of that nightclub job had been its nearness to the world of music. The agent looked up inquiringly.

"He was a busboy," Jack said.

"At the university in Lubbock, then," the agent persisted. "Who were his friends there?"

Jack and I both thought for a while. "There was Tom Perry," I said at last.

Perry? Was this individual still at Lubbock?

I didn't know. "He was a student there last year."

"He and John went into the mail order business together last spring," Jack told him.

The pen wrote. Where did this Tom Perry come from? We didn't know. We'd never met him? No, he was just someone John talked about on the phone.

Well, before college then. What about the crowd he'd gone with in high school? The thought of John going with a "crowd" was so out of character that again I wanted to smile and weep both at once. At Highland Park High School in Dallas John had kept pretty much to himself. "Except for Lynn," I said, "I don't really know of any close friends."

"Lynn?" the agent seized eagerly on the name.

"His girlfriend, Lynn Collins."

17

"Where does Lynn Collins live?"

"They met in California," Jack said. "But I believe she lives in Chicago."

"I think she moved to New York," I said. "At least, John spent Christmas with her there, year before last. She's an actress," I explained to the agent. "She goes where her current play is."

Could we give him a description of Lynn Collins?

Again Jack and I fell silent. We'd never actually met Lynn, though I'd urged John often enough to invite her here. "Anyhow, it's all over," I told him. "They broke up after that Christmas together. It was terribly hard on John."

Was there a picture of Lynn anywhere?

I shook my head. That was another thing I'd kept asking him. "An actress must have lots of photos," I'd say, but for some reason he never showed us one.

And that was all? Those were the only two names we could think of? "What about Jodie Foster?" the agent wanted to know.

"Jodie who?" Jack and I asked together.

"Foster. Jodie Foster."

There was no one by that name in Evergreen, I was pretty sure. I would have remembered, too, because "Jodie" was my own nickname. Jack never called me that, but some of my friends did. Maybe he'd known this person in Lubbock?

The agent didn't think so. Jodie Foster, he explained, was a movie actress.

"Then probably he met her when he was living in Hollywood that time," I said. Funny he'd never mentioned her to us.

The FBI man returned to the kitchen. From somewhere in the house came the muted murmur of a TV set. Through the pass-through we heard the man who had interviewed us using the kitchen telephone.

Suddenly the FBI agent was back in the room. "We have your son on the line," he said. It was so sudden that for a moment I could only stare stupidly at the receiver he held out to me.

I put it to my ear. "John? John, is it you?"

"It's me. Is that you, Mom?"

"John!" His own dear, familiar voice. "Are you all right, John?"

18

"I'm O.K. My wrists hurt a little."

"Daddy's going to an extension upstairs!"

John did sound all right. Calm, unexcited.

What was it about his voice that was so very wrong. . . .

6

JACK:

I grabbed the receiver in the Sells' bedroom in time to hear John say, "No, Mom, I'm fine. Really."

"I'm on, too, John," I said.

"Daddy and I want you to know we love you," Jo Ann told him.

"That's right, son. We're all in this together." I couldn't bring myself to ask what had happened, or why. Maybe I knew I wouldn't get the answer anyway. I told him I was already in touch with a lawyer.

"We'll get to Washington as fast as we can," Jo Ann said.

"The main thing, John," I told him, "is that your mom and I are with you. No matter what's happened, we're still your family. Scott says the same. Diane and Steve, too. And Grandma and Grandpa. You're not alone."

Another voice came on the phone; the man introduced himself as John's temporary court-appointed lawyer.

"How is he? Is he really all right?" Jo Ann asked anxiously. "Was he injured when—during the—" she could hardly bring out the word. "The arrest?"

No serious injuries, the lawyer replied. His cheek was swollen where a man in the crowd had struck him, and there was some chafing at the wrists where he'd been handcuffed.

"Did you know," the lawyer went on, "that your son was arrested in Nashville, Tennessee, last fall?"

"John?"

"At the airport."

"But—John was in school in New Haven, Connecticut, last fall!" I said.

"Well, he was in Nashville on October 9. Tried to board an airplane with a small arsenal. The police didn't notify you?"

The man talked on: court procedures, legal requirements. I scarcely heard. My mind was racing backward to the previous fall, when John had left here to attend that writing seminar. If this man's information was correct, he'd somehow gotten hold of a number of *guns* and ended up in Tennessee, a thousand miles from Yale. How many more bombshells were in store?

". . . bring this case to court before May 29," the attorney was saying.

"I didn't catch that," I apologized.

John wouldn't be 26 until the end of May, the man repeated. In District of Columbia courts, a 25-year-old could be tried as a youthful offender—but that would mean going to trial within the next two months.

I thanked the lawyer for stepping in, assured him we'd come up with permanent counsel as fast as possible. I was glad to retreat downstairs to the sanctuary of the den.

"Arrested carrying guns!" Jo Ann sobbed as I slid the door shut behind me. "Nearly six months ago! Why didn't anyone tell us?"

Outside, the wind was rising, howling through the mountain passes. Inside, our world had blown apart. We'd known John was depressed and directionless—immature was the psychiatrist's word—but never, until the tragedy this noon, had we had the least hint of potential violence. Now it appeared clues had been there all along, only no one had seen them.

Except the police in a far-away city, and they'd simply confiscated the guns—fined John $60 according to the lawyer —and informed no one. . . .

"How did John sound to you?" Jo Ann asked.

I thought back over the phone conversation, trying to put my finger on what had puzzled me. "He sounded better than I expected," I said.

And then I knew. It was what John *hadn't* said. He hadn't seemed agitated, or frightened, or remorseful, or any of the

20

things a person who'd just tried to assassinate the President might be expected to feel. "He sounded—like he always does."

"Yes," said Jo Ann. "I've been trying to figure out what was strange about his voice. It was . . . that there wasn't anything strange about it."

For a long time Jo Ann and I stared at each other across that oversized sofa.

There were two other calls I was glad to receive that long, long evening. The first was from Charles Blair, pastor of the largest church in Denver. Jo Ann and I had never been there, but for over a year—though he couldn't have known this—we'd been watching their weekly televised service.

"Mr. Hinckley?" the voice from Sunday morning was on the telephone that Bill Sells handed across the pass-through. "I just wanted to let you know, sir, that my wife, Betty, and I and our whole congregation will be praying for you and for John."

How he had located us here at the Sells', how long it had taken him to get a call through this ever-busy line, I couldn't imagine. I only knew that when he said he would pray, this man meant it.

The other call was from Governor Richard Lamm whom I'd gotten to know through a project for underprivileged children. The Governor too offered more than condolences. "You'll have to deal with crowds of curious people," he said, "just when you need privacy most." He told me he was assigning us his own two top security aides to accompany us to Washington.

Around ten o'clock that night Sue tried again to get us to eat something.

Jo Ann shook her head. "I couldn't, Sue."

"Lie down for a while, then. The guest room upstairs is all made up. It may be hours before that search warrant is issued."

But though we were both exhausted, going to bed was out of the question. Bill Sells said the media people out front were still clamoring for a statement. He helped us work out a few fumbling sentences trying to express our deep concern for the victims, as well as our intention to stand by our son. Bill carried the statement up to the flood-lit street.

Scott wanted to stay on overnight with his mother and me,

21

but I persuaded him to return to his own apartment in Denver: someone in the family had to show up at the office in the morning to answer the flood of inquiries I knew would start coming in from shareholders and brokers. So about eleven p.m. Scott kissed Jo Ann and headed for his car up on the street. Through the drapes I watched reporters and cameramen besiege him. The wind in the canyons rose until it was a shriek. Jo Ann traced the yellow-and-white plaid of the sofa. The television was reporting that James Brady was dead.

At 2:15 a.m. one of the agents slid open the door from the kitchen. "The search warrant's been authorized by phone, Mr. Hinckley. We can wait for them to drive it up from Denver, or we can get started."

"Let's get it over with."

"Is there a back door to your place?" he asked. "Too many cameras out front." I got out my key to the lower-level rec room entrance and told Jo Ann to try to get some sleep while we were next door, though I knew she wouldn't. Then one by one, six or eight government men and I filed through the Sells' laundry room and out into the whistling black night. The Sells' backyard was ankle deep in snow. Fumbling with the door key in the dark, I felt like a burglar sneaking into my own home.

Because of the hillside our house has a sub-story in the rear. The back door leads into an unfinished recreation room with a pingpong table and my model-railroad layout. There are two other rooms on this lower level, a guest room at the end of the hall, and between it and the rec room, John's small bedroom. I reached in and flipped on the wall switch.

His room was so tidy that I wondered for a moment if Jo Ann had forgotten our agreement. When John wanted to start living at home again, I'd said yes only on the condition that his mother was not to clean up after him. "You don't even change his sheets?" I'd check on her.

"No, Jack. He washes his own sheets, does his own clothes. You know how clean he is."

Glancing around his room now, I nodded. John was a fanatic about hygiene. Not only his room. He washed his hair every day, scrubbed his face till I thought he'd take the skin off.

Twin daybeds, neatly covered in striped spreads, were to the right of the door, a closet with a folding door to the left, an orderly bookshelf in an alcove beyond. Except for the array of medicine bottles on the table between the beds, the room might have been unlived in. The agents filed past me a little apologetically, tracking snow onto the carpet, and began going through the books on the shelves. One man made an inventory of the medicines on the table, while another opened the folding closet doors and drew out a small dark green suitcase.

I hadn't known it was in the closet, but even if I had, what kind of parent would go snooping through a 25-year-old's personal belongings? Just an ordinary looking piece of luggage with no hint of the tragic secrets it had concealed so well.

The agent set the suitcase on one of the striped bedspreads and zipped it open. On the very top, resting on some clothing, lay a pistol box.

The box was empty, the warranty still inside. The investigator began taking other things from that green case. Out came a handful of rifle cartridges, unspent. Out came a black ski mask with holes for eyes, and a pair of scuffed black motorcycle boots. Last of all was a sheaf of paper targets, folded over. The agent smoothed open the top one to reveal the silhouette of a man.

It was riddled with bullet holes.

I stood there trying to stop the room from rocking beneath me. Trying to put the objects on that striped bedspread together with the silent boy who had shared our home . . . and yet shared nothing at all.

On a shelf they found a packet of snapshots taken in Washington four months previously. One showed John sitting on a low wall in front of the White House. Someone must have taken that photo, the agents pointed out: Did I have any idea who?

I didn't. Some passer-by I supposed. I remembered John's showing us those pictures. I knew it was early December because he'd been in Washington when he learned of John Lennon's murder. Nothing in his whole life had affected John as deeply as Lennon's death. He'd taken a train from Washington to join the throng of mourners outside Lennon's New York apartment.

"But you don't know who was with him in Washington? Tom Perry? Lynn Collins?"

I didn't know.

A sampling of books from the bookshelf had joined the pile

of evidence going to Washington. Not a sampling, I corrected myself. My eyes ran over the titles still on the shelves. Books about the Beatles. About chess strategy. Instruction manuals for the guitar. Placed on the bed was a book about the Nazis, a map of Washington, a biography of Ronald Reagan, a book about Lee Harvey Oswald. If I'd ever noticed these titles in John's library, it was only along with all the others. Pulled out and laid side by side, they looked suddenly sinister.

"Is there anything else of John's in the house," they asked me, "or is everything in this room?"

This is everything, I started to say—and then I remembered those cartons out in the garage. I was pretty sure they were just old school papers. Or would have been sure, an hour ago. After what I had seen come out of this orderly bedroom, I wasn't sure of anything at all. I led the party of agents up the short flight of stairs to the first floor and through the side door into the garage. "These are things he shipped back from college," I said, pointing out the unopened boxes stacked along the wall. "And that white car is his."

And there in the icy, unheated garage, the revelations continued. Agents would open a box and pull out a book on *Beginning Spanish*, and another on Adolph Hitler. Instructions on how to care for a cat, and articles on the Kennedy assassination. Anything dealing with violence went into a pile on the hood of the Volare; books on sports and music were returned to the boxes. I stood there, shivering with cold and shock. Some of the boxes held letters from Jo Ann and me. Others contained spiral notebooks filled with classroom notes, as well as essays and poems apparently composed by John. Soon the hoods of the Omega and the Omni, too, were covered with stacks of paper.

It was nearly four o'clock in the morning when they asked me if I had a plastic garbage bag they could carry everything in. I went to the kitchen and got one and watched as they stuffed John's college years inside.

The men headed with the sack to their cars parked in our driveway. In spite of the hour, the instant the front door opened the yard was ablaze with floodlights. I heard reporters shouting questions as the FBI men started up their engines.

I went down the stairs and out the back door in the dark.

There was no way I was going to run that gauntlet of cameras and microphones. No way I could answer anyone else's questions when I had so many unanswered ones of my own.

7

JO ANN:

What could be keeping Jack so long? He'd been next door with the FBI men almost two hours.

In the Sells' kitchen some sheriff's deputies were talking, and somewhere in the house a TV set was on. Over all the sounds was the screaming of the wind. I felt so sorry for the policemen and reporters outside in their cars on this cold night.

My mind went back to our miserable first winter here in Colorado. We'd stayed in a tiny townhouse down in Denver, waiting for spring when we could start building here in Evergreen. Scott was clear on the other side of the world, working on an oil rig. Diane was at SMU in Dallas; John was a freshman at Texas Tech in Lubbock. For the first time since Scott was born there'd been only Jack and me at home: Maybe that's why tensions in our marriage hadn't shown up till then. The weather broke all records that winter, week after week, blowing huge snowdrifts across the roads. I'd never driven in snow. I'd been trapped in that little house, listening to the wind.

Up on the street now, I heard running. Somewhere car engines were starting up, voices calling.

Then I heard the Sells' back door open. I hurried out to the kitchen as Jack came in. His face was ashen. *What happened!* I wanted to ask. *Why were you so long?* But he looked too whipped to put questions to him.

Silently we climbed the stairs. Sue had left a light on in their cheerful green-and-yellow guest room. An embroidered sampler on the wall invited us to "Be at your ease. Get up when you're ready, go to bed when you please."

With the door shut behind us, Jack told me: the empty pistol box, the ski mask, the riddled target. It was too terrifying to take in all at once, but I couldn't ask him to repeat. I had never seen a man as broken as Jack at that moment. "I just saw our son's life go into a trash bag," he said.

Of the things they had found in that suitcase the black pull-on boots were the only ones I remembered seeing. John had brought them and an Army-surplus jacket back from California four years before. I remembered being surprised because John so rarely bought clothes—some California fad, I'd supposed.

We crawled into the king-sized bed and lay listening to the wind, pretending to sleep, each knowing the other was awake. *If I could only really fall asleep,* I thought, *I would wake up and none of this would have happened.*

8

JACK:

Jo Ann wasn't asleep. Her breathing was too shallow. I wanted to say something comforting but no thoughts of comfort came. The battering of the wind against the guest room windows reminded me of my drive to get ahead, to hammer out a good life for my family. . . .

Maybe it was growing up in the Depression. Maybe it was

26

World War II, coming when I was a teenager. At seventeen, with nearly a year of high school still to go, I'd been accepted in the Navy's accelerated V-12 college training program at the University of Oklahoma, completing high school and getting my mechanical engineering degree in less than three years.

Hard work and energy! I played drums in a dance band, earned admission to some engineering honor societies, was elected vice-president of my class, fell in love with a petite and pretty freshman I met on a blind date, Jo Ann Moore.

At twenty I was commissioned an ensign in the Navy and sent to the Pacific. Japan had surrendered two months earlier. I saw Nagasaki, where the second atom bomb had been dropped only weeks before. It was a staggering way for an Oklahoma boy to come of age. And it only increased my conviction that determination could accomplish anything—hadn't it won the war?

In the fall of 1946, age 21, I was discharged from the Navy and took a job with the Carter Oil Company. The pay was only $210 a month—but it was a start in the oil business. When Jo Ann said she'd marry me, I asked my boss for some time off. "Sure," he said, "take Christmas Day."

So Jo Ann and I were married in Oklahoma City on Christmas Eve, 1946, spent Christmas driving across the snowswept prairie toward St. Elmo, Illinois, where I was working. There Jo Ann tried to make a home out of a cold and drafty converted mule barn. The kitchen had an old round top-loading icebox; as the ice melted, the water ran out through a funnel set in the floor. There the water would refreeze, plug up the hole and spread a lake of ice across the kitchen floor.

I had to get up at 4:30 a.m. to be at the oil field by daybreak. Jo Ann would get up to fix my breakfast and pack my lunch pail. She'd pull on bedroom slippers over wool socks, then put my slippers on over hers.

I'd spend the day working with a crew hauling thousands of feet of rods and tubing from the oil wells, separating the sections, repairing them, running them back into the ground. I'd come home stinking and filthy, covered with oil from head to toe and so exhausted I could hardly stay awake through supper.

But we were young, very much in love, full of ambitious dreams for the future. From St. Elmo I was transferred to a bigger job, then another. . . . We moved fourteen times in the first five years. Many months I'd see Jo Ann only occasionally, sleeping most nights in my car at the drilling site, longing to be home with her. I was doing it all for Jo Ann, I believed, to earn the good life post-war America held out to those who were willing to work.

We were in Ardmore, Oklahoma, when Scott was born in 1950, and we decided to stop moving around. Jo Ann would stop moving, that is; drilling engineers have to go where oil is found. But now I had a family to make the weeks away from home worth all the effort. Diane was born in Ardmore in 1953, John in 1955. If hard work could provide our children with a good home and a decent education, they were going to have them.

Someone was stirring down in the Sells' kitchen. Jo Ann and I gave up the pretense of sleeping; it was nearly six a.m. anyhow. We got back into the clothes we'd been wearing when the clock of ordinary life stopped running. It seemed years and years since that pistol went off in Washington. It was not yet a day.

At the stove Bill Sells was making coffee. He turned with a smile: "I have some good news for you. Jim Brady's still alive! They're calling it a miracle."

Jo Ann began to cry, while my knees went so weak I had to sit down at the kitchen table. The President was off the respirator, Bill went on; McCarthy and Delahanty continued to improve.

Later that Tuesday morning there was more good news. Vince Fuller telephoned from Washington to say his law firm would represent us. He and a couple of associates were heading out in a few minutes for the Marine base in Quantico, Virginia, where John had been transferred sometime during the night. I asked Mr. Fuller if he could arrange for us to speak to John again and he said he'd make the request.

It seemed to me we spent most of that second day on the telephone. The most routine thing was suddenly complicated. All Jo Ann and I wanted to do was get to that Marine base as fast as we could. But it appeared that a number of government agencies were now involved.

Strangers came and went at the Sells'; the crowd on the street continued to grow. Our statement to the press, far from satisfying them, seemed to have whetted their appetites—it looked like more reporters and camera trucks up there than ever. Notes of encouragement were passed in to us from friends and neighbors not permitted through the police cordon.

Vince Fuller arranged a telephone call from Quantico. John's responses still seemed to Jo Ann and me strangely . . . bland. They'd kept a bright light on in his cell all night, so that he'd gotten no sleep. But the fact that he was in a cell at all, and the reason for it, seemed scarcely to have registered with him.

Anyone leaving or entering the Sells' house had to run the gauntlet of reporters. Our doctor and his wife, Em and Sue Harvey, bringing dinner over, were besieged. By bedtime I was past caring. For 32 hours we'd been hiding out at our neighbors; we had to get back home. The only thing that worried me was Jo Ann's picture getting into the papers. "Anytime a public figure is shot," the Secret Service had cautioned us, "we have to be on guard against a chain reaction."

It was too late to do anything about me. They'd gotten half a dozen photos of me coming over here yesterday: Bill said they were in today's papers. Jo Ann and I couldn't look at a newspaper.

But I didn't want to have to worry every time Jo Ann went to the Safeway. Earlier that day the two Sues—Sue Sells and Sue Harvey—had gone over to our place to get us a change of clothes and the evening news was carrying the sensational, though erroneous, scoop that "the mother of John Hinckley returned briefly this afternoon to her home."

"How are we going to get over there without Jo Ann ending up on tomorrow's front page?" I asked the others. The press was dug in for a second night—and this time they were watching our back door too.

"Why don't I go up there and talk to them one more time," Bill Sells offered. "I'll tell them you're two tired, grieving parents who need privacy. Appeal to their sense of decency."

Bill was back in a few moments to report that the media people had agreed to let us cross the yard without annoyance. We said our goodbyes, then Bill led the two of us across the dark snowy lawn.

We were halfway there when a blinding light flashed in our faces and a man emerged from behind a pine tree. Bill has a short fuse like I do. He grabbed the reporter around the waist, lifted him right off the ground and spun him around: "Get off this property and leave them alone!"

Bill saw us safely inside our house and asked again if we didn't want him to stay. But Jo Ann and I chiefly wanted to be alone.

Bill left and I bolted the front door. I couldn't even look down the six steps to the lower hall where John's room was. We turned the other way, up the short flight to our own bedroom.

In front of the TV the ironing board was set up, a basket of my shirts beside it. On the bed was an open suitcase. Until that minute I had forgotten that this was the day we were to go to Guatemala to help provide water for some Indian villagers.

9

JO ANN:

Our house was so cold. I turned up my side of the electric blanket and lay there thinking of all those people sitting in their cars up on the street. At last I got up and got us both sleeping pills from the medicine cabinet.

In the morning the crowd was still there. It was Wednesday, the first day of April, the second morning after the shooting. April Fool's Day, I thought. Only . . . there was no one to laugh and say it was all a horrid make-believe.

Friends and officials soon filled the house. The captain of the Colorado Highway Patrol and Governor Lamm's aide arrived and outlined plans for the trip to the Quantico Marine Base. It was incredibly complicated. Five government agencies would be involved, the highway patrol, the Governor's men, the FBI, the Secret Service, and the District of Columbia police. The hardest part, evidently, was going to be getting us out of this house and onto an airplane unobserved, and then getting us off the plane at the other end and out to Quantico without being followed by the media.

It seemed there'd been threats against Jack and me by anonymous telephone callers. I couldn't believe there was any real danger, but the captain shook his head. "Sure, ninety-nine percent of it is bluff, but we can't afford that one-percent chance."

The phone kept ringing. Bill Sells came over and took on the job of answering it, as he had the previous two days at his own house. One of the calls was from Billy Graham who had just come from the President's bedside. "He has a strong constitution," Dr. Graham told us, "and a strong faith."

A supportive call came from Dr. Richard Halverson, Chaplain of the United States Senate. An order of Catholic nuns in Arkansas telephoned to tell us they were praying. Everyone seemed to want to do something to help. Neighbors continued to bring over food through that siege-line of cameras and sound-trucks. Jack's barber called to say that if Jack needed a haircut he'd come here to the house. Several 24-hour prayer chains were organized around the community.

We got a call through again to John at Quantico, telling him we'd be there as swiftly as the authorities could agree on travel arrangements. We spoke several times to my folks in Oklahoma City, and to Diane and Steve in Dallas. Their friends too were rallying around, but both households were also getting an occasional hate-call from people who didn't identify themselves.

It made me wonder how much Bill Sells was concealing from us. Diane phoned from a friend's number: She and Steve, with little Chris and tiny Stephanie, had had to leave their home when a Dallas TV news program not only showed pictures of their house but announced the address over the air.

The overwhelming response on the part of strangers, however, was empathy. "I held my breath, Mrs. Hinckley," one caller told me, "until they released the name of the young man. You see, I was so afraid it was *my* son."

Telegrams poured in too, all of them—at least the ones Bill passed on to us—assuring us of prayerful concern. And the flowers! The first ones came from Ithaca, New York; the card

31

read simply, "Our love and prayers. A brother and sister in Christ." A bouquet and a note of apology even arrived from the newsman Bill had lifted bodily off our property.

We were overwhelmed that so many people cared—and mystified how strangers knew of our religious beliefs. Jack was active, it was true, in Christian service organizations, never, never dreaming that the giving would flow back to us.

It was 48 hours since I'd switched on the TV at my ironing board. Sooner or later, I knew, I would have to go down to John's room. I walked along the lower hallway and stood in his doorway. His things were thrown everywhere—clothes strewn over the beds, heaps of books on the floor. I forced myself to go in and start straightening up.

It was a strange feeling to be picking up John's things. We'd given him complete privacy here in this room—except. . . .

One day last October I'd come home to find him whitefaced and sick after swallowing too much of a tranquilizer a doctor back in Lubbock had prescribed for him. It was presumably an accident—yet I couldn't shake the fear that possibly it *wasn't* accidental. From that time on, hating myself for being under-handed, I had slipped into his room each day to check the number of Valium pills in the bottle by his bed. And now they were telling us that John had been arrested that same month, October—at Nashville airport. I wondered suddenly if those handguns had been right here in this room all the while I was coming in to check his medicine.

As I straightened the striped bedspreads, my hand felt a piece of paper wedged between one of the beds and the wall. I drew it out and felt a lump in my throat at seeing John's familiar handwriting. It was a sheet of lined yellow paper torn from a legal-sized pad, covered on both sides in an almost illegible scrawl. Whether it had lain against the wall for some time or slipped down there night before last when the FBI was going through his things, I didn't know. Across the top was a title:

I Read The News Today, Oh No!

I sank down on the bed and began to read.

> *John Lennon is dead and people continue to laugh and dream and live . . .*

Oh, listen to the comedian tell his jokes . . .
The audience is laughing so he must be amusing,
but I'm not close to a smile. John Lennon is dead!

Seventy-five thousand people with brains are
watching the all-important football game . . .
Isn't it fun and exciting! No, no, no a thousand
times. A man died on December 8, 1980 and nothing
will ever be the same . . .

For an entire week after the assassination
of John Lennon I cried like a sick baby . . .
What I cannot comprehend is the fact that
people are trying to carry on with life now.
What's the use?

In America, heros are meant to be killed. Idols
are meant to be shot in the back. Guns are neat ·
little things, aren't they? They can kill
extraordinary people with very little effort.
But don't say a word about it to the NRA.

John Lennon died a couple of weeks ago and I
did too. Bang, bang, we're all dead. The stupid
earth keeps revolving and the stupid people keep
the faith but they are actually walking corpses.
Everyone is dead.

Ronald Reagan never missed a beat. Of course he's
not in favor of gun control. How can you make a
world move without guns, guns, guns?

I think the Charter Arms people are so clever
to produce guns that are so small, and yet have
the capacity to kill famous people.
Every red blooded American
should send a valentine card to the good folks at
Charter Arms, and the good folks at the NRA.

Speaking of red blood, I heard from an eyewitness
that the stuff was coming out of Lennon's mouth
and body at an alarming rate after he was shot.

*And all it took to produce such a spectacle was
a little toy gun and an American pulling the
trigger.*

*I am an American and boy am I proud! Let's see
how many more idols we can wipe off the face of
the earth . . .*
The dream is over.
I died. You died. Everyone died.
America died. The world died. The universe died.

Did God die?

*The God I was told to believe in would never have
permitted the murder of John Lennon. God didn't
die. He never was alive in the first place.*

10

JACK:

I'd gotten up Wednesday morning feeling better after a night in
my own bed, more able to cope with the logistics of the trip to
see John. My frame of mind, however, proved to have nothing
to do with it. As the morning passed and official complications
multiplied, it swept over me that Jo Ann and I were no longer
private individuals with personal choices. Everyone and his
brother now had a say-so in where we went and when.

An elaborate get-away scheme for our trip to Washington
was being worked out by the officials, with Bill Sells to act as a
decoy to keep the press busy out front, while an unmarked
highway patrol car picked up Jo Ann and me on the street

behind our house. But afternoon came with nothing settled, and by mid-afternoon—over 48 hours after John's arrest—it was clear we would not get away today at all.

To me it was a classic case of too many government agencies. Governor Lamm's security pro assured me it was all necessary. "If you're spotted leaving here," he jerked his thumb toward the street above, "those media folks are going to chase you to the airport, alert their pals at the other end, and make the problem of the security people all along the way ten times harder."

He was right, I knew. And yet what about our problem? What about a family needing to get to a son in trouble? Now that they'd taken a million pictures of the place, why didn't the press move on? "Can you tell me," I asked the security man, "what is so fascinating about an ordinary house on an ordinary street?"

"I wouldn't call it ordinary, Mr. Hinckley. This is a pretty nice neighborhood."

"I could show you a dozen fancier ones nearby."

"That's not the point. A guy who shoots the President is supposed to be a loser. Not a kid whose father owns an oil company."

"I *run* an oil company, a small one at that," I corrected him. Jo Ann and I owned just six percent of it.

"Well, in the papers they've got you with money coming out of your ears. You're supposed to live in a mansion."

I glanced around at the dream house Jo Ann and I had built seven years ago. It was a handsome contemporary, with a cathedral-ceilinged living room and three levels making use of the hillside lot, but a far cry from a mansion. I thought back over the years when I'd worked around the clock, missed out on time with my family, borrowed and scraped to get Vanderbilt Energy Corporation started. I thought of the pressure I'd put on Scott and John to do better, better, always better at school—Diane got A's without prodding—so that they too could get out and compete in the all-important world of business. "Success" was all that mattered.

Until November 20, 1977.

That was the day, here in this house alone, when I'd turned over to God my life, my possessions, my family—confessing to Him how hollow my goals had been.

Now, four years later, I was perceiving that they were worse

35

than hollow. The success I'd given so much for was turning our home and family now, in our time of tragedy, into a kind of public freak show. . . .

I phoned Vince Fuller in Washington for the fourth or fifth time that frustrating Wednesday; he and I were now Vince and Jack. Vince suggested the Jefferson Hotel near his office, whenever we finally got to Washington; his office could handle room reservations.

I told Vince about the strange piece of writing Jo Ann had discovered in John's bedroom. "What baffles me about it, Vince, is that Lennon was shot in December. To read this thing, you'd think John detested guns. But if that really was John they picked up in Nashville in October, why—he was carrying guns himself."

"I'm afraid it was John all right, Jack."

Vince wanted us to bring that sheet of paper with us, along with anything else we found, in the garage or his room or anywhere, that we thought might have a bearing. Especially he wanted Jo Ann and me to recall everything we could remember about John's early years. "Think back to the very first time you noticed anything unusual. I believe you have other children?"

"Two," I told him. "Both older."

"Well, try to recall any way he was different, as a child."

In accordance with Vince's request, I spent some time Wednesday evening going through the boxes out in the garage. The FBI had carted away a huge bagful of stuff, but far more remained. It would take quite a while to sort through it all. Upstairs, Jo Ann found some letters John had written home from college, and packed them to take.

It was Thursday morning before the elaborate arrangements for getting us to Washington were complete. We were booked, under other names, aboard a Piedmont flight bound for Cincinnati and then on to Washington's National Airport. The non-stops from Denver all landed at Washington's Dulles airport, and that's the place the press would be watching. Assumed names, secret routes—it still seemed impossible all of this was happening to us.

As for getting us out of the house unobserved—the problem that had everyone most worried—the highway patrol was to bring an unmarked car to Medinah Drive at the foot of our lot. Just before eleven a.m. Bill Sells was to go out front with some kind of innocuous announcement for the press while Jo Ann and I escaped out the back door. Bill would then return inside here to answer the phone and keep up the appearances of an occupied house. The plan even called for Sue Sells to come over an hour later carrying lunch.

Twenty minutes before this count-down was to begin, Vince Fuller telephoned from Washington. "John's been moved from Quantico," he said.

Apparently he had been transferred earlier that morning to a place called Butner—a federal penitentiary somewhere in North Carolina. "They want to do a psychiatric evaluation, and Butner has the facilities."

Vince urged us to come ahead to Washington anyhow; security was all in place at both ends, and we needed to talk. He'd find out meanwhile about visiting arrangements at Butner: "You can get to North Carolina faster from Washington."

Jo Ann and I were crushed. After waiting three days to satisfy officials, still another delay before we could get to John. The doorbell rang. It was Bill Sells with a copy of yesterday's *Denver Post*. We still hadn't been able to make ourselves pick up a newspaper. "Sue and I thought you ought to know about this now," Bill said, "before you see a paper on the plane or somewhere." On the front page of Wednesday's *Post* was a huge four-column photograph of three young men in Nazi uniforms. **JOHN W. HINCKLEY, JR., FAR RIGHT,** read the bold-faced caption, **STANDS WITH OTHER MEMBERS OF NEO-NAZI PARTY IN ST. LOUIS IN 1978.**

"That's not John! It doesn't even look like John!" we both exclaimed. Except that the young man was clean-shaven with short blond hair, there wasn't the slightest resemblance.

The Evergreen man, (the captioned continued) the suspect in Monday's shooting of President Reagan and three other men, was a card-carrying member of the Party from March 1978 until November 1979, when his membership was terminated.

"That's a damn lie!" I exploded. "They'll have to print a retraction! They'll have to put it in a box right on the front page, like that lousy photo."

I really believed, then, that a retraction would receive the same prominence as an original false statement.

There wasn't a thing in the world we could do at this point: out the back window I could see a nondescript green sedan waiting down on Medinah Drive. It was Bill Sells who had a suggestion: "I've got to tell those reporters *something* when I go out front—why don't I say I'm protesting that phony photograph on behalf of the family?" He looked at his watch, then made his deliberate way up the driveway. Even as the front door closed behind him we could see the media people moving in. For once their zeal was working for us.

Jo Ann and I ran downstairs and through the rec room. Our suitcases were waiting by the door. I snatched them up and we started down the steep back yard, hidden by the house, slithering along the snowy slope beneath the Ponderosas. We heard the motor of the green sedan start up.

We dove into the back seat. At the first intersection a car pulled out of the side street and followed us. Twisting around, I saw it trailing three car lengths behind. "Patrolman," our driver explained. "If anyone's followed us, the trooper back there will slow down and cut him off."

We were headed, this first leg of the trip, not for Stapleton Airport but for our friends the Harveys. The get-away plan involved remaining at their house for a couple of hours in case our departure had been observed: "First place reporters would check would be the airport."

Sue Harvey had a heaping plate of sandwiches waiting for us. Maybe it was the sense of being on our way at last, but in spite of the false photograph, in spite of knowing we would not see John this evening after all, for the first time in three days Jo Ann and I ate a real meal.

Shortly after two o'clock, two different unmarked cars pulled up at the Harveys, one to transport us to the airport, one, again, to head off any would-be follower. In the first car, in addition to the driver, we were happy to see the two Colorado security men who were to accompany us on the trip east.

11

JO ANN:

While Jack kept up a conversation with the Governor's men in the car, I was grateful to be left alone with my thoughts. I was remembering the last time I'd made this trip to the airport, just eight days previously, with John dejected and silent beside me.

He didn't understand, not really, why he couldn't go on living at home, although he'd reluctantly agreed months ago to the "plan" worked out with the psychiatrist. The plan called for John to have a job by the end of February, his own living arrangements by the end of March. For the last three weeks he'd been living in a cheap motel and, we believed, looking for work in Denver. Now he'd brought his car up to Evergreen to leave it in our garage, and asked me to drive him to the airport. He'd decided to go job-hunting in Los Angeles, he said; he liked California better than Colorado. But what he would prefer to either, I knew, would be to forget the "plan" and move back in with us.

At the airport check-in he'd hauled his suitcase from the back seat and spoken for the first time since we left the house. "I want to thank you, Mom, for all the things you've done for me all these years."

As though, I thought in panic, he was saying goodbye for good! Ever since that "accidental" overdose of Valium, back in October, the fear that John might harm himself had never been far from me. "John plays on your fears," the psychiatrist would remind me, "uses them to manipulate you." That was part of the plan too: Jack and I were to present a united front, not let John work on my sympathy when he got me alone.

39

There in front of the airline terminal I'd swallowed to keep my voice steady. "You're very welcome," I told him stiffly. Then I'd driven away before he saw the tears.

I'd cried all the way home, repeating to myself what the doctor had told us. "John will try every trick in the book to get you to change your minds. In the long run, however, he'll be grateful."

But . . . there had been no long run, I thought in the back seat of that government car. Five days after he and I had made this drive down to Stapleton Airport, John was somehow on the east coast instead of the west, somehow pointing a gun at the President of the United States. . . .

The car drove us right onto the runway, to the foot of a stairway in the tail of a Piedmont Airlines 727. We were the first passengers aboard, given the last row on the plane, with Jack in the window seat, me in the middle, one of the security aides on the aisle. The other aide sat across from us next to two empty seats—in one of which a very special friend would be traveling.

Dale Morris was a full-bearded man in his fifties who'd become a kind of unofficial minister-at-large to the entire Evergreen area. He'd been a top salesman at IBM when he discovered that his "real work" was being neglected. So he simply quit. He now ran a service business, supplying hot coffee to Denver office buildings, and leaving him free to go where, in his words, "God can use me." Postponing a score of other commitments, he'd agreed to come with Jack and me on this journey east.

He was coming down the aisle now, with the boarding Cincinnati passengers. He gave us a cheery wink as he slipped into the empty window seat across the aisle.

A few minutes after take-off, a woman started back toward the toilets. Casually, the security aide on Dale's side got to his feet and stood in the aisle, all six feet five inches, 280 pounds of him screening Jack and me from view. I think that was when I realized how very seriously these men were taking their job.

I unfastened my seatbelt and struggled with the button in my armrest: apparently the seatbacks in this last row did not recline. Jack said Vince Fuller had asked about John's early years. Had there been problems at birth? Had he been different in any way from Scott and Diane?

I closed my eyes. But try as I would, I could remember nothing special about John's first months. He was a beautiful baby—plump, healthy, easy to care for. No problems learning to walk or talk. Jack and I had always said how fortunate we were that we'd had no worries with any of our children. The only traumatic thing I could recall was the fire three months before John was born. . . .

We'd been living with our two small children in the first home we'd ever owned, a four-room frame house in Ardmore, Oklahoma. When I became pregnant for the third time we knew we'd have to have a larger place. Late in February we took Scott, not yet five, and Diane, just two, to my folks in Oklahoma City while we packed books and crated dishes for the move to our new house.

That cold, windy morning, a friend invited Jack and me to leave the clutter for an hour and come to lunch. We had the floor furnace in the old house turned up as high as it would go; as we went out the front door a gust of wind must have blown some wrapping material over the hot grating. We were sitting down to eat, clear across town, when a neighbor telephoned to tell us our house was on fire. We rushed home to find fire trucks all over the street, smoke pouring from the front windows.

I went into shock. Suppose the children had been there. Suppose I'd been with them *alone*. Jack had always been my safety—"my rock"—I called him. Every time I realized that he might not have been there, I started shaking again.

I worried that the emotional trauma of the fire might somehow damage the baby I was carrying. But John was born not a day early, husky and healthy.

Well—perhaps *one* day early, if I'd had any say in the matter. Ardmore had built a new hospital that year, due to open May 30. Local merchants announced gifts and discounts to the first baby born in the new maternity wing. We had as good a chance as any of being the fortunate family, but John arrived at 11:29 p.m. on May 29.

He and I were transferred two days later to the new hospital. Since John had been exposed to the outside world in that brief car trip, he was not placed in the nursery with the other newborns, but in a little room by himself. Only a coincidence, of course . . . but sitting in the back row of the airplane almost

26 years later, I thought suddenly that this isolation had been somehow symbolic. Alone . . . separated from his peers . . . years later this was to become John's pattern.

"May I take your tray?"

I looked up to see the stewardess reaching for my untouched supper. I pushed my tray table upright. This couldn't be the kind of thing the lawyers in Washington were interested in hearing. John's birth, his early years, had been absolutely normal as far as I could recall.

It was as the plane began its descent into Cincinnati that a little scene flashed into my mind. A tiny episode I hadn't thought of in years. Mother and I were shopping in a supermarket when John was maybe four. Mother glanced down at the small towheaded boy clinging to me. "That's one child you'll never have to worry about losing in a crowd!"

I had looked down too and chuckled. John was clutching my skirt in his little fist as though life depended on it. "It's not the store where I usually shop," I explained. Even as I said it I was aware that neither Scott nor Diane had ever stuck so close, unfamiliar place or not.

That was all—nothing really. Just a fleeting memory of a child who wasn't especially adventuresome. Certainly nothing I ever worried about. In fact with two lively older children to keep track of, I was grateful that my third was such a stay-at-home. . . .

12

JACK:

My knees were jammed against the seatback ahead. I could hardly wait for Cincinnati and the chance to stretch my legs, but when the plane landed the security men asked us to stay in our seats. Dale offered to go into the terminal and get me a paper but I didn't want one. I couldn't understand my violent aversion to seeing John's story in print. Maybe I had a subconscious conviction that if I never saw it down in black and white, it wouldn't really have happened.

All at once I knew what this slow, mournful progression across the country reminded me of. It was like a trip to bury someone you loved. Like that journey in the winter of 1949, traveling on the train that was carrying my mother's body back to Meriden, Connecticut, for burial in the family plot. Jo Ann, pregnant with Scott, had stayed in Oklahoma, but my sister Avilla and our stepfather, Kib Brooks, whom Mother had married when I was eight, sat across from me on the long, long ride. We were mostly silent, then, as now, the silence of people coping with grief too fresh to share.

Mother's death should not have come as a surprise; she'd had a slow, agonizing battle with cancer. But for all those years she never told me what was wrong, because of the stigma attached to the disease. Cancer, in the 1940s, was a condition you didn't talk about.

She'd wanted so much to see the child that was on its way—wanted so much for it to be a boy, so that she could know the name Hinckley would be carried on. Mother had been so proud of that name. Avilla had taken the last name

Brooks when Mother remarried, but Mother insisted I remain a Hinckley, and I agreed.

Now I'd had to deny that name to get on an airplane. . . . I wrenched my mind away from the present, tried to concentrate on John's early experiences as Vince had asked. His childhood had been absolutely normal, as far as I could recall. He was a handsome, blond, rather shy little guy—maybe a little less rambunctious than the other two.

The fact was, I'd been so wrapped up with career problems when John was small that my recollections were a little vague. In 1956, when he was one, I decided I'd never get ahead until I made the plunge into my own business. I set myself up as a petroleum consultant. No customers. To keep food on the table, I tried all sorts of side ventures—building storm shelters, digging swimming pools. Nothing worked.

At last I faced the fact that I'd have to go back to working for someone else—any work, anywhere. The two oil centers were Dallas and Denver. I tried Dallas first, because it was closer. I'd go into one of the mammoth new skyscrapers and write down the names of every oil company listed in the lobby directory. Then I'd take the elevator to the top floor and work my way down by the stairs, knocking on endless doors, presenting my qualifications.

For weeks I stuck to this routine, scarcely seeing my family. Running out of prospects in Dallas, I tried Denver. I was noting names and trudging down stairwells there when one night I found a telephone message from Jo Ann slipped beneath the door of my closet-size hotel room. A job offer had come through in Dallas.

So in November 1958 we moved. We'd been in Ardmore ten years by that time—happy, fulfilling years for Jo Ann. We both knew the uprooting would be hard on her. Just how hard we never dreamed.

The size, the speed, the impersonality of Dallas seemed to throw her into a kind of immobility. She dreaded stepping outside our rented house. When necessity forced her to the grocery store she fought waves of panic all the way, often having to flee, leaving her shopping cart in the aisle.

Struggling to learn a new job, I was impatient with these "imaginary" problems. "You just need to get away from the kids for a few hours," I'd tell her. But if I talked her into going

44

to a movie, we might have to leave halfway through the film. If we went to a restaurant, she'd often lose the meal in the ladies' room.

Alarmed at last, I insisted she go to a doctor. He found nothing organically wrong, assured us the anxiety attacks would decrease as she adjusted to her new surroundings. And so they did. We bought an attractive house in the University Park section of the city—though the $22,000 price meant additional pressures on me. Jo Ann made friends in the neighborhood, became active in her Altar Guild, joined a bridge club and got involved at the children's schools.

But I found myself wondering as the plane taxied to the runway for the second leg of our trip from Cincinnati to Washington, what effect all this might have had on impressionable young John—my business ambitions and being uptight all through his first years, then Jo Ann's unhappiness, to which I'd been so blind, those early months in Dallas. The other two children were in school by then, out of the house much of the day. Could Jo Ann's fears and anxieties have been communicated to our little boy at home?

But even if all this was true, I thought as the plane took off for the second time, there'd apparently been no lasting damage. John had started school, with no special problems, was an above-average student, a top scorer in "Y" basketball and a star quarterback for the White Bombers, his elementary school "Y" football team.

I couldn't quite understand Vince Fuller wanting us to poke about in a perfectly ordinary childhood for some supposed clue to something that happened twenty years later. I remembered the fantastic birthday parties Jo Ann gave for John at the end of May each year, the house filled with happily screaming kids. I remembered the Indian Guides "tribe" that John and I had joined, a group of eight or ten fathers and sons sitting cross-legged in a circle for several hours each month, wearing feathered headdresses and solemnly weaving belts out of leather.

The Guides were sponsored by the YMCA and several weekends a year we'd drive to a "Y" camp to sleep on iron cots and eat half-cooked food scorched over an open fire. I could still see John's eyes shining with excitement in the firelight—and I'd made life-long friends among the men in the group. Surely it was nonsense to try to link the tragedy in Washington with anything in John's typical suburban childhood.

Then a long-forgotten remark by a neighbor came to mind. "John never opens his mouth over at our house. We call him Silent John."

It was the first hint we'd had that John felt ill-at-ease away from home. Jo Ann began watching with this in mind and reported that, sure enough, he seemed reluctant to leave his own yard. If his playmates came over, fine. But if none appeared, he would not go looking for them.

It's shyness, we told each other. He'll get over it. Like his solemn little face. It was a family game, trying to get John to smile. I remembered the photographer who had come to do a family portrait going through every giggle-producing antic in his repertory. Scott and Diane were weak with laughing but John's steady, serious gaze never altered. "We're mean to tease him," Jo Ann would say. "If he doesn't feel like smiling, that's his business."

It was inconceivable to me that he could be unhappy. Why, our kids had everything—a yard to play in, a TV set in the living room, water-skiing on weekends with our outboard motorboat. We were the family whose American dream had come true.

Looking back, I realized that the dream had had an enormous price tag. Oil is the riskiest, most unpredictable business in the world and no doubt I'd brought its tensions home with me. Almost from the day we moved to Dallas, the company that had hired me was in trouble. A year and a half later it went bankrupt. By then, however, I had contacts in the city; within a week I had a job with a Dallas petroleum consulting firm.

And it was there that I pioneered a new concept in the oil business: operating oil and gas wells for the owners on a contract basis. It filled a need in the industry and the demand for our service grew.

By 1965, when John was ten, I decided I was ready to become an independent oil producer. I was forty that year, the age at which ambition suddenly demands a timetable. The trouble was, it costs hundreds of thousands of dollars to buy leases and drill a well. Though I knew how to find oil, even with repeated trips to money sources in New York I could not raise the necessary drilling funds. For the second time my efforts to go into business for myself ended in failure.

Ironically, meanwhile, the consulting and operating service flourished. In 1966 I sold our home in University Park and bought a larger one on tree-lined Beverly Drive in fashionable Highland Park. It was a big old place built in the 1920s and badly in need of repairs and a paint job, but the seller accepted a small down payment and gave us a second mortgage.

The kids were then sixteen, thirteen and eleven, and for them the house had two particularly appealing features: its own swimming pool—the first private pool ever built in Highland Park, we were told—and a fully equipped commercial-style soda fountain.

Scott and Diane adored it. John—well, John never showed much emotion about anything. Like the kids' car, for instance. In June the year we moved to Highland Park, Scott got his junior driver's license and approached me on the subject of transportation. Scott's point was well taken: Without a car in that neighborhood you were pretty much marooned. Together we researched second-hand cars and settled on a green '65 Mustang.

It was a delighted boy who drove his own automobile into the driveway with his younger sister dancing in excitement on the front steps. The understanding was that the Mustang was to pass to each child in turn on his sixteenth birthday. So John too had a personal stake in the car; yet I remembered that he hadn't even come out of the house to see it. He's only eleven, I'd reminded myself; driving probably seemed a long way off.

It was in that house on Beverly Drive that Jo Ann and I had our first worried talk about our third child. It wasn't even all that worried. Looking back now, of course, knowing what had happened three days before in Washington, every memory was magnified. At the time it seemed like a conversation any parents might have about any child.

"I think John feels very lonely at his new school," Jo Ann remarked at bedtime one evening. John was the only one whose schooling had been affected when we left University Park, since Scott and Diane were already in the senior and junior high schools that served the whole area. But John, going into sixth grade, had had to transfer away from Hyer Elementary where he'd made a name for himself in sports.

"No one ever comes home here after school with him either," Jo Ann went on, though the pool and the soda fountain had become a magnet for Scott's and Diane's friends.

"Give him time," I said. I was too tired by bedtime to listen to what seemed like trivial problems. It was a beautiful home, a fine school. John was like his mother—when he adjusted to the new surroundings he'd be perfectly all right. . . .

13

JO ANN:

The *Fasten Seat Belt* sign was on for Washington, the lights of the city glittering below. The security man turned to Jack and me: "Stay in your seats when the plane lands. We'll be the last ones off."

Passengers got up and rummaged for their things in the overhead bins, then inched forward toward the front. When the aisle had emptied the stewardess came back and opened the door in the tail of the aircraft. Stairs unfolded with a whirr and we walked down them, legs stiff after hours of sitting. We'd boarded the plane in Denver at 3:30; here in Washington it was eleven p.m.

What looked to me like a whole fleet of police cars were drawn up on the runway behind the plane. Jack and I climbed into the back of one of them, Dale Morris and the two Colorado security men into another, and our little caravan joined the stream of taillights speeding along the Potomac. Then we were on a bridge crossing the river, the Jefferson Memorial looming white and lovely on our left. I had been to Washington only once nearly thirty years before, on the first vacation Jack and I ever took.

The Washington Monument rose towering above us, floodlit and brilliant. The police escort swung left and suddenly there was the White House. Behind its stately fence it had a deserted look. The man who should be living there was in a hospital bed; the First Lady in an adjacent room at the George Washington University Hospital. And somehow at the root of all the pain and dislocation was our son John.

The police convoy sped up a broad avenue and pulled up at the Jefferson Hotel where a lady met us at the front door and led us directly to the elevators, bypassing the registration desk. As we rode up to the sixth floor she introduced herself as Rose Narva, the hotel manager.

The sixth floor corridor was filled with policemen in blue District of Columbia uniforms. Mrs. Narva led us to a corner suite overlooking a narrow alley at the rear of the hotel. There was a large living room, a bedroom for Dale and one for us, with a room for the two Colorado aides down the hall. An enormous bouquet of flowers, Mrs. Narva's own gracious welcome, greeted us in the living room.

From the phalanx of police out in the hall and the speed with which we'd been whisked through the lobby downstairs, leaving the hotel was clearly out of the question, so we ordered sandwiches sent up to the room. I hated even to think what this suite of rooms must be costing. I also knew Jack was determined to reimburse the State of Colorado for every penny it cost to send the two security men with us.

For now, though, my only concern was continuing on our way down to North Carolina to see John. But when would that be? A message from Mr. Fuller said that he and others from his law firm would come here to the hotel room in the morning, so our trip to the prison evidently wasn't scheduled before afternoon.

For another hour that night Jack and I sat up, looking back over John's junior and senior high school years, trying to remember everything the attorneys might want to know. "Didn't he seem happier," Jack asked, "after he got used to Highland Park?"

It was true. After that lonely sixth-grade year in a strange school, he'd entered junior high and found himself with many of the kids he'd been with since kindergarten. He was elected president of his seventh-grade homeroom; later he was chosen to manage the football team. I remembered how delighted Jack and I had been that this quiet, gentle boy was receiving recognition, like his more outgoing brother and sister.

"But he never really got involved in sports again," Jack recalled. "Not as a player."

That was true, too. Our second Christmas in the new home on Beverly Drive, Jack had given John a tennis outfit—racquet, shoes, shorts and shirt. I don't believe John ever took the things from the box.

But in general John seemed to get along fine in junior high. He never had large numbers of friends like Diane and Scott, but one of the fellows from his class would occasionally come home with him to use the pool. Or he'd go with a couple of others to a movie or a rock concert. He didn't seem to feel the need of great crowds of people around. "Which is O.K.," Jack and I would reassure each other. "We shouldn't expect all our children to be the same."

Thinking back, it was when these classmates began to date that John found himself increasingly alone. He was far too shy to ask a girl out. Maybe his complexion had something to do with it. He had no more than the normal crop of adolescent pimples, but he was constantly medicating his face and trying new products.

Whatever the reason, he increasingly spent the evenings upstairs in his room. I worried especially on weekend nights. "I hate to think of him up there alone," I'd say to Jack, "listening to those awful Beatles records."

We'd try to coax him downstairs to join us in the living room. When Bobby Fisher became an international celebrity, John began poring over chess books. Jack would often suggest a game in the evening; John always declined.

We tried not to worry about the lonely evenings, reminding ourselves that Scott too had been a "late bloomer" when it came to girls, doing very little dating, really, until he got to college. The lawyers were going to ask about the ways in which John had been different, but what constituted "different"? Almost every family I knew had someone like John in it, a little more solitary, a little more introverted than the rest. Wherever mothers gathered, we discussed two problems. The noncommunicative child and the baffling appeal of rock music. I worried about John as a teenager, but I didn't know any mother who didn't have worries equal to or greater than mine.

14

JACK:

A lack of *realism*. That's what concerned me about John as he reached senior high school, lack of any concept of what it took to get ahead in the real world. College, for instance. Scott was already at Vanderbilt University in Nashville. When Diane decided on Southern Methodist, I thought it might spark John into thinking about his own choice, just two years away.

"College isn't all that important for a musician," he said.

I wasn't going to get into that old argument again; he knew my opinion of rock music as a career. "O.K., John, but it can take years to get started in the music field. How are you going to support yourself in the meantime?"

Silence. John never gave me much of an argument, just waited out my pep talks. Or I'd try to get him to think realistically about his own field. "John, how are you going to make it as a performer when you can't even *read* music?"

"A lot of rock stars can't read music."

I resisted the temptation to say that their music sounded that way. "But John, knowing the basics of theory and harmony can't *hurt* a music career. Why don't you take some lessons? Get an informed opinion on how good you are."

John had never once played his guitar for his mother and me. Though he spent hours every day sequestered in his room doggedly plunking away, he was too bashful to perform even for the family. And this was the guy who was going to stand up in front of a vast audience and wow them with his music.

I know Jo Ann thought I was insensitive to John's feelings,

but actually I empathized with him more than she could ever know. Scott had finished Highland Park High School before John entered, but I knew what it was like to have a brilliant and popular older sister just ahead of you. Avilla outshone me at everything. A straight-A student, she was also a tall, blonde beauty: queen of Dartmouth College's winter carnival, featured in *Look* magazine.

Except that Diane was petite, like Jo Ann, she reminded me in many ways of Avilla. Diane was blonde, bright, bubbling—head cheerleader, vice-president of the school's popular mixed choir, Homecoming Queen nominee, member of the National Honor Society, voted by her classmates one of the "Four Favorite" senior girls. In high school John was fated to be "Diane's little brother," as I'd been Avilla's.

Perhaps that's why I did things with John I'd never done with the older two, taken him with me on trips, just the two of us. I remembered bringing him here to Washington one time when I had a business meeting, exploring the city together afterward on a tourmobile.

I hadn't been as strict with John, either. I'd been far more demanding with Scott, scolded him, spanked him a lot more often. By the third child I'd become less of a perfectionist. If it had been Scott in this terrible trouble, I'd be searching my conscience in agony now, wondering if my sternness, even occasional harshness, had been a factor. I hadn't been half as tough on John.

Didn't need to be. John was an obedient, well-behaved child—*subdued* was the word that came now to my mind. A conscientious child. I thought of the care he'd lavished on our two handsome alley cats, Hunk and Titter, feeding them, brushing their long orange fur until they looked like the aristocrats they definitely were not. About the only thing I ever recalled reprimanding John for was playing his phonograph too loud.

If I had any guilt about the kind of father I'd been for John, it was that I had failed to praise him when he did something well. But I hadn't praised Scott or Diane either. I'd never understood the importance of a father's praise—probably because I'd never experienced it. Never once could I recall Kib Brooks complimenting me. To any achievement his response was invariably: "That's O.K., Jack—but you can do better."

As his high school graduation approached and John still had made no move to apply to a college, Jo Ann and I requested some sessions with his guidance counselor. John, typically, was mostly silent during these interviews, but they did produce the name of a school. Texas Tech, the counselor told us, was well liked by the kids from Highland Park who went out there. It was not as competitive, perhaps, as a private school, but those who wanted to could get a top-notch education there in Lubbock.

"Why do I need to go to college?" John asked afterward.

"We've been over and over this, John," I said. "College is insurance. It doesn't mean giving up your music, just adding some basic business skills."

Total silence.

"And Lubbock isn't that far from Dallas," I went on. "You could get here to see Diane at SMU on weekends." I'd made up my mind to move our office from Dallas to Denver, as soon as John was out of Highland Park High School, and I knew John hated the idea of leaving Dallas as much as Jo Ann did.

It was curious. After having such a terrible time adjusting to the move from Oklahoma, Jo Ann now loved Dallas, while—except for a few close friends—I was sick of everything about it. The summer heat, the empty country-club lifestyle, what seemed to me to be a social-climbing, dollar-worshiping set of values—though I certainly had no other values to put in their place. I yearned for the cool beauty of the Colorado mountains.

"You say you don't want to leave Texas," I went on to John. "If you go to Texas Tech, you won't have to."

John was scratching Hunk under the chin. He didn't look up.

We had many similar discussions, if these monologues of mine could be called discussions. And in the end John reluctantly agreed to enter Texas Tech in the fall of 1973 as a Business Administration major. . . .

15

JO ANN:

Friday morning we had breakfast sent up to the suite in the Jefferson for us and Dale Morris. It was a shock, opening the door for the room waiter, to see policemen standing in the corridor and know they were there for us.

I bathed, dressed, and still there was an hour to wait before our lawyers arrived for this first face-to-face meeting. How grateful we were for Dale's suggestion that we start the day with prayer. Together we thanked God for the continuing recovering of the President and the other injured men. Jim Brady was miraculously still alive, and showing some improvement. We asked God to alleviate the pain of the victims, to comfort their families. For ourselves, we hardly knew what to ask, except for wisdom greater than our own in knowing how to help our son.

What a contrast between Jack and Dale! Dale's brown eyes above his black beard radiated peace. "That's in God's hands," he'd say when one of the enormous unknowns of our situation loomed before us. Jack's sapphire blue eyes, so concerned, so worried, were the eyes of a man who had taken the weight of this whole tragedy on his own shoulders.

Shortly after nine o'clock there was a knock at the hall doorway and we let into the suite four people who were to become tremendous figures in our lives. Stocky, powerfully built, dressed in a conservative pin-striped suit, Vince Fuller all but gave off sparks of energy and optimism. Behind him was a quiet-mannered, good-looking graduate of Yale law school, in his mid-thirties who introduced himself as Gregory Craig, and following Mr. Craig two still younger lawyers, a man and a woman both still in their twenties. We hardly took time to shake hands before we asked how soon we'd be leaving for North Carolina.

"Not till tomorrow morning, I'm afraid," Mr. Fuller said.

Tomorrow! I wanted to cry out. Why . . . that would be Saturday—and this awful thing had taken place on Monday! Five *days* before we could see our son! Mr. Fuller was explaining about prison procedures, the length of time required to process new arrivals, facts that made no sense at all to my impatient heart. Dale tactfully headed out to look up some Washington friends. Jack sent down for more coffee.

Then he and I began the review of John's life for the four lawyers. We described his uneventful childhood, his shyness around strangers—so like my own—his increasing loneliness as his friends began to date.

Young Mr. Craig looked up from his notepad. "So the first signs of trouble came in early adolescence?"

Trouble? "Absence of trouble" was nearer the truth. "My friends used to tell me how lucky I was," I told him. They were lying awake nights wondering whose car their children were driving around in. Whether they were drinking, taking drugs. "John never made us worry that way."

"But he did go to Texas Tech," Vince Fuller asked, "that fall after he graduated from high school?"

"Yes." First he'd come out to Denver with Jack and me, and helped us get settled in a little townhouse. Then Jack drove him to Lubbock in time for the fall semester.

"How did he feel about it?" Mr. Fuller wanted to know. "Was he excited? Scared? Resentful?"

Jack thought for a minute, running a hand through his thinning hair. "It was always hard to tell how John felt. He didn't express his emotions. I remember he was upset when he found out freshmen had to live in dormitories. He'd wanted his own place, off campus."

John had had a succession of roommates that first year, and complained about all of them. One studied late at night. Another was black; John had never been around people of other races. Another roommate was "too countrified."

Listening to John's constant dissatisfaction each time he

55

phoned home certainly hadn't helped me with my adjustment to my own new surroundings. As the lawyers' questions continued, my mind went back to that tiny townhouse in Denver that first bitter-cold, windy winter, with Jack trying to conceal from me the seriousness of his business crisis.

The previous April, with our house in Highland Park sold, and the transfer of Jack's business headquarters to Denver all set up, the New York firm raising his drilling capital went bankrupt. This was Jack's third attempt to launch a firm of his own—and for three years it had seemed to go well. Now he was left with a mountain of obligations and no way to meet them.

So the move to Denver in August 1973, which I had been dreading in any case, took place in an atmosphere of terrible tension. In September John left for Texas Tech. Scott had finished college and was working on offshore oil drilling rigs in far-off Indonesia. Diane was still at SMU in Dallas.

Jack and I were alone and he was working late every night in a desperate struggle to keep his doors open. Tension for Jack invariably settled in his back. That fall it was so bad he could not stand up without holding the back of a chair, straightening slowly like an old man. No wonder he was often impatient and irritable. I couldn't burden him with my own anxieties, and I had no one else to talk to.

There was even a crisis with one of the cats. Hunk and Titter were past middle age now, perhaps ten years old, and in October I noticed that Hunk was having difficulty breathing. I located a vet in the Denver phone directory. The doctor diagnosed cancer; nothing could be done except to try to keep the old cat as comfortable as possible.

On his weekly telephone call home from Texas Tech, Hunk's health was always the first thing John asked about. When he came to Denver for Thanksgiving, he rushed first to the cat, asleep in a corner of the townhouse living room. "Hello, old Hunk Dory," John said, stroking the thick orange hair. Hunk raised his head, got painfully to his feet and yawned—the first time I'd seen him do that in a month.

John's presence was like a tonic to the ailing animal. All weekend John held Hunk in his lap. Sunday we put an unenthusiastic son on the plane back for Lubbock. Early Monday morning Jack went into the living room to find poor old Hunk dead on the cushion John had placed on the floor for him. It was almost as though the old cat had stayed alive to say goodbye to his best friend.

I couldn't bring myself to telephone John knowing how upset he would be, so I wrote a letter instead, breaking the news as gently as possible. When John phoned home next, however, his reaction was . . . actually there wasn't any reaction. I was amazed: he'd doted so on that big alley cat. I was the one who finally brought it up: "I'm so sorry about Hunk, dear." There was a moment's silence. "Yeah . . ." he said at last.

The big excitement that Christmas was Diane's engagement. Big, handsome Steve Sims was a football player at SMU. He and Diane made a striking couple, Steve dark-haired, broad-shouldered, six-feet-four; Diane so blonde and barely five feet tall. Steve was graduating in May: They wanted to be married in Dallas right after graduation, before their SMU classmates dispersed.

Jack insisted we go ahead and plan the wedding Diane had dreamed of, financial crisis or no. The wedding would be at St. Michael And All Angels Episcopal Church, where Jack had been a vestryman and usher and I'd been on the Altar Guild. Diane decided on eight attendants in spring pastels, and eight ushers in black tails and white gloves, including John, and Scott who would be flying in from Asia.

In the flurry of excited telephone calls between Diane and me, there was the regular weekly phone visit with John. Invariably the news from Lubbock was negative. John had arrived late for registration after Christmas to find all the good second semester classes filled. A few weeks later he'd had to drop a course, bringing his already-low total of twelve hours down to only nine.

"What was the trouble?" Jack wanted to know.

Nothing really. John had just fallen behind in his assignments. He felt it would be better to get a "W" for withdrawing than an "F" for failing.

I remember that there were some heartfelt words between Jack and John over the importance of effort. The words, actually, were mostly from Jack's side. Remembering his own first year at Oklahoma—a year younger than John—taking his final semester of high school and two years of college-level engineering simultaneously, Jack had trouble comprehending how anyone could find twelve hours of courses burdensome.

57

John's relief at being back in Dallas was touching to see—even though for the wedding he had to part with T-shirt and jeans long enough to appear in rented black tie and tails. His freshman year at Tech was over, and we were not surprised, when the wedding festivities ended, to hear him announce that he was staying in Dallas for the summer rather than returning with Jack and me to Colorado. He found a job at Gordo's pizza place and a furnished room nearby. Clearing tables and sweeping floors wasn't an awfully challenging job, but Jack and I were pleased at John's initiative in landing it.

Every day that summer of '74 Jack and I were making the long drive up the eastern wall of the Front Range from Denver to Evergreen, to oversee the building of our new home. We'd brought with us the crystal chandelier that had come with the house on Beverly Drive, to hang in the new dining room. For the living room I bought a new brown armchair for Jack, two smaller ones for the other side of the fireplace, a sofa in a patchwork of browns and rusts to go between them.

To me, however, the focal point of the house were the three large portrait-photos I'd had made at Neiman-Marcus in Dallas when each child was eighteen. I was so proud of all three! Dark-haired Scott leaned casually against a desk, hand in the pocket of a navy blue business suit. Diane, ash-blonde hair falling below her shoulders, held her hands in the lap of a long white dress. John, uncharacteristically formal in a brown suit, stood beside a globe of the world, the wood of the studio backdrop bringing out the deep honey-blond of his hair.

How fortunate Jack and I had been, I thought; through all the turmoil of the 1960s to have never a moment's anxiety about any of them. All three out of the nest now, the child-raising years behind us. I had the builder construct three free-standing panels along one side of the living room where those portraits could smile at us each time we entered the room.

On Labor Day 1974, just a little over a year after we moved to Colorado, our dream house was finished. We left the tiny townhouse in Denver and moved up the mountainside to Evergreen. In spite of Jack's continuing business struggle, it was a time of achievement for us both—a long way away from that drafty mule barn in St. Elmo 28 years before.

Only one thing cast its shadow over moving day. Two weeks

earlier John had called from Dallas to say he'd decided not to return to Texas Tech for his sophomore year that fall.

"What in the world do you intend doing?" Jack had exploded.

He intended, it seemed, to go on working at Gordo's.

"The rest of your life?" Jack pressed him. "That's the kind of job you'll be stuck with, you know, without a college education."

I hated these arguments over the phone—these lectures of Jack's, more accurately. "Is it the school?" he asked John. "Do you want to transfer somewhere else?"

No, Texas Tech was O.K. It was just that he thought he'd stay on in Dallas for a while. Nothing we said could change his mind. John had turned nineteen four days after Diane's wedding—old enough to work instead of going to school if he chose to.

"You'll see," I tried to soothe Jack. "He'll go back to college after he's had a little time on his own." The sons of a number of my friends had dropped out for a while. "He'll get more out of school in a year or so."

Jack was not convinced. "This is a competitive world. If you don't stay with it you get left behind."

16

JACK:

Staying with it. . . . That summed up everything my experience in business had taught me. I remembered all through John's high school years how I'd kept traveling to New York, trying to raise drilling money. I'd check into some cheap uptown hotel and learn the subway route to Wall Street. There, I'd change a five dollar bill for a roll of dimes and stand in a telephone booth hour after hour, dialing every stock brokerage house listed in the Yellow Pages. Perhaps one call in twenty resulted in a face-to-face interview and a chance to present my proposition. Then I'd return to my two-foot square "office" and continue the routine.

It was years before a New York brokerage firm at last agreed to raise the money I needed—the same firm whose bankruptcy three years later precipitated the crisis the year we moved to Colorado. If I'd ever had any doubts about the importance of staying ability, those first two years in Denver ended them. Twenty times over, Vanderbilt Resources would have failed if Arnold Nass in the Dallas office, and Ivonne Ellison, my administrative assistant at the new headquarters, had not been as determined as I was to save it. We'd been forced to sell our best assets, fire other employees who'd become close personal friends, plead with creditors, claw and scratch just to keep out of bankruptcy ourselves. Many mornings when I drove to my office I wasn't sure I'd still have a company by the end of the day.

And here was John, dropping out of school because there were a couple things he didn't like about it. . . .

"But he did go back?" Greg Craig's question brought me back to the living room on the sixth floor of the Jefferson Hotel where four lawyers were following the family's history. "John did eventually return to Texas Tech?"

"Yes. He stayed out just the fall semester." Maybe the boredom of the pizza job or the realities of minimum-wage living finally got through to him. At any rate, when John joined us for Christmas 1974, the first in our new home in Evergreen, he announced that he intended to return to Lubbock in January.

Jo Ann and I were delighted. "You'll enjoy it much more now that you're a sophomore and can room by yourself," Jo Ann told him.

Sure enough, soon after reaching Lubbock, John phoned to say he'd found an off-campus apartment. A few weeks later a letter came to say that he was playing some tennis. To me, that was even better news. It just wasn't healthy for a young man to sit around as much as John did. I even indulged in a little fatherly self-congratulation: Maybe that gift of a tennis racket, so many Christmases before, had planted a seed of interest after all.

On a Sunday telephone call in late February, however, he mentioned that he'd had to drop an accounting course. It seemed he'd had to leave the lecture room several days running.

"What was the trouble?"

"I felt dizzy and my arm hurt. Pains all the way down my writing arm. I'm going to have to give up tennis, too."

"Have you seen a doctor?" Jo Ann wanted to know.

No, the arm was all right as long as he didn't use it too much.

That spring, 1975, I reached a major decision with the business. Our difficulty had never been in knowing how to find oil and gas; the problem was always lack of money. There was one standard, obvious way to get the operating funds we needed: Bring in public shareholders. This meant first of all preparing the mountain of documents required by the Securities and Exchange Commission—the most demanding, time-consuming project we had yet attempted.

At the end of May, with a year and a half of college now behind him, John wrote that he was returning to Dallas to take a summer job again at the pizza joint. On May 29, John turned twenty; a week later was my own fiftieth birthday. To celebrate, Jo Ann and I went for a week's vacation to Hawaii.

And along with me in my suitcase came a book: *Mere Christianity* by C. S. Lewis. A stranger choice for reading on a romantic tropical island would be hard to imagine. But try as I would I could not escape the tugging of that book. Something strange was happening to me, something I didn't understand at all. After 25 years as a faithful Episcopalian—vestryman and weekly communicant, churchgoing had suddenly lost its appeal. It wasn't just the Episcopal church. I shopped around at others in the Evergreen area and failed to find the mysterious something that I was looking for at any of them. Even the "Hunger Task Force" which our diocese had launched, though I'd taken an active personal part in it, failed to touch some need inside me.

Then in the *Reader's Digest* I came upon a reprint from *Mere Christianity*. It was an excerpt from the chapter on "Pride"

61

and almost every sentence seemed to ring home. Actually, the book was on our own shelves; my sister, Avilla, had given it to me years before, and I had read it then without excitement. This time, the power in its pages literally transfixed me; I carried it everywhere with me; compelled by Lewis' logic, terrified by where it led. Could a person *really* do what Lewis described: Surrender himself and everything he had to God? I knew *I* couldn't, and yet I couldn't put the book aside and so I lugged it along on our holiday in Hawaii.

How, I wondered, did you go about taking your hands off the controls of your life—and the lives of those you cared for? Diane's husband, Steve, for example, that great loving bear of a man, with a mind as quick as his smile, how could I "turn him over" to God without doing everything in my power to see him get ahead? In the year since their marriage he'd been knocking himself out trying to sell commercial real estate in the middle of a recession, working at night waiting tables in a restaurant. Steve could go straight to the top if he got into the right field at the beginning of his career.

With his salesman's skills, it seemed to me, that field was insurance. My mind began running down my contacts in that profession, people I could put Steve in touch with. That's how it went all through that fiftieth birthday trip: reading about a life of trust and surrender, closing the book to figure the best ways of getting ahead.

And of course, once back in Colorado, the Securities and Exchange prospectus consumed me entirely. The government requirement of "total disclosure" meant months of meetings, phone calls and correspondence, and all the skills of Arnold Nass, Ivonne Ellison and our Dallas lawyer, Joe Bates. Amid the clattering typewriters at Vanderbilt, Lewis' sublime propositions in *Mere Christianity* seemed mere daydreams.

All that summer John phoned us faithfully every Sunday night from Dallas; he'd rented a one-room efficiency near the pizza place and seemed contented enough, but I worried that he hadn't even tried to find better-paying work. The job at Gordo's didn't even cover his living expenses; we had to continue his allowance through June, July and August. It wasn't the money I minded. It was just that I remembered how Scott, every summer while he was in college, had knocked himself out to earn money ahead for the school year. He'd worked on road crews around Dallas—the highest paying work around—backbreaking labor in the brutal Texas sun, fiercely determined to earn his own way as soon as he could.

With the end of August I found myself growing tense as we waited for John's Sunday night call, fearing he'd announce as he had last year that he wasn't returning to school in September. But John returned to Lubbock on schedule for the fall semester and Jo Ann and I drew a sigh of relief.

It was a good fall all around. Steve had taken my fatherly advice with good grace and was applying at insurance firms in Dallas. Scott was back from his third trip around the world, having worked on off-shore drilling rigs from Scotland to Singapore. The large firm he worked for had assigned him to company headquarters in Houston—but I, meanwhile, was edging closer to the dream I'd scarcely admitted to myself. The dream of having one of my sons join me in business. I'd never mentioned it to either of them, but maybe because I'd never known my own father, it was the greatest thing I could imagine. John had made his distaste for the world of business pretty clear. But if we ever got the go-ahead from the SEC, and if we grew as I then expected we would, maybe it would be time to approach Scott.

With the money he'd saved on his off-shore jobs, Scott had bought himself a new car. He telephoned that fall, 1975, to say he'd been to visit John in Lubbock and promised him his old car, a snappy-looking red Camaro that had originally been mine. "I'm going to put four new tires on it first, and get some work done on the engine. It's five years old and—well, you know John and cars."

John's indifference to anything mechanical was a constant source of amazement to Scott and me, both mechanical engineers. When the green Mustang had passed from Diane to John, he'd mostly left it sitting in the driveway on Beverly Drive, leaving it to me to take care of repairs and maintenance, until finally I'd gotten rid of it. I was touched that Scott would spend several hundred dollars of his own money to see that his younger brother had transportation.

John drove the Camaro to Denver for Christmas that year, the second in our Evergreen home. We'd become close friends with our next-door neighbors, Bill and Sue Sells. It was a mountain tradition to make your own permanent Christmas wreath out of the big Ponderosa pine cones. Bill drilled holes for toothpicks in hundreds of them, Jo Ann and Sue put the wreath together, on the wheel of styrofoam I had mounted on a plywood backing. The finished wreath, over five feet in diameter, was a knockout against the natural moss rock of the fireplace wall.

Why couldn't the whole season be this way, I wondered, everyone working together. Instead, as Christmas approached each year, Jo Ann drove herself to exhaustion cooking and baking, sending out hundreds of cards, wrapping scores of gifts. "Why don't we skip gifts in the family?" I'd suggest. The same for the elaborate Christmas dinner: "We'd rather have hot dogs and have you with us in the living room."

But because her mother had done it that way there had to be turkey and dressing, six vegetables and two kinds of pie. John played Santa Claus that year as always, passing out the packages heaped beneath the tree. I couldn't remember when I'd assigned that role to him, but it was many years before, when I first began to notice that, unless given some such part in the activities, he'd hang back, leaving the limelight to his brother and sister.

Most of his Christmas vacation that year, I was spending ten- and twelve-hour days at the office. In the evenings, though, I noticed that whenever neighbors dropped by, John would bolt down the stairs to his room. "I didn't know those people," he'd explain next morning.

"Well, if you'd hang around, you'd get to know them. You'll never make friends sitting down in your room."

He wanted to switch to the Liberal Arts program at Tech. But a Liberal Arts degree, I pointed out, wouldn't mean very much at a job interview.

By December 31, the requirements for the Securities and Exchange Commission were complete at last. On January 1, 1976, Vanderbilt became a publicly owned company. We were a minuscule operation in the mega-business world of oil, but now that we could sell our stock to the public, the sky was the limit.

Scott had agreed to come with the new company, Steve had accepted a sales job with a Dallas insurance firm. John had agreed to stay with Business Administration at least another semester. The year 1976 was going to be great.

17

JO ANN:

I was almost as nervous as John, as he backed his red Camaro out of the far side of our three-car garage in early January and crept up the steep driveway en route back to Lubbock. We'd had a snowfall the day he was due to return to school and he'd stayed two extra days until the roads were clear. John hated winter driving as much as I did.

He arrived safely but the delay over the snow storm made him late for registration: once again it seemed that all the good courses were filled . . . Jack hit the ceiling when I reported this.

"I know, dear, but it wasn't his fault that he was late getting back."

With each phone call the rest of that winter, tension seemed to build between Jack and John—tension that passed in turn to Jack and me. In March John informed us that once again he'd dropped a class rather than receive a failing grade. Jack dressed him down over the phone while I tried to explain to John that it was actually his father's pride in him that was speaking: Jack simply wanted him to live up to his potential.

"Maybe," I suggested to Jack that night at dinner, "you shouldn't have held out for the business courses. If John hates those subjects, how can he do his best?"

Even as I spoke the words, I saw the hurt in Jack's blue eyes. "Why is it always my fault?" he asked. "Why don't you blame John just once!"

Neither of us was hungry after that.

Jack was opening a division office in Houston; he planned to go there by car one time in April, so that I could go along and we could stop off to see John. I started setting aside some odds and ends for his apartment—dishes, a throw rug.

One unusually warm noontime early in the month I walked up the driveway and crossed Brookline Road to our rural mailbox. Sue Sells was out, too, sweeping the last of the old snow from their brick walk.

"Hi, Sue!" I called down from the street. "You don't even have enough there for a snow man!"

Most of us in Evergreen were new to the mountains and could never get used to snow that lingered so late. In the mailbox, along with the usual bills and department store specials, was a letter from John. I was relieved: He'd missed his customary phone call on Sunday.

Back in the living room I settled down on the patchwork sofa and hurried through the rest of the mail. I always saved letters from the children for last, so I could dwell a little longer on them.

The first rays of the afternoon sun were streaming through the tall south windows, highlighting the enormous Christmas wreath over the fireplace. We'd meant to take it down after the holidays, but it was so big we couldn't find any place to store it.

John's letter was written as usual on ruled school note paper.

"Dear Mom and Dad,
    By the time you receive this letter I will no longer be in Lubbock. I have dropped out of school. I know you'll never understand, but I'm too miserable here to take it any longer. I honestly won't blame you if you get mad and cut me off . . . I'm sorry I'm doing this to you . . . I only hope someday I can make you proud of me."

No forwarding address, no hint as to where he planned to go, what he planned to do. I looked at my watch—maybe there was still time to catch Jack before he left the office for lunch. "Jack and Scott just stepped out," the receptionist told me. "Let me see if I can catch them at the elevator."

In a moment Jack's voice was on the line. "Oh Jack!" I said, forgetting all the gentle ways I'd planned to break the

66

news, "John's left school and he doesn't say where he's gone."

Of course there was nothing Jack could do, except spend an anxious day. Why couldn't I have waited until evening to tell him, I berated myself. Why did I handle every crisis by running to him?

That night we telephoned Diane and Steve in Dallas, on the faint hope that John might have gone there, but they were as surprised at the news as we. We talked with the manager of the apartment building in Lubbock who confirmed that John had moved out a few days earlier, but could tell us nothing more. No, he didn't know any tenants with whom John had been friendly.

School authorities knew nothing either. And so all we could do was wait . . . a day. Two days. A week, then two weeks. Every time the phone rang, every time the mail truck stopped at our box, my heart stood still.

Scott thought we should notify the police: "There can't be that many 1970 red Camaros with Texas plates."

But John was almost 21. He was not a child. In leaving school he'd done nothing illegal. It was a bid for independence, Jack and I told each other over and over. If we called in the police, it would announce to him and the world that we didn't trust him.

If he couldn't handle school for the present, that was O.K.—that's what we longed to tell him. Why had he thought he had to go off in secret, automatically assuming we wouldn't understand?

When the weeks stretched into a month, Diane joined Scott in urging us to notify the authorities—if not the police, then the Missing Persons Bureau. Jack concurred. It was I, strangely, who held out for waiting a little longer. It was May now: Mother's Day was two weeks off. Since the first Mother's Day creation he had made for me in kindergarten, John had never failed to remember the occasion. Wherever he was, he would not forget.

As the date drew closer, my daily vigil at the mailbox grew more agitated. And then one noon, three days before Mother's Day, six weeks since that devastating letter, there was John's handwriting on a large white envelope. I tore it open right up there on the street.

FOR YOU, MOM was printed above a contrite and apprehensive looking skunk.

> At times I've been a STINKER
> In fact a PEST indeed—

I didn't bother to finish the printed greeting, but turned the card over. On the back was a three-paragraph note:

Dear Mom and Dad,

   I hope this card finds you both well and in good spirits, despite your impossible younger son. I've taken a cozy, inexpensive apartment in Hollywood, Ca. I live about 3 blocks away from the famous Hollywood & Vine corner and two blocks away from Sunset Strip. I was very lucky to find such a location because I am within easy walking distance of about 30 of the most famous music publishers in the world. I'm trying to sell some of my songs. I've got two appointments next week to see music publishers. I've also met a guy who wants to start a group with me. But with my limited funds, I don't know if I'll be able to or not.

   I hope you're not too disappointed in me for dropping out of school so suddenly without any notice or anything. I *do* feel bad about being so inconsiderate. But one thing which is very important to me is the fact that for the first time in years I am happy.

   Isn't being happy the most important thing in life? And since I'm happy, I hope it makes you happy or at least tolerant of my actions.

> Love,
> John

I read it through tears of relief, then read it again, then ran down to the house to telephone Jack. There was no return address on the envelope, only a Los Angeles postmark. But John was alive, and pursuing his dreams. Of course his happiness made us happy!

Our only disappointment was that he continued to exclude us from his new life. We longed to send *him* a card on his 21st birthday, May 29, perhaps to enclose some cash, which he apparently needed. We wondered what he was living on, since he didn't mention a job.

After the Mother's Day card, more news-less weeks passed. Once more I found myself haunting the mailbox.

"He wouldn't be impossible to find," Jack pointed out the second week in June, as we discussed once more the advisability of flying out there. "Three blocks from Hollywood & Vine and two from Sunset Strip—how many apartments can there be in that area?" And yet . . . the unwritten message on the card, both of us felt, had been: *Leave me alone for a while. This is something I need to do all by myself.*

At four o'clock on Saturday, June 12, the mail truck pulled up to our box. Jack was showering after eighteen holes of golf. I hurried up the driveway—and there in the mailbox it was. A five-page letter from John! And on the last page, in all-caps, an address, at long last. But . . . what was this written above it: "my address was. . . ."

Was?

Hastily I skimmed the first page ". . . I am in trouble . . . without food . . . someone broke into my room—stole my possessions. . . ."

I ran down the driveway. Sitting together on the side of our bed, Jack and I read the letter:

Dear Mom and Dad,

Through a series of sorry circumstances, I am in trouble. For the past 2½ weeks I have literally been without food, shelter, & clothing. On May 14, someone broke into my room and stole almost all of my possessions. (My clothing, my suitcase, my guitar, some cash, even my razor.) I was out at a music studio attending a music class, and when I returned, everything was gone.

May 14 . . . just after he had sent the Mother's Day card, then. . . .

With some money that was hidden under the bed I was able to stay another week in my apt. but since May 21, I have been homeless. I've been too proud and embarrassed to contact you until now, but I'm forced to, because it's beginning to get out of hand. You don't know how badly I wanted to make it on my own, but this is ridiculous. I'm becoming an absolute physical wreck.

The only possessions I now have are 4 shirts and 1 pair of pants & a pair of shoes. I carry them around in a pillowcase. At night I have to sleep on picnic benches and the ground. The last two nights I've been sleeping on the roof of an apartment building. This sounds like something out of a B movie, but I swear to God it is the nightmarish truth. Your son, for the past 2½ weeks has had to walk up to strangers and ask them for spare change, so I can eat.

Although physically I am being ravaged, my spirit has not yet been broken. I honestly feel that I could achieve success here, if I only had half a chance. In the past 2 months I've had two important appointments: one with a record manager at MGM Records, and one with a record producer at United Artists records. I played them some tapes of some of my songs. The producer at United Artists was very impressed with one in particular. He replayed it 4 different times, bringing in different people to listen to it. He wants to take my song and get professional musicians to record it for a demo tape. I could not just hand over my song to him, though, because I have not yet had it copyrighted. I was in the process of going through the copyrighting procedures when I got robbed.

What I'm trying to make clear to you is this: Even though I'm sleeping on an apt. house roof and eating one meal every other day and haven't had a bath in 3 weeks, I'm still in good spirits because I honestly believe there are great possibilities here. I've never had a feeling like this before.

I realize that many of my actions in the past few months have been inconsiderate and certainly don't warrant your helping me out, but I can't emphasize to you enough how badly I want to stay here and try to become someone you can be proud of.

I'm now 21 and I believe that these next few months and year will be the most crucial in my life. You don't know how grateful I would be if you could give me limited financial support and a great deal of moral support during this critical period.

I know it's asking a lot after the way I've treated you, but please help me out.

70

You can write me at my old address, because I'm going to the Post Office and fill out one of those cards telling them to hold my mail there. Even though it might be risky, please send cash. No bank in this city will cash a check for me now. One important lesson that I've learned from this mess is that as soon as I can get my feet back on the ground, I am going to get another steady job, just so I'll always have some cash handy. I've learned the hard way that a steady job is a *thousand* times better than roaming the streets with these hunger pains.

On the other hand, if you feel that being robbed is just what I deserve for the way I've acted, I'll try to understand.

> Love,
> John

Then followed the old address. I was in tears long before this final page. Frightened too. This very minute John was sitting hungry on a park bench, his belongings beside him in a pillowcase. . . .

What could we do, a thousand miles away? After waiting over two months to have an address for him, now this cry for help arrived on a Saturday afternoon when the post office, bank—everything—was closed until Monday morning.

"And we still don't really have an address," Jack pointed out. "Even if we could scrape together some cash, whatever we have in the house, maybe ask the Sells—how can we mail it off to some former apartment number on the chance that the post office will hold it for him?"

He was dressing hurriedly as we talked, though what we were to hurry and *do* we hadn't yet figured out. "Why didn't he phone us?" Jack kept asking. "He could certainly get hold of a dime and reverse the charges."

Then Jack thought of the 7-Eleven. "Don't they sell money orders?" He gunned the car up the drive while I sat down and tried to compose a coherent letter to send with whatever Jack managed to get. *Telephone when you get this,* I wrote at the top of the page.

I told him how sorry we were about the robbery, and tried to reassure him that we were not down on him because he'd left school—only distressed that we hadn't known where he was for so long. "You never gave us a chance to encourage you in your new venture, which is what Daddy and I both want to do."

I heard the automatic garage door open and ran to see what luck Jack had had. "Got the money order!" he said. A hundred and ninety-five dollars was the largest amount they would write. "I'm going to send a twenty-dollar bill along with it," Jack said, "in case he has trouble cashing it. If he'd only called—we could wire money through Western Union."

I scribbled a hasty close to my letter and Jack took off for a neighboring town where he thought the post office had a late Saturday pickup. While he was gone I wrote John again, in case our first letter didn't reach him. I said all the same things, urged him again to call the minute he received it, and stuffed into the second envelope all the bills I had in my purse.

We took the second letter to the post office in Evergreen and once more settled into the dull ache of waiting. Sunday . . . Monday . . . "When's the soonest he could get the letters?" I kept asking Jack. My worst fears had proved terrifyingly true: sleeping on rooftops, begging money for food, prey to who knew what kind of twisted individuals who take advantage of homeless young people. I couldn't understand why he didn't sleep in the Camaro instead of on a park bench. "Maybe he feels safer out in the open," Jack thought. "Or maybe he sold it to get cash. But then he could pay the rent, buy clothes, everything. The new tires Scott put on it are worth that much."

Jack tended to be more positive about the crisis—or pretended to be for my sake. "This may be just the shock it took to make a realist out of him. Look what he wrote about finding a job."

John's call came on Tuesday evening. Jack picked up the phone from his armchair by the fireplace, I from the wall in the kitchen. The operator hardly got out the words, "Would you accept a collect—," before we were both saying, "Yes, we will, operator!"

We hadn't heard John's voice since early April, and here it was mid-June. We all talked at once. "Where are you calling from?" Jack wanted to know, and "Have you eaten something, dear?" I asked.

John was calling from a phone booth outside a McDonald's

where he'd just eaten. He had received both letters. Sure enough, as Jack feared, they had not been held at the post office, but left in the hallway outside his old room, where he'd gone back daily to look.

"Wouldn't you have been better off in the car than on a rooftop?" I asked.

"Car? Oh you mean the Camaro. I don't have it any more."

"What do you mean?" Jack asked.

At the kitchen phone I bit my lip. I'd hoped that—after so long—Jack wouldn't let himself get exasperated.

It seemed that John had sold the Camaro back in Lubbock. That was where the plane fare to Los Angeles had come from—with enough left over to live on for several weeks.

"Why in the name of heaven didn't you *drive* to California?" his father asked. "Then sell the car out there, if you were going to. You can get a lot more for an automobile out on the coast."

Of course Jack was right, but why bring it up, I thought, since the thing was already done? As we hung up the phones that Tuesday night, with John promising to keep in touch, I had the feeling that we understood one another no better than before.

18

JACK:

Jo Ann felt that I overreacted about the Camaro, but my reaction was mild compared to Scott's. Having put so much of himself into getting the car ready for John, he was appalled that John would sell it without a word to him. "You know John and money. I'll bet some dealer paid him about half what it was worth.''

But we were in touch! Actually, I was tremendously proud of John. Rock music wouldn't have been the field I would have picked for him, but it was the one he wanted and he was going all-out for it. Hang in there, John! I found myself cheering.

We began getting regular letters from Los Angeles, just as we had from Texas Tech, with the enormous difference that John sounded enthusiastic. About the music anyhow. His efforts to find a job continued to be frustrating:

June 25, 1976

Dear Mom & Dad,

I am writing this letter on a Friday afternoon, after a long day of job hunting. I am really beginning to get discouraged. In the past week, I have been to well over 100 restaurants, supermarkets, record stores etc. looking for work. . . .

On the brighter side, a few days ago I had an appointment with the producer at United Artists. He seems to be quite interested in me and my career. . . . He's about Scott's age and he is very knowledgeable about the music business. . . . He pointed out that the songs I write seem to be perfectly suited for duos. I never really thought about it, but he is right. He thinks it would be a good idea if I found someone else who played guitar and sang harmony, and form a duo. . . .

He also seems to feel that loud rock bands have had their day, and are on the way out.

Hooray! I greeted this information.

And of course if I tried to go solo, I wouldn't stand a chance. Again, I agree.

Hooray once more! Obviously John had been able to hear from this United Artists fellow what he could never have accepted from me.

He explained to me that since I have so little actual experience, I need to form a duo and start performing. But what made me feel the most optimistic about this

74

whole project is that he said he would like to manage and produce me and my future partner.

I told him that if I began this project I would have to forego getting a job for a while because of the time problem. He then told me that within two months I would be making more money than I would ever see working a 9 to 5 job. Now, I'm trying to be realistic about this. I know just because he says I'll be earning lots of money doesn't mean it will positively happen. This is the basis of my dilemma. Should I go all out and give everything I've got toward this project, or should I pass it up and keep looking for a job. I'm just scared if I pass it up I'll never have such a good chance again.

I would appreciate your thoughts on this important subject. Please keep in mind, the only reason I'm out here in Hollywood is to try and attain some success with my music and this could be a golden opportunity I've been looking for.

Write soon.

Love,
John

We'd written back, of course, enclosing more money and congratulating him on the interest expressed at United Artists. I reminded him, though, of his resolve, those hungry days after the robbery, never to be without a steady income. He telephoned soon afterward to say he'd taken a job going door to door for a photography studio, offering coupons for portraits at half-price. My heart went out to him, remembering how I'd hated knocking on doors cold turkey. Once more I admired his stick-it-out spirit.

Jo Ann was especially delighted by a piece of news in mid-July. John had a girlfriend. "I met her in a laundromat," he told us over the phone, his voice squeaky with excitement. Jo Ann and I exchanged winks: That was John all right. He might be down to his last quarter, but it would go to keep his clothes clean. Apparently they'd started talking as their things whirled around in adjacent dryers. She was a young actress named Lynn Collins.

Every call home from then on was filled with Lynn. Her California sojourn, apparently, was a college graduation gift from her family. They were quite well off, we gathered. "And they're behind her career all the way."

On August 14 he wrote,

Tomorrow, Sunday, I am going with Lynn and a male friend of mine to his brother's beach house at Malibu. . . . I've always heard how nice it is at Malibu Beach, so I couldn't turn down an invitation like this.

Later, John phoned to tell us the day had been all that he hoped. The better he got to know Lynn the more he liked her. "She seems to care about my career as much as her own."

He was still hoping, he wrote, for something to come of the United Artists contact:

Good news! Next Wednesday I'm going into the studio to cut a professional demo of 2 or 3 of my songs. The fellow at United Artists that I have been associating with has been promoted to another position so I'm now working with new people. . . . At first the record manager didn't want to put up the money. I told him I had a verbal agreement, and he said he would get back to me.

After the songs are recorded I will try, with their help, to place them with a publishing company. . . . After that the public demand for my songs will be so incredible, I will be paid $100,000 in royalties and I can then retire to a mansion in Beverly Hills.

I was glad to see that John was able to laugh at himself in the midst of studio run-arounds. But while he joked about future fortunes, his present finances were ceasing to be a laughing matter. For two months now, since he'd supplied us an address in mid-June, Jo Ann and I had been sending him a weekly survival sum, with the understanding that at the same time he was to hold down at least a part-time job.

Now, as far as I could figure out, he wasn't working at all. The photo-coupon job hadn't paid enough to be worth his while. "For all the work I was doing," he'd written in early August, "I made $1.00 an hour. That's ridiculous."

I heartily agreed. But he'd said nothing since then about looking for an alternative, better-paying job. Was it good for him, I worried, for us to keep sending money month after month, with him supplying nothing?

Toward the end of August a member of my board of directors happened to mention a friend of his out in California who manufactured school jewelry—class rings, fraternity pins, that sort of thing—and who was looking for salesmen. I got excited. John could sell to kids his own age, work weekends if he had rehearsals or auditions during the week. I asked my friend to put in a good word for John.

At home I shut myself in my study to compose what I knew would be a difficult letter to my son. I wanted John to know that his mother and I were behind him on his choice of career, every bit as much as Lynn's folks were behind hers. The first thing we'd done, after we learned about the robbery, was send money for another guitar. That ought to tell him, better than words, where our hearts were.

We felt it was time, though, I wrote, for him to work harder at becoming self-supporting. I pointed out that summer was nearly over; many young people would be going back to school, which should mean that jobs would open up. I proposed three more months of the present arrangement, after which we'd hope that he'd be earning his own way. "Now don't worry about starving to death," I reassured him, "because we obviously won't let that happen." I told him about the jewelry-selling job and asked him to follow through.

John didn't have much to say about my letter when he phoned next. He'd called the jewelry manufacturer as I requested, and informed the man that he was already working—though he was vague about the nature of his job. Then came a letter dated September 2, 1976:

Dear Mom & Dad,

I'm telling you, when it rains, it pours. Since I talked to you Tuesday night I have had nothing but trouble.

#1 After I got through talking to you, I got in our elevator to go back up to my room and guess what? The elevator got stuck inbetween floors. I pushed the alarm button for 20 minutes before anyone responded. In all, I was stuck in that stupid elevator for 2 hours. I'm glad I don't have claustrophobia.

#2 While at work Wednesday, I began having severe eye sting attacks. I'm sure this L.A. smog is the reason.

I've had to quit work early both yesterday and today because of the problem.

#3 Today I went to the United Artists people and they told me quite coldly that my songs would have to be put on a waiting list. That ticks me off. The last time I talked to them they were optimistic and now they act as if they couldn't care less.

#4 Last night as I was walking home from Lynn's this old pathetic wino kept following me and finally he grabbed my arm. I elbowed him in his stomach and made a quick exit, fearing he might pull a gun on me or something.

Ah! but there's more.

#5 If I had been in a normal mood, I probably wouldn't even have gotten mad, but I had been with Lynn and we practically broke up. So I wasn't exactly in a good mood walking home.

Yes #6 is that Lynn and I are apparently through. No more comment on that.

So it's been a wonderful two days! I can't remember when I've had more fun. Now if you'll excuse me, I think I'm going to go and kill myself. (Just kidding . . . I think)

I'm afraid the entire weird, phoney, impersonal Hollywood scene is finally getting to me. Since United Artists all of a sudden seems to have lost interest, I think I'll take my tapes to some publishers myself.

Love,
John

I couldn't blame John for feeling discouraged by the on-again off-again treatment in the music world. But behind the specifics of the situation I was afraid I recognized an all-too-familiar pattern. A string of bad breaks, a physical ailment. John, I guessed, wouldn't be staying in Hollywood very much longer.

Sure enough, in mid-September he telephoned with more reports of shoddy treatment from the recording studios. He was glad he'd saved some of the money we'd been sending because a really "great break" had just opened up "in Boulder, Colorado, of all places!"

It seemed there was a new rock group forming in Boulder where John had a chance to get in right at the beginning. "So next time you hear from me I'll be 25 miles from home!"

We were glad he'd be living nearby, and said so. Neither Jo Ann nor I had felt comfortable about Hollywood. It was just that, since he had launched his noble experiment out there, I'd yearned to see him make a go of it.

Jo Ann was convinced he was leaving because of Lynn. In Hollywood they'd keep running into each other—probably be using the same laundromat. John's next phone call was indeed from Colorado. But not from Boulder. He was at Stapleton Airport in Denver: Could one of us come get him?

Jo Ann and I made the hour's drive together, trying to decide on how we should react to this newest change in plans. If John wanted to live at home, we agreed, it should be with the understanding that he'd either attend a local college or find a job. "Of course," we kept reminding ourselves, "he may still be planning to go to Boulder." Perhaps he'd just come on a few days early to see us. That was the good part: it had been nearly nine months since we'd laid eyes on him, not since he inched the Camaro up the driveway in January to drive back to Texas Tech.

Just outside the terminal, sitting on his suitcase with his new guitar across his lap, was John. One look at his face and I knew I mustn't press him about his plans. This had been his Great Adventure, his bid to lead his own life his own way. It hadn't worked and I wished that we had the kind of father-son relationship that would let me put my arms around him and tell him how much I hurt for him.

Instead, we drove up the mountainside talking about everything else under the sun. "What was Malibu Beach like?" Jo Ann asked, and "How's Titter?" John wanted to know.

We were turning into Brookline Road when I asked about the rock group in Boulder. "When do you start rehearsing?"

"The group's off," John said.

It was all he ever told us about the "great break" that had brought him back to Colorado. Neither Jo Ann nor I ever brought up the subject again.

In the hotel living room in Washington, Vince Fuller stood up, arching his shoulders to loosen his back. We'd been going over

79

John's history for nearly three hours. The letters from him that Jo Ann had brought along had disappeared one by one into Vince's briefcase.

"So," said Vince, "it was four and a half years ago that John left California." The FBI, he told us, pursuing the possibility of a conspiracy, was interested in contacting everyone John had known out there. Could we think of any other names?

We couldn't. "But Lynn Collins might," I said.

Vince glanced at Greg Craig, who looked hastily down at his notepad. I guessed that Greg had been in touch with Lynn already—and that her testimony wasn't altogether in John's favor. Perhaps, I thought, Lynn and John had lived together, though John had always spoken of *his* apartment and *her* apartment, as though underscoring the fact that they lived apart. I appreciated Vince's trying to shield us, if that was his gentlemanly intent, but after the horror of Monday did he really think we'd be upset by such a revelation?

Vince broke into the awkward silence. "What were John's plans that fall, after he returned to Colorado? Did he intend to stay with you, or go back to school, or what?"

That, of course, was the very question we had asked ourselves. . . .

19

JO ANN:

John apparently had no specific plans that fall of 1976, other than stroking Titter as long as the cat would sit in his lap (which was all day) and playing his guitar. I'd hear him behind the closed door of his room plinking away at the same few chords. He'd taken to wearing sunglasses, a green army fatigue jacket and a pair of black pull-on boots. It was an outlandish getup, but I realized I mustn't be surprised by anything that came from California.

I was relieved that he never appeared in those clothes when Jack was home—grateful for anything that avoided confrontations between them. I could watch Jack's impatience mount as the days passed and John seemed to be making no plans at all for the coming year. He was 21 years old, and in the three years since he'd started college had completed only four semesters.

"He's been home three weeks," Jack said to me one night, "and I don't think he's looked at a single *Help Wanted* ad. It's too late for school. Is he just going to hang around and do nothing?"

"He's had a tremendous disappointment with his music," I reminded him. "And with Lynn. He's still licking his wounds."

"The way to get over disappointment is to get out, find a job!"

The problem was, there were few jobs in Evergreen. That meant looking in Denver and John didn't want to drive my car in the city. And so I ended up taking him, day after day, an hour down the mountain and an hour back, answering ads. Eventually he found work as a busboy in a nightclub. Jack and I had actually gone dancing a couple of times at Taylor's; beyond packing people in so tight you could barely breathe, it was a perfectly respectable place.

Even if he'd still had the Camaro, John would never drive after dark. Across the street from Taylor's was a one-time motel, now turned into "apartments," where he took a room for $150 a month. It was a dismal place with concrete block walls and peeling linoleum floors. I brought down a few furnishings from the house, and kept him supplied with homemade cookies and an occasional casserole.

My chief concern, though, was what he was doing for friends. Jack would stop off a couple of times a week, driving home from the office, and reported that he usually found John asleep. His job did keep him up till the wee hours, of course. He told us he sometimes took the bus downtown to use the Denver library. But it seemed an awfully bleak existence for a young man.

On John's days off his father or I would go for him and drive him up to Evergreen. There I'd try to get him to come to the Club with me where he might meet people his own age. He'd shake his head. He preferred to stay in his room, catching up on his sleep or strumming that guitar. Music and an occasional movie seemed to be his only recreation. I remembered, one time that winter, he asked me if I'd seen a film called *Taxi Driver*.

I hadn't. "What's it about?"

"It doesn't matter," he said.

For five months John cleared away tables and swept floors at Taylor's until any fantasy about getting into the entertainment business through the back door was thoroughly dispelled. Neither Jack nor I was surprised when at the end of February he informed us he was quitting; what caught us totally unprepared was that he planned, with the money he'd saved out of his paycheck, to return to Los Angeles.

"But John," his father argued, "what makes you think they won't give you the same runaround as before?"

"That's how you have to do it in the music business, Dad. You have to keep coming back every six months."

In spite of our misgivings, John flew back to California on the first of March, 1977. My secret hunch was that he was really going to try to patch things up with Lynn. In either case, it was an even more decisive failure than the first trip. Within two weeks he was phoning to ask for plane fare home. The "stupid" music studios weren't taking any newcomers; the "dumb" producers wouldn't even talk to him.

Sitting there in that sixth floor suite at the Jefferson Hotel, reviewing John's life year by year for the lawyers, I suddenly saw that abrupt second journey to Los Angeles as the alarm-signal it should have been. This was more than just the floundering of a young man trying to find himself; it was the cry of a child who's lost his way.

Jack and I never heard.

When John came back from California talking about return-ing to Texas Tech, we took it, in fact, as a sign that the crisis was over. The year of experiment was behind him. The Hollywood dream was "out of his system." The unskilled job at Taylor's had pointed up the need for a college degree. In his gratification, it was Jack who suggested John switch from the

82

business course to the College of Arts and Sciences: "I expect you'll be a lot happier."

We couldn't figure out whether John was a sophomore or a junior or what, that summer session of 1977. He'd been out of school over a year, since his sudden departure for California in the spring of '76. When he stayed on at the close of summer school to enroll for the '77 fall semester, Jack and I told ourselves that the whole California episode had really worked for the best. Our son had finally grown up.

20

JACK:

I was delighted when on his own, that fall in Lubbock, John shopped around for a secondhand car and got a good buy on a used Toyota Corona. John showing a practical side—another positive result, I felt, of the previous year's hard lessons.

My business was also going well. In the nearly two years since we'd gone public, Vanderbilt Energy had taken off just as I anticipated. That fall we were mentioned in *INC*. magazine as one of the one hundred fastest-growing companies in the entire country, and among the ten most cost-efficient. Our stock had climbed from about $.75 per share when it was first listed in January 1976, to around $3.50 by mid-November 1977.

On the surface, everything seemed fantastic. In April Diane and Steve's first child was born; Christopher's portrait taken when he was six months old beamed from my office desk. Jo Ann was happy and involved in Evergreen. Scott was daily proving more valuable to the company. John was back on track in college.

How to account for that strange emptiness inside me? The business success I'd struggled for, now that it was happening, was strangely hollow. Going to the office each day was suddenly a chore instead of a challenge. At home tensions were mounting between Jo Ann and me. We could hardly talk without quarreling. She accused me of being too critical of both her and John; I felt she encouraged him in the ailments and other excuses he was again coming up with for not getting better grades. Even tennis had ceased to be fun. I won the men's senior singles and mixed doubles championships at the Club, then quit playing.

Nothing had zest in it anymore. My copy of *Mere Christianity* was underlined now on almost every page. The book seemed to say I'd been looking in the wrong places for satisfaction. But if family and career, sports and volunteer work weren't the places, what was?

I remember it was a chilly late November evening. Jo Ann was visiting her parents in Oklahoma City and I was alone in the house. I'd built a fire in the living room beneath our year-round wreath and was sitting in my armchair thinking about the emptiness of my life and how miserable I was. I recalled some words of C. S. Lewis: God doesn't want my good works, my possessions, or my good intentions—He wants *me*.

And all at once, unexpectedly, unimaginably, I found myself out of my chair and on my knees by the coffee table, whispering words I scarcely comprehended. "Lord, take my life . . . take everything I am. . . . I commit myself to You."

I spoke the words; I meant the words; but I did not understand them. I had no more idea than before *how* one turned over the direction of one's life. It was an act of my will, not my mind. With my mind I would have said it was impossible for a personality as controlling as mine to give up any ounce of that control.

With my mind, too, I would have said I already *was* a Christian—had been for years. Now I saw that I had never had a personal relationship with Christ: I had only been religious. When I got up from my knees in our living room on November 20, 1977, I was a Christian in a totally new way. How new I could not begin to imagine.

● ● ●

John had begun preparing us in his weekly phone calls, for the fact that he was growing a beard, correctly guessing that his mother and I would not applaud the idea. What we were not prepared for, when he arrived home for Christmas, was the excess weight. He must have put on forty pounds since returning to Lubbock. His face, framed in sideburns, beard and moustache, was round as a moon.

Eight-month-old Chris was the delight of that Christmas season. John especially adored him, crawling around on the floor with him, holding him on his lap, patting him to sleep: "Just like he does Titter," I teased Diane.

And yet . . . it was not a happy Christmas. Jo Ann as usual was tense and exhausted from weeks of preparation, while I was newly and painfully aware of the contrast between the birth of the Savior whom we were presumably honoring, and our materialistic celebration. Working with the Hunger Task Force, I'd seen areas of Denver I'd never known existed. Now, in addition to the food program, I joined a ministry to skid-row down-and-outers, going down Sunday mornings with three or four other businessmen to conduct services in a decrepit old store front "mission."

When John phoned home that spring term it was increasingly to report physical ills. "I keep waking up in the middle of the night with something in my throat." He was losing so much sleep he was afraid he was going to fail History.

As usual, Jo Ann was sympathetic, I was exasperated. Kib Brooks had raised me to believe grown men didn't bellyache about their health. John was a man now—should be. At term's end he'd be 23.

At the end of March he phoned to say he needed an operation. "I *knew* something was wrong with my throat, and now this doctor says I should have a tonsillectomy right away."

Next day Jo Ann called the doctor in Lubbock. When I got home that night she met me at the top of the hall stairs with a baffled frown. "Jack, the doctor in Lubbock didn't know what I was talking about! He never told John he needed surgery."

We stood staring at each other with the children's teenage portraits smiling down at us. It was good news, of course, medically. But why would John make up such a story?

When we confronted him with the doctor's statement, John

sounded as confused as we were—said he was sure he'd heard the word "tonsillectomy." The throat complaints continued—joined by others. Pain in his arms, his legs, his chest, his head. Even Jo Ann's patience was wearing thin. And yet, of course, we couldn't rule out the possibility that the problems had a physical base. Overweight alone, I thought, might account for a lot of it.

He missed so much class time with various ailments that once again he had to stay on for the summer session. In September 1978, after four consecutive semesters at Lubbock, he arrived at Steve and Diane's announcing that he was going to look for work in Dallas that fall rather than return to school.

He landed a job at a print shop and found an apartment nearby—a single room with an icebox and a hot plate, Diane reported. With Steve's help, the Toyota managed to keep running, and John would come by their place on his days off to play with little Chris.

Then one night on his way home from work, John was waiting at a red light when some guy without a penny of insurance plowed into the rear of his car. No one was hurt, but the Toyota was badly damaged—and John's enthusiasm for driving, never great, now even less. Instead of driving to Colorado for Christmas as he'd intended, he came by plane.

Again Jo Ann and I were startled and dismayed by his appearance. His normal weight was around 160; he must have been well over 200.

That fall Vanderbilt had purchased another small independent oil company, nearly doubling the size of our operations and keeping me on the run. Jo Ann and I had also bought a condominium on a golf course in Solana Beach, California, just north of San Diego. It would be a good rental property, I reasoned, when we weren't using it—yet with the increase in our income our first responsibility should be to others. I'd stepped up our giving to big organizations like World Vision, a Christian relief agency, and Food for the Hungry, and the Christian Aid Mission, but with the guilty certainty that that was not enough. We should be going, ourselves, where people were hurting.

The possibility that someone was hurting much closer by, right beneath our own shake-shingled roof, did not occur to me. Of course I knew John was having his problems—but with enough effort and self-discipline he'd lick them. My whole activist, achiever philosophy blinded me to needs that weren't visible. Drought, famine, unjust social conditions—they were enemies we could see and tackle.

John's personal growing pains were resolving themselves anyway. After being away from school that fall, he was planning to return to Texas Tech after Christmas. He flew back to Dallas with the three Sims to pick up his Toyota and drive the crippled vehicle back to Lubbock. On January 1, 1979, Diane telephoned from a friend's house. Two days before, she said, an ice storm had brought down the electric wires in their neighborhood. All day December 31 she'd waited for the heat and lights to come on. By five o'clock she knew she had to get little Chris out of that cold house.

"When I called our friends, they said of course bring John, too. But Daddy, he wouldn't go. John stayed all by himself in that pitch-black, freezing house. And it was New Year's Eve!"

I didn't understand the sudden shudder of fear which ran through me. "Well," I tried to reassure us both, "you know how John is about strangers." But that picture continued to haunt me. John alone in an icy, dark room.

John just sitting there.

John alone.

Diane phoned next weekend with the end of the story. John had stayed on with them in Dallas a few extra days waiting for the roads to be free of ice, then set out for Lubbock in the Toyota. At seven that night he reappeared at the Sims' front door. His car had skidded off the road about an hour out of Dallas, landed in a ditch, and it had taken him that long to walk to where he could call a wrecker and wait for them to haul it out.

It really did seem like John got more than his share of bad breaks. Diane said he'd flown back to Lubbock after selling the car for practically nothing. Doubtless, after these delays, he'd find the best courses filled again. "When he telephones," I promised Jo Ann, "I won't say a negative word."

21

JO ANN:

But instead of phoning, John wrote a letter. He addressed it to
Solana Beach, California, where we'd gone for a mid-winter
vacation. It started off as a typical John letter, full of
complaints about his health:

> Lubbock, Texas
> Jan. 17, 1979

> Dear Mom & Dad,
>   The year 1979 has been delightful so far, I've had two
> colds, a backache, an earache. . . .

Then came a surprise:

> Things will be nicer here in Lubbock in a few days. I
> have a friend coming to visit me this Friday the 19th. My
> California girl friend Lynn Collins is coming all the way
> from Chicago for a week's stay. . . . She desperately
> wants to get out of Chicago for a while, I guess you've
> been hearing how bad the weather has been up there.
> Anyway, with her unlimited financial resources, she's
> decided to visit me here in balmy Lubbock. I've bought a
> new pair of slacks and sports coat so it really must be a
> big occasion!
>   I guess I'll have to show her Lubbock from the inside of
> a taxicab. I just haven't had time to look for a car. Maybe
> I could rent a car from Hertz for a week.
>   By the way, I've lost 13 pounds since leaving Ever-
> green. All without exercise.

Have fun in California. I'll call sometime next week.

Love,
John

Jack and I were tickled to see John looking forward to something. I slipped a $20 bill in an envelope to help cover the cost of the new clothes. All week we waited eagerly to hear how Lynn's visit had gone. As usual there was no telephone in his off-campus apartment, so he had to initiate all calls.

At last a long bubbling letter arrived in Solana Beach:

Lubbock, Texas
Jan. 25, 1979

Dear Mom & Dad,

What a great week this has been. Hectic, hectic and more hectic!

Last Wednesday, two days before Lynn's arrival, I got sick as a dog due to my fasting. I lost about 18 pounds, but I don't recommend it as a way to lose weight.

Well I was feeling fine when Lynn arrived on Friday night. I was able to rent a car for a good price, so I was there at the airport to pick her up. Actually she had changed very little, considering it had been 2½ years since I had last seen her. I was a bundle of nerves until I finally set eyes on her and then everything was perfect from then on.

We've *never* seen her, I thought, wondering again why John would never even produce a picture of her. The letter went on, ecstatically relating all they'd done from the moment they dropped her suitcase at the Hilton hotel. Proudly he described the roles she'd landed in three recent Broadway productions, and her current work with a Chicago repertory group.

Saturday night we went to a disco, although I protested this idea very much. We had a big brunch Sunday and then watched the Super Bowl. I wasn't going to miss that game for anything! Lynn doesn't care too much for football.

After John's classes Monday morning they'd gone to a

shopping mall where Lynn spent $150 and John bought an ice cream cone.

We didn't do much Tuesday except talk, talk, talk, and talk. I took her to Steak & Ale for dinner. I went over to her room Wednesday morning for more talk and packing, then drove her to the airport at noon.

Well, I have now had time to digest everything that has happened over the past few days. This is the greatest thing in the world but it does present problems. Lynn has been gone about 24 hours and I am very depressed. It was only two months ago that Lynn was almost completely forgotten by me, only because I thought I would never see her again. But now that we have exchanged these letters and spent time together again, everything has changed!

I simply don't know how I am going to survive here in Lubbock without her. I know it sounds very maudlin, but unless you have been in my shoes for the past few years, you won't be able to understand how I feel.

Well I better finish now before I drown in my misery. Have a safe trip back to Evergreen.

Love,
John

We were sorry, of course, that he was experiencing such a letdown, but delighted that the week with Lynn had been all that he dreamed. I even felt a twinge of wistfulness, reading how they had talked and talked. Jack and I seemed to be finding less and less to say to one another. . . .

Instead of enjoying the golf, which is why we'd bought this winter vacation home, Jack was spending hours every day inside, reading religious books. I couldn't understand what had come over him since what he called his "conversion" two years before. Any time he was having fun, nowadays, it seemed to me he felt guilty—as though Christians were supposed to go around in sackcloth and ashes.

The deepest Christians I knew—people like my sister-in-law, Shirley, and Avis Lee in Evergreen—were also the most joyful. It wasn't that they were indifferent to the needs of others, Avis's prayer group cared for people all over our area. You didn't have to look overseas to find families in need! But the more Shirley and Avis loved God, the more they loved their families and their friends, too, while Jack seemed dissatisfied with everything and everybody.

We got back to Evergreen the first week in February to find a startling—and confusing—letter from John waiting there. He and Lynn had apparently decided over the telephone to go to California and live together, or at least near one another, right away, without waiting for John to complete his final year at Tech. He was clearly anticipating massive objections on our part—and he was quite right. Still, it hurt us that he would cast us in the role of automatic opponents without even hearing our side.

Feb. 1, 1979

Dear Mom & Dad,

Well, I called Lynn this morning and found out she has decided to move to California for my benefit. She knows I don't want to live in Chicago or New York and she wants to be with me *now* so she is leaving for California in a few days. She prefers the stage of New York to the screen of Hollywood, but she is going to Hollywood just to suit me.

So what do I do? I know exactly what you want me to do. And you know what I want to do. And I know what Lynn wants me to do.

It is a choice of Lynn or Lubbock. To me, there is no choice. Lynn couldn't care less whether or not I have a college diploma. She knows I want to be a songwriter and she has heard my songs and believes I have talent. But most of all, she just wants to be with me and vice versa. Why is this so hard for you to understand?

In my nearly 24 years, there has been exactly one girl that has cared anything at all for me and now you want me to tell her to just forget about it for a year, until I can get a degree which will be meaningless in my life as a song-writer.

She is sacrificing a stage career on Broadway so she can be with me in California. It would be the greatest and most unnecessary risk of my life to let her go there alone; Hollywood is just crawling with guys that will be trying to pick her up.

It is an absolute miracle from heaven that Lynn is still

single and cares for me! And I'm supposed to tell her to keep her eyes closed for a year in Hollywood while I diligently earn my degree a thousand miles away.

Well, this is my dilemma. I care nothing for school and everything for Lynn. So why should there be a dilemma? Because you think a piece of paper is more important than a potential lifetime relationship. I don't understand it. I swear to God I don't understand it.

Lynn wants to be with me now, with or without diploma! I just heard her say that an hour ago. I'm going to call her back tonight and tell her to go ahead and get settled in California. I'm going to tell her that I will stay here in Lubbock for now and we will all just see what happens.

John

The last sentence was especially puzzling to Jack and me—as if John foresaw such adamant resistance on our part that he had already accepted defeat. How frustrated we were that there was no way we could telephone him and reassure him that though, indeed, we disapproved of what he contemplated, we understood his feelings. I went straight to my desk upstairs in our bedroom and wrote, urging him to call home. Our chief fear was that he would simply take off for California, as he had three years earlier, giving us no address. I asked him not to let this happen again, asked him to keep the lines of communication open, no matter what he and Lynn decided to do.

And then, of course, I enumerated all the things parents worry about—asked what kind of a job he hoped to find without a degree, or whether he expected Lynn to support him. I reminded him that he'd mentioned nothing about marriage, inquired whether Lynn's parents knew about the proposed arrangement.

"I *do* understand that you and Lynn are in love," I wrote, "and I think that's great." I told him he was wrong, if he thought his father and I cared only about a diploma. "As you said, it's only a piece of paper." But a piece of paper that could be important to his and Lynn's future.

It couldn't have been a very coherent letter, but maybe it helped him think things through a bit, because when he eventually phoned he said no more about quitting school. "If you two really love each other," Jack tried to comfort him, "a few more months apart isn't going to change things."

We were grateful that John and Lynn had listened to us—but we yearned for a return of the kind of enthusiasm he'd shown at the time of her visit. He sounded down on himself, down on life, that spring. What worried us most was his interest in some right-wing political group there on campus. We'd been so grateful when our children escaped the student violence of the sixties, now here was John talking about demonstrations. From what he told us, the group was twisting Christian slogans to suit some warped racist philosophy.

I sent John the only really angry letter I'd ever written him. I didn't like to throw his poor academic performance in his face, but he *was* failing a number of subjects: "Since you have so much time to spend away from your studies, I suggest you do a little Bible reading, praying and churchgoing."

Whether it was the time devoted to this group, or some other reason, once again it was the old pattern of missed classes and "incompletes." Once more, the summer of '79, John stayed on in Lubbock to make up the work. It was six years since John had entered Texas Tech. His goal was to graduate, finally, in June 1980, and yet, as he entered the fall '79 semester, we began to wonder if he was going to make even this long-postponed goal.

Once again, every phone call brought new woes with his health, new problems with getting his assignments in on time. Jack and I were increasingly concerned about him . . . and increasingly and perversely taking out our anxiety on each other. One thing we both agreed on was that, while he was home for Christmas, we'd get Em Harvey to give him a thorough physical.

But John didn't come to Evergreen that Christmas.

He phoned about the middle of December to say that Lynn Collins had invited him to spend the holidays with her in New York. The timing was particularly good, he went on, because his novel was finished now and, this way, he could make the rounds of New York publishers himself.

He'd mentioned a couple of times that he was working on a "whodunit" and Jack and I had sent him writer's manuals and other books to encourage him. "But John," I said, "I thought Lynn lived in Chicago."

93

She did, John said—that is her family did. Lynn, he explained, had landed a really big part in a show opening on Broadway in a few weeks. "I won't be staying with her, Mom, don't worry," he added hastily. "She knows this guy in New York who can put me up at his place."

"How are you going to pay for a trip like that?" Jack wanted to know. "I thought you were broke."

All fall at Tech John had been after us to let him sell some of his Vanderbilt stock. We'd given stock to each of the children, back when it wasn't worth much more than the paper it was printed on. Now, several years later, it had some value. John couldn't understand why we wouldn't let him have access to his shares, as Scott and Diane had to theirs. We'd tried to explain that his brother and sister were out of college, working and buying homes, used to managing money.

If this made him angry, typically he hid his feelings. But he'd found various ways all that semester to remind us what a hand-to-mouth existence he was leading. "If you can't make ends meet in Lubbock," Jack asked, "how are you going to swing a trip to New York?"

Well, it seemed the only part of the trip would require cash-out-of-pocket would be bus fare as far as Shreveport, Louisiana. Lynn was there for her grandfather's funeral; they could drive her car the rest of the way together.

John was obviously determined to go, and there wasn't much we could do to stop him—except to tell him how much we'd miss him. It would be the first Christmas he had not been home. The ritual of passing out the packages when the day arrived was hollow for us all without him. He hadn't even given us a number in New York where we could call him. All Christmas Day we expected him to phone, at least to speak to his nephew, who was now nearly three. But there was no call, that day or all the following week. "I hope he's all right," I'd worry aloud a dozen times a day. "New York's such a big, unfriendly place."

We were a mighty relieved family when he finally phoned to say he was safely back in Lubbock—on time, for a wonder, to register for the spring term. Christmas in New York had been fantastic. He'd met a lot of Lynn's "showbiz" friends, and a couple of publishers acted interested in his book. No, he didn't have a copy to send us; he'd had to leave both the original and the carbon with the agent who was helping him. But it had been a great trip. It was going to be twice as hard, now, to settle down to school.

Not only hard, it turned out. Impossible. Every letter home in January told of missing classes. Again the principal problem seemed to be his throat. He went back to the ear-nose-and-throat man he'd seen earlier, the one I'd spoken to on the phone at the time of the false-alarm over the tonsillectomy. But a barium-swallow turned up nothing.

Remembering what a hard time he'd had adjusting to school after Lynn's visit the previous January—threatening to chuck it all and go to California—we told ourselves the low period would pass. It did not, however, and at the beginning of February we suggested he come home to let Dr. Harvey have a look. He wasn't keeping up with his schoolwork anyway.

Jack and I were appalled at his appearance when he stepped off the plane in Denver—pale, puffy-faced, at least sixty pounds overweight, with barely enough energy to walk to the car. I took him next morning to Em Harvey who gave him a complete physical, including every test he could think of.

"I won't have the lab results for a day or two, Jo Ann," Em told me, "but I honestly can't find anything wrong—except for the weight, of course." John, at five-feet-ten, weighed in at 230 pounds on Em's scales. "That's enough to make anyone feel lousy."

To be on the safe side, though, Em referred John to an internist in Denver, and also recommended that we take him to Saint Luke's Hospital for a throat scan. John's most persistent complaint was "pressure" when he swallowed, "like something's there." He also spoke of a "rocking" feeling in his head for which a doctor in Lubbock had been giving him an anti-vertigo medicine.

John went with a kind of pathetic eagerness to these various appointments, clearly hopeful that someone, somewhere would have the answers. Once more, however, extensive tests failed to reveal any organic cause for his problems; the Denver doctor agreed that getting off weight was a priority. Em outlined a strict diet. With low-cal meals prepared by me and daily pep talks from Jack, John took off ten pounds in three weeks.

And began talking about going to Dallas. . . .

95

Although Jack and I had lived in Colorado for six and a half years, Dallas remained home for John. He'd missed too much of the spring semester at Tech to graduate in June. "But maybe I could get a job in Dallas till the summer session starts."

"Better than sitting around in Evergreen," Jack agreed. He had a brainstorm about a car for John, too, after his bad luck with the Toyota. The company had a Volare in the Houston office that had too many miles on it for the kind of tough driving the landman put it through, but should be fine for getting around Dallas and Lubbock. Jack bought the car from the company and paid John's airfare to Houston to pick it up. This time Jack hung onto the title papers; he didn't want John selling the Volare for half its value when he needed a little quick cash, as he had the Camaro.

In a few days John called from Steve and Diane's to say he'd driven safely from Houston. As so often before, Steve threw himself into John's job search, tirelessly coming up with leads and contacts. When John telephoned to say he'd been hired by a Dallas newspaper, Jack glowed with pride in him: "Maybe he really has found his field in writing!" "Are you staying on your diet?" I'd ask each time he called, and he'd assure us that he was.

All the news seemed good—so good that subconsciously, I believed, both of us were steeled for the inevitable pinprick in the current balloon. Sure enough, before long problems at the job began to emerge. They'd switched him to the night shift. They were giving him only cut-and-paste jobs. They were cutting back on his hours.

In any case, the stay in Dallas was never intended to be more than temporary; at the end of April John returned to Lubbock for what we all hoped would be his final semester.

22

JACK:

We had brought the review of John's life up to one year before the present, and all of us were ready for a break. I telephoned room service to order a late lunch sent up.

Jo Ann and I were glad for the chance to get to know the younger two members of the Williams & Connolly team a little better. Lon Babby and Judith Miller had been mostly silent listeners as Vince Fuller and Greg Craig threw questions at us—but it was clear that Lon and Judy were missing nothing. Neither looked much older than John. I wondered what these high-achieving young people thought of his aimless college years.

Lunch arrived; I still couldn't get used to the sight of policemen in the corridor. As we ate I thought back over the previous twelve months, trying to get events in order in my mind. It was difficult because I'd been away so much this last year. Not just the usual business travel, but trips for various overseas relief efforts. I'd gone twice to Guatemala on village-water projects, flown to Florida to help World Vision set up housing for Haitian refugees.

I did recall that shortly after John quit the job at the Dallas paper to return to Lubbock, he'd phoned to ask for a loan—a small one, under a hundred dollars—to help him get started in business.

"Business?" I was so surprised I almost dropped the phone. John had never shown the least interest in anything so mundane. It seemed that a friend of his on campus, Tom Perry, was doing so well in a mail order business that John had decided to try it too.

I don't know when I'd felt more encouraged by a development in his life. His novel was apparently continuing to make the rounds of New York publishers, but that had always seemed to me a long shot. Here was something actually within reach, a small business he could carry on after graduation if it did well. I gave him my enthusiastic backing, urging him to be business-like and write up regular reports as I did for my investors. Early in May we got a letter from him bursting with a new kind of self-confidence.

May 4, 1980

Dear Mom & Dad,

I don't mind telling you that the time and effort I have put into this mail order business has been substantial. It really takes a huge amount of research to come up with a useful, lucrative product. Writing the perfect classified ad without wasting any words is agony. I've spent this entire weekend searching for good places to advertise and last night I wrote up my "report."

In the beginning I will be advertising in 5 national magazines, three monthly and two weekly. The total price for the 5 classified ads is $75.00.

On Friday I registered my business for a ten year period, so I now officially own my own business. I am the president of LISTALOT, an ingenious name. I will be listing a lot of things. Get it? And it's a good idea to have a one word title, so my company name is perfect.

I am offering two different types of information: (1) the names and address of the top 75 country music stars fan clubs and (2) how to set up your own mail order business. I think I have come up with some cleverly worded ads, so now I just have to wait and see what the response will be.

In the meantime, I'm going to help Tom with his company, since he is expanding. Until I get some of my own profits, I hope to be sharing in some of his profits.

I re-registered at Tech on Friday.

Love,
John

The enclosed electric bill was just forwarded to me. As of today I'm broke so please pay it.

I would have paid ten electric bills with pleasure, to see John so motivated and positive. It seemed to me that both of the items he was offering stood a good chance. My only fear was that the time devoted to LISTALOT could mean falling behind in schoolwork, which happened all too easily with John.

His phone calls home all May and June continued to report progress in his business. He'd taken out a post office box where readers of the ads could write, and opened a bank account to keep LISTALOT funds separate. For once I let myself believe that the cycle of high expectation, cruel disappointment would not be repeated.

It was with a lighter heart than I'd had in months that I accepted the invitation of an investment banking firm to spend ten days in Europe at the end of the summer. They would set up meetings with European investors for the presidents of five U.S. companies, including Vanderbilt—even pay some of the travel expenses. It was a flattering offer, reflecting our company's growth.

I needed some encouragement; at home I couldn't seem to do anything right. Jo Ann and I differed over so much—even the best way to serve God. Our unhappiness with each other was so acute that we'd started seeing a husband-wife team of Christian marriage counselors. In their consulting room we could discuss things more calmly than at home, but the issues didn't go away.

It was to try to improve our relationship that, when the European trip was suggested, I told the sponsor I'd like to bring Jo Ann, though none of the wives was coming along. "We'll go a week early," I told her. "Travel by ship, just you and me."

She was as thrilled as I hoped she'd be, started packing weeks ahead of the August 22 sailing date. The cloud over the summer, as always, was concern for John. My worry about his juggling both business and school proved more than justified. By early July he was seeing a Dr. Rosen in Lubbock who prescribed a medication for stress.

"What kind of drug is it?" we asked over the phone.

"It's called Valium."

I saw Jo Ann stiffen with alarm. "Valium is habit-forming," she told John.

As soon as he hung up, we dialed the Harveys and caught Em at home. He was guarded, it seemed to me, in his opinion. He told us that not a great deal was known about the mood-altering drugs and, yes, Valium could occasionally be addictive, "but in the dosage you say John is taking I certainly wouldn't consider it cause for alarm."

23

JO ANN:

A few days later, however, we learned that John was not on one drug but two. Dr. Rosen had apparently also prescribed a mood elevator, Surmontil, in addition to the Valium, to combat John's depression. John had begun to complain again of pain in his writing arm. His ears bothered him: he couldn't hear the professors. His legs hurt so badly at times he couldn't even walk from the school parking lot to the lecture room. Once again the pattern was repeated—he was going to get failing grades in his courses unless he dropped out.

Jack was horrified. "How can you consider quitting, this close to graduating?"

As for LISTALOT, there was never any news, and eventually we stopped asking about it. After the initial excitement, John's mail order business seemed destined to die on the vine like all his other projects.

Jack's disappointment was so deep we couldn't even discuss it; it became just one more of the topics we avoided in the interest of peace. Mealtimes at our house were becoming pretty silent affairs. Why, I wondered, when Jack and I loved each other so much, were we unable to reach out to each other?

I felt there was no point in John's staying on in Lubbock when he wasn't even going through the motions of getting an education, and at length Jack agreed. "But you're not going to stay home and play nursemaid to a 25-year-old. You're not going to miss out on this trip to Europe."

To salve John's ego over this inglorious homecoming, we told him it would help us to have him keep an eye on the house while we were away, water the plants and look after Titter. So in August 1980, John drove the Volare home, still an undergraduate, still without a career direction. At least, we were pleased to see, he'd stuck to his diet, taken off some of the excess pounds. Jack had a suggestion for while we were gone: "I'd like John to have a session or two with Darrell Benjamin." Dr. Benjamin was the psychologist retained by Vanderbilt to help evaluate prospective employees. "Get a professional opinion—find out why John can't stick with anything he starts." Since medical tests had failed to explain his succession of ailments, it seemed like a reasonable next step.

The trip on the immense *Queen Elizabeth II* was wonderful. We had a table for two by a window and danced every night. We needed that peaceful interlude. Once ashore it was six cities in five countries in ten days, with Jack occupied day and night. We flew home September 10, to find the house in good shape—and John full of a plan to attend some kind of writing seminar at Yale University. He'd mentioned something of the sort before we left, but Jack and I had been stung too often by these brief enthusiasms, to pay much attention.

"Did you see Dr. Benjamin?" Jack asked him.

Yes, they'd had two sessions together.

"Did he give you any tests?"

There'd been no tests, and John was noncommittal as to what they'd discussed. But the fact that he'd driven all the way down to Denver to keep the appointments, I felt was encouraging. John too must be relieved to have a trained, objective person in the picture. From here on, we'd have help in making decisions. . . .

24

JACK:

The first thing I did when I got back to the office after our European trip was to phone Darrell Benjamin. "You've seen John twice—what do you make of him? Why can't he stay in school, or stick with a job?"

"I think it's what you've been saying all along, Jack. The guy's simply immature." John would never get his act together, Darrell felt, until we cut the apron strings. "Agree on some kind of plan for John's becoming self-sufficient. Put it down in writing."

It was so much in line with my own thinking that I wondered why I hadn't done it before. To my surprise, John was immediately enthusiastic. He knew the very proposal he wanted to suggest. If we'd agree to underwrite the seminar at Yale, starting in just a few days, he'd pledge to work as he'd never worked before, "till I can make a living at writing."

"How can you qualify for Yale," I asked, "when you've failed the last several semesters at Tech?"

The writing workshop, he explained, wasn't actually *part* of Yale, it just took place *at* Yale—used their classrooms. He'd seen an ad for it in a writers' magazine. It would last five weeks, each one on a different kind of writing. Fiction, movie scripting, and so on. "I'm going to take my novel. That agent in New York is just sitting on it."

"You know what *I* think?" Jo Ann said later that evening. We were having dinner at the Club, just the two of us, John as usual having begged off. "I think Lynn's tied up in this. There must be writing schools right here in Denver—but New Haven's close to New York.''

If that was the appeal of going east, John didn't mention it; he'd only said how much he wanted professional guidance with his writing. ''O.K.,'' I said, next morning at the breakfast table noticing how Jo Ann's plants in the window had made a cheery miniature jungle out of that corner of the kitchen. ''Let's figure out the cost. What's the tuition?''

John couldn't remember exactly; he thought about $2,000, including room and meals.

''Then there's the air fare to New Haven. Say $2,300 total.'' My proposal was that I sell enough of his Vanderbilt stock to cover it. I didn't feel much like putting family funds into another educational venture for John when we'd sent him to college for seven years only to have him drop out just short of a degree.

John didn't even wait to hear my reasoning. Selling some of his shares was a great idea. Anything that would let him attend that school, I had a feeling, would have been fine with him. That same day I started the necessary paperwork for the stock sale. At noontime, passing a bookstore on my way back from lunch, I went in and thumbed through a bunch of writers' magazines. I found no ad for any writers' seminar in New Haven.

When I asked John about it that evening, he couldn't remember the name of the magazine. He'd cut out the coupon and mailed it in, then tossed the rest of the issue. He couldn't understand why the registration forms hadn't come yet.

''Well, give them a call, John. You don't want to arrive in New Haven, like you have in Lubbock, and find the courses already filled.''

Next night he reported the phone conversation. ''That dumb woman in the registrar's office lost my application. There are only three days left, so I had to give her all the information over the telephone.''

September 17 was when classes started, he reminded me, while the sale of his stock required several days to clear. Would we be willing to advance him $500 for the air ticket and his first few days living expenses, to be paid back when the sale went through?

I said I'd talk it over with his mother.

25

JO ANN:

I felt of course we should lend John the money, encourage him in every way we knew how. It wasn't as though John were a spendthrift. He didn't care *enough* about money—never wanted anything new to wear.

Which is why I was surprised when he asked me now if I'd go clothes-shopping with him. It strengthened my suspicion that Lynn Collins was behind this sudden desire to go to school in the New York area. Of course I went with him gladly—anything to get him out of bluejeans.

We must have gone to every department store in west Denver, fighting all the other back-to-school shoppers. John didn't want just any new clothes, it turned out, he was searching for specific items. We looked at scores of jackets before he found the one he had in mind. And shoe stores! "Boots? For New Haven?" I asked. Not only that, they had to be pull-on boots trimmed with metal rings, and they had to be black. When at last we located *the* boots, I was puzzled to find they were exactly like the ones he'd brought back from California four years earlier.

The long day's shopping trip was certainly worth it, I thought, when John came upstairs on the morning of the seventeenth dressed for his flight east. The new clothes, along with the loss of nearly forty pounds, revealed the handsome young man he really was. I was almost alarmed by the speed of the weight-loss; so eager did he seem to look his best he'd almost stopped eating, the last few days.

Jack was worried that John was building up his hopes too high, that if his writing failed to impress these experienced instructors, he'd be plunged again into self-doubt and depression. He'd tried to draw an analogy with his own field: An oilman, he told John, has to be ready to abandon a well that proves to be a dry hole. In the same way, John should be prepared if writing *wasn't* the right career. "Like me when we drill for oil, you won't know till you try. But you have to know when to quit—and have another option in mind, if that happens."

The most obvious option, John and Jack agreed, would be to return to Lubbock in January. "A businessman will always set aside some of his capital for that fallback position." The sale of John's stock had brought $3,600; Jack showed John how to budget it to cover the weeks at Yale, with $1,200 in reserve to re-enter Tech, if that became necessary.

The night before his departure, John had summed up the understanding in writing:

CONTRACT AND/OR AGREEMENT, SEPT. 16, 1980

I will receive the sum of $3,600 in check, taken from my stock. This money is intended to last from Sept. 17-Feb 1.

If I decide to go back to school in January, I should have approx. $1,000-$1,200 remaining in mid-January for schooling.

As soon as I receive the check and set up a bank account, I will repay the $500 borrowed for travelers checks.

And I do pledge to try and make the coming weeks as productive as possible. It's now or never!

Thank you for the money and one more chance.
(signed) John W. Hinckley, Jr.

Jack was taking John to the airport on his way to work. It was with a feeling that our 25-year-old was on the right track at last that I waved him and Jack up the driveway.

I was wrong.

This time there wasn't even the customary month or so grace-period before the bad news began. John phoned after only three days to say he hated New Haven. The town was dirty and industrial, the students were sloppy, everything was horribly expensive. It was the familiar prelude, Jack and I were sure, to the announcement that he was going to quit. Jack had a meeting the next day in California with the people at World Vision. He drove off to the airport as discouraged-looking as I'd ever seen him.

I looked at Jack now, sitting on the hotel sofa next to Vince Fuller, hating the part of the story I had to tell next, hating for Jack to have to learn about it this way—this episode I'd hoped he'd never discover. But Mr. Fuller said that in order to help us they had to know "everything."

With Jack in California I was alone when John's next call came. "Are you liking New Haven any better?" I asked, though I was afraid I knew the answer. New Haven was O.K., he guessed. He wouldn't know. He was calling from Stapleton Airport; would I drive down and get him?

"You're calling from *where?*"

"From Denver, Mom. Can you come and get me?"

"But John, you just left! Not even a week ago. What in the world are you doing back here?"

"There are some things I didn't do."

I drove down to Denver utterly mystified. Nor did John's explanation on the way back to Evergreen make the situation much clearer. I gathered there was a bank account in Lubbock he had to close out, presumably the one he'd opened for LISTALOT. "But why didn't you do that before you left school? And . . . if it's in Lubbock, why come to Denver?"

Because, he told me, his airline ticket was between New York and Denver—the only way he could get the cheap round trip. And he'd been too sick the last few weeks in Lubbock to round off his affairs there. Ordinarily I was sympathetic with John's health problems, but this time I found myself more angry than understanding. "So you've taken an expensive air trip to get a few dollars out of the bank in Lubbock— something you could handle through the mail! Your father's been absolutely right not to let you handle your own stock. You just don't think!"

John looked as surprised as I felt, to hear me talk this way. It was as though I had relied on Jack to play the heavy-handed parent, while I expressed the tenderness both of us also felt. In Jack's absence I was having to represent both realities.

John had retreated into silence, his habitual response to being "lectured." All I could draw out of him was that, yes, he still intended to take part in the writing seminars at Yale. This week, he'd discovered on arriving in New Haven, was registration only; actual classes didn't start until next week. "With what it costs to live there, I figured there was no sense hanging around after I'd registered."

My chief anxiety was that Jack would come home early from California and find our son back in Colorado. "You can stay here tonight," I said as the garage door slid open. "Daddy may be home tomorrow and I don't want him even to know about this hare-brained trip of yours."

True to my word, the next morning I drove him back down to Denver. Since his ticket to Lubbock was not until the following day, I dropped him at a Motel 6 and scored another point by refusing to pay for the room. "How am I going to get to the airport tomorrow?" John asked. I opened my mouth to say, "That's your problem." Instead I told him, "I'll come and take you." Cutting apron strings was obviously going to be a learning process on both sides.

Still, I felt I'd gotten a message across. I was glad for that, and glad I'd been able to keep the whole escapade from Jack. . . .

I looked up, now, to see how he was taking this belated revelation. He was staring at me across the antique coffee table at the Jefferson Hotel, shock and hurt in his eyes. But Jack had had so much on his mind in September. Last summer and fall thousands of Haitian refugees were pouring ashore on the beaches of Florida. Jack had returned from California and left again almost immediately to help set up a refugee center in Miami.

I was always lonely when Jack was away. Sue Sells and other thoughtful neighbors asked me over and Scott and Diane kept in touch by phone. The last day of September Diane received a post card from John mailed in Washington, D.C. Apparently the seminars still hadn't started in New Haven, so he'd taken the train down for some sightseeing. "It's a weird card," Diane told me over the phone. "He says he's been hit over the head by reality for the past two weeks and he doesn't like the feeling."

"I'm afraid it's girl trouble," I told her. I confided my theory that he'd chosen Yale to be near Lynn. "I'm afraid it sounds like the romance has hit a snag."

John wasn't communicating with me—hurt, I supposed, at my unwelcoming attitude. But a week or so later Diane heard from him again. This time the post card was addressed to his three-and-a-half-year-old nephew, telling Chris his Uncle John was coming to see him.

"Does he say he's dropping the seminars, Diane?"

"Not exactly. Just says New Haven is the worst place on earth, and he'll see Chris very soon."

"Maybe he'll come while I'm visiting you," I said. I was planning a trip to Dallas the following week.

John, in fact, got to Dallas before I did. He phoned Diane on Friday, October 10, to ask if he could stay with them. Diane, Steve and Chris were taking off that weekend to attend a football game in Waco with Steve's parents, but Diane told John where she'd leave the key.

Vince Fuller looked up from the notes he was making on a yellow pad. "Did you say John telephoned his sister on October 10? The day after he was arrested in Nashville?"

There on the sixth floor of a Washington hotel, two worlds came together in my mind. On the one hand the world of family comings and goings; on the other, the world revealed to us this past week. The arrest in Nashville airport, the confiscation of three handguns. Then . . . John hadn't been calling Diane from New Haven at all, but fresh from his encounter with the Nashville authorities.

He'd found the Sims' key, been there at their house when Diane and Steve and Chris got home Sunday night. I got to Dallas three days later. I took the airport bus to the north Dallas terminal to find John there to meet me along with Diane and Chris. Actually, it turned out John had not come to meet me, but was on his way out to the airport himself. We had just three minutes to talk. I tried to find out where John was going but it was impossible over Chris' howls. Diane and I gave John a hurried hug, unwrapped Chris from his legs and waved him off to his waiting bus.

"John seemed like his mind was a thousand miles away," I said to Diane as we drove to her house.

"I know," she said. They hadn't pressed him about the writing course in New Haven because he obviously didn't want to talk about it. "He wouldn't even play with Chris, just stayed in the guestroom with the door shut."

He'd gone out looking for work, briefly, Monday and Tuesday, she went on. "Then he heard you were coming today, and he thought we'd be too crowded with both of you, so he took off."

"But where was he going? Didn't he say?"

Diane thought he was going back to New Haven for the start of another seminar. Poetry, maybe. But that night at dinner, Steve said John had talked about returning to Los Angeles. *Lynn,* I thought. *Just as sure as we're sitting here, Lynn's back in California. . . .*

26

JACK:

Vince Fuller, once he'd started something, was like a bulldog with a bone; Jo Ann and I had been answering questions now for five hours. The four lawyers held a whispered conference. "We'll call it a day," Vince announced. "Tomorrow you're flying down to North Carolina. We'll pick it up again the day after."

He filled us in on the arrangements for the trip to see John in the morning. Once more police would see us directly onto a plane, while from Raleigh-Durham airport a government agent would drive us to the Federal Correctional Institute at Butner. Technically, Vince explained, John wasn't supposed to have any visitors at all during his psychological evaluation. "But we've asked for an hour's visit. Also some time for you with the prison staff before your return flight."

An hour? Only an hour? And it was clear that even this concession had taken some doing by our lawyers.

"But," Jo Ann asked tremulously, "we can see him again right away, can't we?"

Vince shook his head. "Not these first few weeks, I'm afraid."

That night the Colorado security men, who'd been following the TV coverage in their room down the hall, had good news to report. Jim Brady was making headway in his heroic fight for life. Today, four days after the shooting, President Reagan had had his first solid food.

On Saturday we were up for an early breakfast in the room. Dale Morris was coming with the Governor's men and us to North Carolina. Dale spent much of his time these days visiting men behind bars as part of the Prison Fellowship program headed by Chuck Colson; he would meet with Butner inmates.

Hotel manager Rose Narva knocked on our hallway door at 7:30 a.m. and led us past the current shift of policemen in the hallway to the elevator, then through the downstairs lobby to an unmarked patrol car parked in front of the hotel. Once again we were driven right onto the airport runway and put aboard the plane ahead of the other passengers.

At Raleigh-Durham airport we were met by a beautiful young blonde who introduced herself as "Charlie" and kept our minds off our destination with stories of her adventures as an undercover drug agent. At the start of the long driveway leading through a wooded area to the prison, a number of television cameramen were waiting. We were waved past the guard station so fast that we were inside the restricted area before I realized they had been watching there for us.

"How did they know when we were coming?" I asked.

"They didn't," said Charlie. They'd been staking out the prison for days, she said, knowing that sooner or later we'd be bound to show up.

Butner Federal Correctional Institute was a collection of modern one-story buildings behind a double row of high chain-link fences. Charlie parked the car in front of the administration building and took us inside to meet Warden

Ingraham and his staff. Afterward, Jo Ann and I were taken into a small room to be photographed. From there we were screened through a metal detector somewhat like the ones at airports, then led by a prison official with the unlikely name of Jesse James across some grounds to a small separate building. Somehow I had not been prepared for the elaborate security: Four guards accompanied us, walking behind us, in front and on both sides.

We stopped outside the little building while a guard unlocked the heavy metal door. John, Mr. James told us, was the sole inmate of this eight-cell unit; the other rooms had been cleared to maintain him in isolation. He led us through several more locked doors and into a small concrete-block cell. In one wall was a glass see-through, on the other side of which a guard was stationed. The room contained three blue molded, fiberglass chairs and a stationary exercise bicycle.

Then John appeared in the doorway. Maybe it was the size of the guards on either side of him, but John looked so small. That was my first reaction. Small and young—almost a child, certainly not a man who would turn 26 the next month. He was wearing a bright orange beltless jumpsuit, with blue canvas slippers on his feet. He looked pale, but he was clean and fresh shaven and . . . something else. Something about his mood I couldn't quite put my finger on.

John hung back near the door, perhaps embarrassed by the setting, perhaps daunted by the scrutiny of the guards, who had left the room but were following every movement through the window. Oblivious to everything else, Jo Ann hurried to him and threw her arms around him. Afterward I did too, folding him in a bear hug for the first time I could recall since he was a chubby little towhead.

What do you say, the first time you see your son after he has done the unthinkable? Why did you shoot the President, son? Of course you don't. Instead, as we'd done a number of times on the phone since Monday, we told John we loved him: No amount of anger or revulsion could change that. And that we intended to see this thing through together.

He seemed appreciative. And yet somehow I had the feeling that even here, dressed in that prison uniform, reality had not sunk in. Whatever that indefinable change in his bearing, it certainly didn't seem like remorse or apprehension.

111

We gave him a Bible and letters from Scott and Diane and his grandparents. We didn't talk about the shooting. That was like an abyss yawning at our feet: One step and we might never regain the solid ground which permitted us to function, an hour at a time. We asked about his cell. It was a replica of this one, he told us, but with a bed and a table. He described his transfer here by helicopter from Quantico Marine Base outside Washington.

I urged him to read his new Bible. "John, you've gone to church and Sunday school all your life," I began awkwardly, hyper aware of the watching guards. But I was finding out, I told him, that reciting prayers in church was not the same thing as coming to God directly with our needs. I asked him if he'd like to do that now, with us.

John nodded. Sitting in those straight-backed chairs under the unblinking scrutiny of the men beyond the glass partition, the three of us joined hands and bowed our heads. Jo Ann and I prayed for strength for us all, for guidance, for forgiveness. Repeating the words after me, John asked God to take charge of his life. Expectancy—was that what I'd been sensing in John? Almost a . . . buoyancy?

Mr. James was at the door of the bare little room to tell us the hour was up in what seemed far less. Jo Ann hugged John again, then I did. Why had I ever been shy about such things? Then we followed Mr. James into the bright North Carolina spring. Short and strained though the visit had been, both Jo Ann and I felt infinitely better. Seeing him, touching him, was like releasing a breath we'd held for five endless days.

"I'm so glad we prayed with him," Jo Ann said. "He seemed . . . relieved, afterward. Didn't you think so? As though he'd laid down some terrible burden."

A chill went through me as Jo Ann spoke. I knew what it was that had puzzled me from the moment John appeared, that quality I couldn't put my finger on. Relief. She was exactly right. As though he'd gotten some monkey off his back.

But Jo Ann was wrong about the timing. The relief was there before we ever began to pray. . . .

27

JO ANN:

This time the reporters at the end of the long prison drive were ready, cameras catching our departure. Charlie stepped on the accelerator as media people scrambled into their cars. Soon they closed the gap and fell in behind us, a little motorcade trailing us the thirty miles back to the airport.

Back in Washington a police car was again waiting at National Airport to meet us. So was the press. Their counterparts in North Carolina had obviously phoned ahead. Press cars followed us back to the Jefferson where Rose Narva again led us at a sprint to a waiting elevator.

Upstairs in our room we took off our shoes and began making phone calls—to Scott in Denver, to Diane and Steve in Dallas, to my folks in Oklahoma City. Physically, we were able to tell them, John seemed well; emotionally, remarkably calm—a lot calmer than I felt after the chase by reporters at both ends of the return trip. We'd been up since 5:30 that morning and all I wanted was to crawl into bed. First, though, there was something I had to do: I had to write to the four victims and their families.

Until I'd seen John, time had had a curious suspended quality. Now I knew I had to try to express our grief at what our son had done. I sat at the dainty antique desk in the hotel bedroom for a long time, groping for words. Forgiveness? How could I ask the Bradys to forgive? The assurance that Jack and I were praying for them? Wouldn't that sound insufferably pious? Soon the floor was littered with wadded stationery.

Jack burst into the room a little after ten o'clock: "Can you believe they're showing the Jefferson on TV? Dale's been downstairs—says there's a camera truck parked on 16th Street and spotlights playing all over the hotel."

Neither Jack nor I could yet bring ourselves to turn on a TV set, but the Colorado men, watching the late news in their room down the hall, had rapped on our door to report that CBS was proudly announcing the whereabouts of John Hinckley's parents—not only the name of the hotel, but the fact that we were on the sixth floor. It would make the job of protecting us, the security men pointed out, that much more difficult.

It was past midnight when I finally got down a letter that expressed at least a little of what I felt. I copied it out four times, personalizing each one, before I went to bed.

In the morning I read the letters over and they were awful. Stiff and formal and not at all what I meant to say. Dale Morris suggested prayers again in the living room. Afterward, while we waited for the lawyers, I wrote all the letters over.

With the four lawyers this time came a distinguished-looking white-haired man whom Vince Fuller introduced as the head of the psychiatric department at Georgetown University. In addition to the evaluation which government doctors would carry out at Butner, Vince felt we should get independent opinions from some private psychiatrists. Dr. Steinbach was giving up his Sunday morning to come here and listen to John's history, after which Vince hoped he would give us the names of some qualified men who would be willing to make the necessary trips to North Carolina. For Dr. Steinbach's benefit we swiftly reviewed what we'd told the lawyers.

"You say John exhibited flat affect from fairly early?" Dr. Steinbach inquired.

"Flat what?"

"Flat affect." It meant, the doctor explained, a kind of numbing or muting of emotions, an inability to feel great joy or great sorrow. "You say you never saw him angry, for instance?"

"That's right," Jack recalled. "Never angry, never excited."

"And do I understand," Dr. Steinbach asked, "that you eventually took him to see a psychiatrist?"

Yes, we told him. There in Evergreen.

"John came back to Evergreen from New Haven?"

"Indirectly." I told Dr. Steinbach about my brief crossing-of-paths with John in the North Dallas bus terminal in the middle of October. I'd stayed on four days with Diane and Steve, hoping all the while that John had returned to New Haven for the next segment of the seminar—suspecting, however, that he'd been headed for Los Angeles and Lynn Collins.

To my surprise, the day after I got back to Colorado, John too arrived in Denver.

I was alarmed when Jack brought him home from the airport—John looked so haunted and hopeless. After dinner the three of us sat down in the living room, Jack in his "throne" as John called his father's big brown armchair, John in one of the smaller armchairs on the other side of the fireplace, and me in the middle—figuratively as well as literally—on the patchwork-leather sofa. Always trying to be the peacemaker, trying to support both of these men whom I loved so much, trying to keep Jack from being critical and John from retreating into silence.

As near as we could understand, the entire $3,600 from the sale of John's stock—and the never-repaid $500 loan, too—was gone. Money that was supposed to have lasted four months had been frittered away in one. Spent, we supposed, running to and fro between New Haven, Washington and Dallas (and that bizarre trip back here to Evergreen, which at that point I was keeping from Jack). About the arrest in Nashville ten days earlier for trying to carry handguns aboard an airplane, neither of us of course had the slightest inkling, at that time. To us it was the old story of inability to stick with what he started.

"What are your plans now?" Jack wanted to know. "Since you seem to have given up the writing seminars."

John had no plans.

"I mean, would you like to stay here in Evergreen? Get a job somewhere in the area?"

John hated Evergreen.

"Then where *do* you want to go?"

John didn't know.

Looking utterly frustrated, Jack got up and went to his study. John dragged himself down to his room complaining of a headache. I sat alone for a while, then went up and knocked

115

on Jack's door. "I'm so worried about him, Jack. I've never seen him this low."

"What can we do that we haven't done?" Jack asked despairingly. "He's had every medical test there is. We've tried to let him pursue his own interests. Nothing seems to help."

"I know." And then I said aloud the word I'd been skirting with my mind all evening. "Do you think maybe he ought to see a . . . psychiatrist?"

It was a scary word to both of us. No one we knew went to a psychiatrist.

"I'll phone Darrell Benjamin in the morning," Jack said. "See if he can recommend someone."

"Someone close by," I suggested hopefully. With winter coming, the roads between Evergreen and Denver would be treacherous—and I didn't need to ask who'd be doing the driving.

Dr. Benjamin came up with the names of two psychiatrists, one of them right in Evergreen, a Dr. John Hopper. The earliest evening appointment Dr. Hopper could give us—so that Jack could be present too—was a week away, October 28. Before then an event occurred which moved my anxieties into a new gear.

John had lapsed into his old pattern of hanging around the house, shutting himself in his room with his guitar. I played bridge that day, getting home around three in the afternoon. John met me at the door, pale and frightened-looking.

"Where've you been, Mom? I'm sick. I've been throwing up all day."

"It must be this 24-hour virus."

He shook his head. "It was the pills I think. I think I might have taken too many."

It was all he would say, but the words lodged like a sliver of ice in my heart. An overdose of Valium . . . just how accidental had it been? John knew his father and I were upset with him for failing to live up to our "contract," and he was depressed over the experience at Yale. He didn't say he'd gone there to be near Lynn, but I was convinced that that was at the bottom of everything. How glad I was that we were getting outside help for him at last.

Two evenings later, on October 28, Jack, John and I drove

into Evergreen's little business district. We located Dr. Hopper's office in a low-rise redwood professional building and Jack parked the Omega around back. Secretly ashamed of my feeling, I was glad that no one would see us parked here. Dr. Hopper was not as forbidding a personage as I had feared. Tall, slender, warm-mannered but professional, his face had a habitually concerned expression, as though the problems people brought to him became his problems too. The four of us talked for a while, then John and the doctor were closeted in his inner office for an hour. They emerged into the waiting room having agreed on a second session two days later.

The following week I drove John to two more appointments, watching for any sign that his spirits were improving. He remained so withdrawn and listless, however, that I started doing something I hated. When John came upstairs in the morning—never until after Jack left for the office—I'd take a pile of sheets down to the laundry room and step surreptitiously across the hall to check the number of Valium pills in the bottle on his bedside table. I had to search to find it among all the other bottles there: Surmontil, Drixoral for his allergies, aspirin, Tylenol, Bufferin, huge jars of vitamins. Four Valium pills a day, the prescribed number, were all he seemed to be taking.

Now that John was under a doctor's care, Jack felt free to go ahead with a trip to Africa planned five months previously in connection with the world hunger crisis. How could we have imagined that another kind of crisis was taking shape beneath our very own roof? What could have tipped us off before the breaking point was reached?

Thinking back, here in this hotel sitting-room, fresh from seeing John in a prison cell, knowing that a week earlier he had fired a gun at the President of the United States, it seemed almost impossible that we could have missed the danger signals that must have been there. But there were such normal-seeming explanations, I told Dr. Steinbach, for John's case of the "blues." His inability to finish college. A falling-out with his girl. The failure of LISTALOT. Disappointment with the seminars.

"Why, anyone would be discouraged," Jack would say. "That's why he's got to get out and get some successful experiences under his belt."

117

But every new suggestion of Jack's was rejected before the words were out. John wouldn't go for a walk with his father, wouldn't even stay in the same room with him. Sometimes John would spend the afternoon upstairs, usually, I noticed with surprise, choosing Jack's "throne," sitting there by the hour with Titter on his lap. The minute he heard the garage doors open he'd head for the stairs. I'd beg him to wait. "Daddy's home, John. You and he haven't had a visit in a long time."

"Dad doesn't want to talk to me," he'd mumble from the stairway. "He doesn't even want me in the house."

I could understand the appeal of Africa to Jack, under the circumstances, see why he wasn't eager to stay at home where he and I weren't communicating all that well either. Yet I was dismayed at being left to cope with John's problems alone. Just when I needed "my rock" most, Jack was going away.

28

JACK:

I couldn't honestly have said which was the stronger drive, to help people in drought-stricken Africa, or to get away from Evergreen. John acted as though my presence was an affliction to be endured and Jo Ann gave me no support at all. Everywhere else, it seemed, my efforts at caring were received with eagerness. World Vision wanted me to spend the month of November working in Kenya, Zimbabwe and South Africa, and I was ready to go as soon as the presidential election was over on the fourth. I was convinced that with Reagan the Republican Party had the best chance in years.

Jo Ann and I went to the polls early. John stayed in his room. He came upstairs that evening, though, to watch the returns on TV, Titter in his lap. As Reagan's totals mounted he seemed as elated as I was. "Maybe there's hope for the country yet," he commented.

Before I got off for Africa, Jo Ann and I had a private session with Dr. Hopper to find out if he was getting anywhere with John. At 25, he told us, John was still dealing with issues of adolescence. I liked the man, felt he was sincerely trying to help. But we didn't need to pay a psychiatrist to hear that John was immature. He pointed out that Jo Ann and I were giving John different messages—but I knew that too. If Jo Ann would just stick to what we'd decided and not make things so comfortable for John around home, he might be showing some independence by now.

"But Dr. Hopper," Jo Ann objected, "John isn't well! His legs are weak and he gets dizzy spells." Twice when she'd been with him in a public place—a shopping mall once, and another time at the Denver Art Museum—he'd gone so white she'd been certain he was going to faint. "He needs a job where he can sit down."

I left for Africa on November 9 with nothing resolved. Nothing ever got resolved where John was concerned. As for the tensions between Jo Ann and me, if we tried to discuss them we'd end up arguing—and then I'd get the silent treatment. I was actually more worried about my marriage than about John, now that he was getting a psychiatrist's help. Jo Ann's and my problems went far deeper than any disagreement over our younger son—back to a difficulty in communicating that had begun years earlier.

What a difference with the team from World Vision. We traveled thousands of miles, worked in the most primitive conditions in total harmony, starting each day with prayer before sunrise. To talk about Jo Ann I felt would be disloyal, but in those early morning sessions I often mentioned John. Several times I was embarrassed to find tears coming as I spoke my son's name. But no one here seemed to mind; little by little I let out my sorrow and sense of defeat. At home I was supposed to be the strong one.

Three weeks was a long time to be away. Every day I missed Jo Ann more. Maybe it will be different between us now, I thought as the return flight neared Denver on December 1. Maybe Jo Ann and I can start off on a new footing. I half hoped John wouldn't be at the airport with her, so we could have the drive home, just the two of us.

John was not at the airport. John was not in Evergreen either. He had left the house 24 hours earlier.

29

JO ANN:

I argued and argued with John when he started talking about leaving. "At least wait till Daddy gets back. It's only a few more days."

When he wouldn't, I talked to Dr. Hopper. The doctor felt that John's desire to get out of Evergreen was probably healthy—a sign of independence. John's idea was apparently to go to Washington, D.C. I didn't understand the pull of that particular city—but at least, the doctor reminded me, John would be doing *something*.

Before Jack left he'd made John promise to spend at least some time each day looking for work—and of course that left me the one to see he lived up to it. I'd turned into a real nag, constantly after him to get out of his room. It was the phenomenon I'd noticed before when Jack was away: Without his father to fuss at him, I became the critical parent, driven almost to distraction by the sight of John moping about the house.

Maybe Washington was right for him. Evergreen certainly wasn't. Maybe it was Lynn again, maybe her current play was there. Or maybe John just had warm associations with the city where he and his father had visited together, years before. And so, I'd driven John down to the airport on November 30, the day before his father was due back from Africa.

"How did he pay for the ticket?" Jack wanted to know next day, when I told him the news. "Did you give him money?"

"Of course I didn't!" I didn't know what money he'd used—it was one of the things that had puzzled me in fact. He must have had some left over, after all, from the $3,600.

The following week there was horrifying news on TV: John Lennon had been murdered in the entryway to his apartment building in New York City by a young gunman named Mark Chapman. There were scenes of the crowd outside the building, interviews with weeping fans. Jack and I had never understood the hysteria over the Beatles, but John idolized them and we knew this would be a bitter blow to him.

Day after day we kept hoping he'd call to say how he was handling it, but a week passed until, on December 16, John phoned at last. He was not in Washington but in New York; he'd taken the train up as soon as he heard about Lennon. I wasn't surprised; I'd actually been searching for his face among the photographs of mourners in Central Park. As we feared, he was in a deep depression. "I want to come home, Mom."

Plane reservations were hard to get just before Christmas; he planned to go standby the following day. I told him to phone us when he got to the airport in Denver; once more I wondered how he was paying for all this travel. Jack and I had agreed to meet with Dr. Hopper before John came home, so that evening we drove over to his office.

"You two need to reach an agreement between yourselves on some reasonable expectations for your son," he told us. "I hear you, Mrs. Hinckley, continually making allowances. And you, sir, would like to see him functioning like an all-American businessman. Somewhere in-between there's a realistic goal, for John, for right now."

We discussed it for a while in his office, continued talking back at home. Christmas, I pleaded, should be a happy time, without pressure. That got Jack started on how the pressure at Christmas came from *me*, how I always tried to do too much, and pretty soon we were in the middle of another argument. Jack did agree, though, not to ask John anything about his future plans till after the holidays. Steve and Diane were coming with three-year-old Chris—that should get his mind off the Lennon murder.

When John walked off the plane next day we hardly knew him. His eyes were red-rimmed and sunken, our fastidious, super-scrubbed John looked as though he hadn't shaved or bathed in a week. "Don't make any cracks about Lennon, Dad," were the first words he said. "I'm in deep mourning."

I saw the hurt in Jack's eyes that John would think it necessary to warn him.

John acted so dazed that once more my fears about drugs were roused. When he was still moving like a zombie two days later, Jack confronted him:

"John, have you been taking drugs?"

It was John's turn to look hurt. "Of course not," he said. "Except the Valium." He sounded so genuinely surprised that I was sure it was the truth. And yet—how could the death of someone he'd never even met leave him so devastated? It was almost as though John Lennon had been more real to him than Jack and I.

30

JACK:

For the very first time I grew alarmed about our son and drugs. I hadn't paid much attention to Jo Ann, truthfully, about the Valium—she always worried too much about the kids. But John was acting so strange, sometimes just staring off into space.

I remembered a recovered alcoholic friend of ours talking

once about Valium addiction. He'd gone to a private psychiatric hospital somewhere in Arizona, which also treated Valium addicts. I telephoned him from the office and he said he'd contact the place for me.

In a little while the manager of the hospital himself called. Yes, they'd had a lot of experience with Valium.

"Valium may not be the only problem," I told him.

"It never is," he said.

I explained that John had been seeing a psychiatrist for various adjustment problems, but that he'd taken off for Washington before they'd accomplished much. That was why hospitalization was often the best answer, the manager said: In a "therapeutic environment" psychiatrists could work with the total person.

It seemed like a drastic step, yet I wondered if it was time to consider something like this. I thanked the manager and drove home to discuss it with Jo Ann. Her relief was touching to see: "I don't think he's getting much help from these sessions with Dr. Hopper," she said.

The one thing remaining was to convince John. It would be a self-committal, of course, which meant he himself must recognize the seriousness of the problem. I lit the logs in the fireplace and we sat there beneath the pine-cone wreath, John in a small armchair facing mine, Jo Ann on the sofa between us. "You wouldn't have to go till after Christmas if you didn't want to," I told him, knowing how much he was looking forward to the Sims' visit. "Mom and I would drive you to Arizona, of course."

At first John seemed reluctant. He denied absolutely that he was abusing his medication. Yet at the promise of help with underlying needs—"things that are bothering you deep down"—I saw a flicker of hope in his eyes. In the end he agreed to the hospitalization.

"What about Dr. Hopper?" Jo Ann asked as we got ready for bed. We'd made an appointment with him for the following day, December 19, to discuss John's getting back into therapy now that he'd returned to Evergreen.

"Go see him, I guess," I said. "Get his input on it." Hopper had had six sessions with John before he left for Washington on November 30; maybe he could explain why Lennon's death had hit him so hard.

Dr. Hopper didn't have much to say about Lennon, but a great deal to say about the hospitalization plan. "Don't do it!" he warned. "I've worked in these hospitals, and I've worked with people who've come out of them. It makes adjustment to the real world that much harder. If you put him in a hospital you'll be making an emotional cripple out of him."

It was an anguished session with Jo Ann and me totally confused. Dr. Hopper was the only one who seemed certain, and in the end we followed his advice. After all, he was the expert. . . .

He'd seen no evidence, Hopper assured us, of Valium misuse by John. "But if you're concerned about it, there's a far less expensive and less potentially damaging way to wean him from Valium than putting him in a hospital."

Dr. Hopper had been working with a technique called biofeedback. He'd purchased a machine to assist patients in learning the procedure and his wife had trained as a biofeedback instructor. "It's a way of getting in touch with our own emotional responses and, eventually, learning to control them." With this approach, Dr. Hopper believed, he could have John off Valium in thirty days.

And so we held another family conference in the living room. When John heard that we'd now decided *against* the hospital, he actually seemed disappointed. "I'm not the only one who can't get his head together around here," he said—and that about summed up the situation.

Steve and Diane were alarmed at John's appearance when they arrived for Christmas. Scott too. Vanderbilt was so busy these days that Scott almost never got up for a meal with us in Evergreen anymore. He hadn't seen his younger brother since John took off for Washington, and was shocked at the change in him. "He's grieving over John Lennon's death," Jo Ann explained, and both sister and brother accepted that; they belonged to the generation that had seen the Beatles as larger than life.

Everyone was extra considerate of John that Christmas, not forcing him to join in the merrymaking unless he felt like it. He spent most of his time with Chris, helping him set up his new train set. He gave Diane a book called *The Mother's Almanac* in anticipation of the new baby due next month. Some days Jo Ann and I were encouraged, feeling he was coming out of his depression. Other times he'd shut himself down in his room, refusing to emerge even when Chris pounded on his door.

Christmas dinner was Jo Ann's usual elaborate production with a turkey and all the trimmings, including rutabaga because they were my favorite, and the chandelier from Dallas sparkling down on us all. Jo Ann made a fetish of taking down and washing those scores of glass pendants every year just before Christmas. In the chandelier's glow I got a sudden look at John, hunched absolutely motionless over his plate, head on his chest, a portrait of despair.

The next moment, mumbling something about not feeling well, he excused himself from the table. He rejoined us after dinner, but that image stayed with me, and I prayed we were making the right decision not to put him in the hospital.

New Year's Eve Jo Ann and I decided not to go out. The Sims were back in Dallas, Scott was seeing the new year in with his crowd down in Denver, and we didn't feel like leaving John alone. Around nine p.m. we got out a bottle of champagne and asked him to join us in the living room, but he guessed he'd stay down in his room. We could hear him playing Beatles' tapes on his cassette player.

"He asked me to pick up some peach brandy for him, of all things, to celebrate the new year," Jo Ann said.

"*Brandy?*" John would never even have a glass of wine with dinner. "And he specifically asked for *peach* brandy?"

"That's what he wanted. I figured I could use the rest of it in cooking."

So there were just the two of us upstairs. I put the unopened champagne bottle back in the refrigerator. Jo Ann and I didn't care much for New Year's toasts anyway. It was a good night to sit in front of the fire and review the past year. Except for John's continuing failure to find a direction for his life, 1980 had been a time of accomplishment. Vanderbilt had had its best year ever, doing nearly $4 million worth of business. That was a drop in the bucket compared with the oil and gas giants, but a source of satisfaction for an outfit that had started ten years before with half a dozen shareholders investing a total of $100,000. I'd prefaced my annual report to our 1,400 current stockholders with a quote from the Bible:

Commit to the Lord whatever you do, and your plans will succeed (Proverbs 16:3).

I was convinced that this was true. Together on New Year's Eve, Jo Ann and I committed the year about to begin to God's keeping.

31

JO ANN:

John came upstairs earlier than usual next morning—I suspected because it was a holiday and his father was home. Jack would get terribly upset when John stayed in his room all morning—though John would explain that he was writing, and "writers need privacy."

"Happy New Year, dear," I greeted him.

"Happy New Year," he said. He'd brought the brandy bottle up with him. He hadn't drunk much of it.

Jack lowered his newspaper. "Did you stay up to see the old year out?" he asked.

"Midnight? Yeah."

"Mom and I must be getting old—we didn't make it."

John went to the refrigerator and got out the bottle of apple juice while I put the peach brandy away in the cupboard.

The next day, Friday, January 2, I drove him into Evergreen for his first biofeedback session. Afterward John described the procedure to me. Electrodes attached to his forehead, and a small thermometer taped to a finger, sent electronic signals to a headset, and also activated a needle on a display panel, so that he could both hear and see his own reaction to various kinds of stress. With these mechanical aids he was to learn a series of relaxation techniques.

Jack and I spent two weeks in California that month, feeling sure that something good would result from these treatments. On our return, however, we found him as morose and uncommunicative as ever. He would sit for hours with Titter in his lap, staring out at the snow-covered pine trees, moving the upper part of his body back and forth in a strange little rocking motion. About the only encouraging sign was that he'd begun going out occasionally to the little Evergreen public library.

Jack and I met with Dr. Hopper on January 23 to discuss the next step. Helping John to get off Valium was only one part of what Dr. Hopper called the treatment plan. More important, in his view, was for Jack and me to decide on goals. Jack thought I differed with him here, but I didn't at all. "We want John to be happier," I told the doctor. "We want him to become self-sufficient," Jack said. That was the same thing, wasn't it? How could a 25-year-old be happy staying home dependent on his parents?

"If he's not going back to school," Jack said, "he ought to find a job and start supporting himself."

Dr. Hopper turned to me. "You agree, Mrs. Hinckley?" When I nodded he went on, "Then the three of you must work out a plan and a timetable for achieving this. Something you'll put in writing and really stick to, this time." It was almost word for word what Dr. Benjamin had said four months before.

Once again, as I had repeatedly since John Lennon's death, I voiced my fear of John's harming himself. Again Dr. Hopper assured us that he did not detect suicidal tendencies in John.

John was unenthusiastic about developing a plan, but then he wasn't enthusiastic about anything. Together he and we agreed on the end of February as the deadline for finding a job (it was then the last week of January). "It doesn't have to be something you intend to stay with the rest of your life," Jack consoled him.

By the end of March, according to the plan, John would be living away from the house. . . .

Our little granddaughter was born on January 30. I flew to Dallas February 6. "John's treatment plan seems to be working," I told Diane as I rocked tiny Stephanie. "He's found work on a weekly newspaper." The paper was in a nearby suburb and the job was to start February 23—actually ahead of schedule.

That evening I telephoned home. "How's John?" I asked Jack. That was the way our conversations always seemed to start.

"I don't know. He's not here."

"What do you mean?"

"He's gone. Took the Volare and cleared out. I found a note when I got home a few minutes ago."

I asked a dozen questions but of course Jack didn't know the answers and got angry with me because I kept on asking. "But what does the note *say*, Jack?"

"Says he'll be back in time to start his job. Says things are too tense here in the house and it's better for both of us if he goes away."

"Jack! Did you say something to upset him?"

"There you go—making it *my* fault!"

It was always this way: John's erratic behavior left Jack and me at odds with each other instead of with him. We made an appointment with Dr. Hopper when I got back from Dallas, feeling we could discuss it more rationally in the presence of a third party. John was so reticent and naive, I told the doctor—I worried about how he managed away from home.

He got himself on and off airplanes, Dr. Hopper reminded me. Again, the doctor felt that John's restlessness might be a positive sign—the stirrings of independence. The important thing for the two of *us* was to agree on how we were going to handle these unannounced departures.

If John wanted to live in a family, or any other group, the doctor went on, he'd have to learn that it was a two-sided arrangement. He couldn't just ignore our wishes and wander off at will, leaving everyone wondering where he was, yet still expect our support. "When John gets in touch with you, I suggest you make him wait at least 48 hours before you let him come home."

Both Jack and I were alarmed at this idea. "It's the middle of winter," Jack protested. "What's he going to do if he has no money and no place to stay?"

"Shouldn't that be his problem?" Dr. Hopper asked.

We compromised on 24 hours. Even so . . . "Suppose it's

the middle of the night?'' I asked. ''And there's a blizzard and he's standing on our doorstep?''

It would have to depend on the circumstances, Dr. Hopper agreed. ''But you've got to get some control over the situation. Otherwise you'll be facing these same problems five or ten years from now.''

Four more days went by. Four days of running to the phone each time it rang. Jack and I went back to Dr. Hopper's. I cried through most of the session. Dr. Hopper still believed John would come back in time to begin work at the newspaper on February 23, then five days off.

''But what if he's sick somewhere!'' I worried. He'd been asking to have X-rays taken of his head, I reminded the two men. He'd mentioned it often enough that I'd gotten Em Harvey to recommend a specialist, but before we could make an appointment John had disappeared.

Nor could I imagine what John was doing for money. I knew Jack suspected me of supplying him with cash over and above the allowance agreed on in the ''plan,'' but I never had.

A troubling thought kept coming into my mind. . . . Beneath the globe of the world in his study, Jack kept some gold Krugerrands which he'd bought as an investment—seven or eight, I thought—worth several hundred dollars apiece. I wasn't sure of the exact number, just that each time I dusted in there, there seemed to be fewer. Doubtless Jack had sold them, or put them in the safe deposit box. To imagine one of our children stealing was so far-fetched I wouldn't breathe my suspicion aloud even to Jack.

As it turned out, Dr. Hopper was right. John came home, in fact, that very night. We were sitting in the living room after getting back from Dr. Hopper's when about ten o'clock the doorbell rang. I was afraid it was the police with news of an accident, and hurried down to the front door behind Jack. A blast of icy air came in as Jack opened it. John stood sheepishly on the doorstep, the Volare parked in the driveway behind him. Of course we pulled him inside.

John wouldn't talk about where he'd been for the past ten days. He was pale and haggard-looking, wanting only to go to his room, refusing the meal I offered to fix. But he was safely home, and for the moment that was all we cared about. The idea of making him wait 24 hours, that had seemed possible in the abstract, had proved out of the question when the time actually came.

A few days later John set off in the Volare for his first day of work at the newspaper, wearing the handsome jacket and slacks he'd bought for Yale five months before. Jack fairly glowed with pride in him: "It was just a question of firmness and patience," he told me as he climbed into his own car. "You'll see a big difference in his self-esteem now."

About 5:30 I heard the Volare pull into the far side of the garage. Minutes passed though, before John appeared in the hall doorway, jacket rumpled, new slacks soiled. They'd told him—or he'd understood—that he was being hired as a writer. Instead he'd spent the day moving paper bales around a warehouse. His legs hurt and his back hurt and he just didn't know if he could go back again in the morning.

Jack's disappointment when he got home seemed almost keener than John's. But he wouldn't hear of his quitting. "You haven't given the thing a chance! Show them they can depend on you in the warehouse and they may give you a crack at a writing assignment."

John wanted to cancel his appointment with Dr. Hopper that night, saying he was too tired, but we insisted he go, and ended up by going with him. Together with the doctor we talked John into sticking with the job at least a while longer. By the end of March, five weeks off, Jack reminded him, the "plan" called for him to be in his own apartment. How could he do that if he wasn't working?

The end of March . . . what a neutral, unexceptional date that seemed to us all, as we planned the future, there in Dr. Hopper's office.

John was subdued and silent as we drove home—but when was he anything else? The annual shareholders' meeting of Vanderbilt Energy was scheduled that week in Phoenix, Arizona, and Jack insisted I come along as planned.

"Just when John's getting started in this job, Jack? Don't you think I should be here?"

"That's just why you *shouldn't* stay. He needs to feel this is *his* job, *his* life."

And so we left for Arizona on February 25.

32

JACK:

The meeting in Phoenix was full of jubilant expectations for the future. Oil prices were climbing right off the charts. Our stock had risen to nearly $13 a share, and the sky seemed the limit. I even got in some golf before we flew back to Denver March 1.

It was dark by the time we got the car out of the long-term parking lot and drove up to the house. The Volare was not in the garage. "Maybe he's seeing Hopper tonight," I said.

Jo Ann hurried inside. I was still getting the suitcases from the trunk when she reappeared in the garage. "Jack, he's gone again! This was on the stairs."

I took the scrap of paper from her and read it beneath the overhead light bulb.

March 1, 1981

Your prodigal son has taken off again to exorcise some demons. I'll let you know where I am in a few days. This is something I have to do even though I know you don't understand.

John

P.S. Titter has been fed today.

"He's right. I don't understand!" I exploded. It was a repeat of all the other disappointments we'd been through with John. The big plans, the new job—the old pattern of quitting.

He was gone, all right. In the kitchen he'd left enough Super Supper and water to last Titter a month. "He shows more consideration for the cat than he does for you and me," I grumbled.

We telephoned Dr. Hopper who suggested that John was testing us: Did we or did we not mean what we said?

It was true. It was as much our fault as John's. When he'd showed up late at night two weeks earlier, after driving us half frantic with worry, had we insisted on a complete accounting? No. We'd welcomed him home, asked few questions. "This time," I told Jo Ann, "he's not going to waltz right back in."

But . . . would there be a "this time"? Again the slow days passed; again the agony of not knowing mounted. In my "quiet time" each morning I committed John, wherever he was, to God's care; by evening I'd be stewing again.

At 4:30 a.m. on Friday, five days after we'd returned from Phoenix, we were awakened by the telephone. I groped for the receiver by the bed. John's voice on the other end. "John? Where are you? I can't hear you!"

Silence.

"John, are you still there?"

Some words I could not make out.

"I can't understand you, John. Speak louder!"

For several minutes I struggled to hold a conversation. Jo Ann had switched on the light and was sitting up in bed. John was in New York, that much I caught. He either hadn't eaten or hadn't slept—maybe both—in two days. The rest was too garbled to follow, interspersed with maddening silences. "John," I said at last, "I can't make out what you're saying. Hang up, get something in your stomach and call back."

For half an hour we waited. The second call went better. He'd had a bottle of Coke, he said, and felt better. He was broke and hungry and wanted to come home.

Jo Ann was all for him coming straight on, but I felt it was take a stand now or never. "John, it's just after five o'clock in the morning out here. We can't make decisions at this hour. Call me this afternoon at the office and we'll discuss it." John hated phoning the office, but he was going to have to start doing a few things my way. We needed time to think, time to consult with Dr. Hopper.

Even before John's afternoon call, I'd backed away from my

132

own stand and arranged for a plane ticket to Denver to be waiting for him at Newark Airport. Dr. Hopper, when Jo Ann and I had telephoned him that morning, had advised against doing this: "How's he going to learn to face the consequences of his behavior if you keep stepping in and bailing him out?"

"But he sounds so bad," Jo Ann told the doctor tearfully. "He's out of money. Where can he stay—how can he eat?"

Jo Ann was right—we couldn't leave him stranded in New York City. Neither, in faithfulness to the plan, did I feel we could let him move back in with us. "We'll get him safely back to Denver," I told Hopper, "then deal with it from here."

To make a point, I bought the airline ticket for the following day, Saturday, March 7. "It won't hurt him to cool his heels in New York one more night," I said to Jo Ann's protests. When John phoned me at the office I explained the arrangements I had made. That evening I learned he'd called Jo Ann twice more, pleading to come home. "Jack, he says if we don't bring him back right away we'll never see him again!"

"He's only trying to scare you," I said.

I wasn't as sure as I tried to sound, and we made an appointment for that night with Dr. Hopper. He urged us not to give in to threats. "If he were my son," he said, "I'd send him $100 and wish him good luck."

Both Jo Ann and I stared at him. We knew him to be a compassionate man who really cared about John. Earlier, in an effort to establish better rapport, he'd suggested a weekend ski trip, just the two of them. John had reacted with panic at the idea, but it showed a very personal interest on Hopper's part.

"It's too late," I said. "I've already bought the ticket."

"And when he gets here?" Hopper asked.

"Once he gets here, out of New York City," I said firmly, "he'll have to make his own arrangements." We talked for an hour. Hopper and I talked, that is; Jo Ann mostly sat and cried.

Saturday morning John phoned the house. He had no money to get to the airport, he told me. How was he supposed to get from Manhattan to Newark?

"John, that's your problem. Why don't you think of these things before you take off on these scatterbrained trips?"

"The busfare out there is $7.50," John said.

"John, people get stranded all the time without money. Go

133

to the Travelers' Aid. Go to the nearest church. Go to the police. I don't know. I can't solve your problems from halfway across the country.''

At last he hung up—and I promptly set about trying to solve his problems. I recalled that one of our board members lived in Manhattan. I telephoned him and he said of course he'd lend John some money.

Inside an hour John called back. ''No one will give me any money,'' he said. I doubted he'd even tried—probably just waited a respectable interval till he could dump the problem in my lap again. I gave him my friend's address. ''How will I get to his—?''

''You'll *walk,*'' I almost shouted into the phone. ''And John,'' I added, ''phone me from the airport so I'll know you got there O.K.'' There I go, I thought as I replaced the receiver, asking him to function as an adult one minute, hovering over him the next.

My mind kept going back to a troubling conversation with Scott the previous afternoon. Scott had just returned from a meeting with our geologist in Dallas. When he stepped into my office, though, he closed the door behind him. ''This isn't about business,'' he said.

While he was in Dallas he'd spent the night with Diane and Steve, and the three of them had done a lot of talking about John. ''We think he needs to . . . be in a hospital, Dad. He just keeps going down. Sure, I know about Lennon last Christmas—but it's more than Lennon. John just doesn't seem like he can cope anymore.''

I got up to stare out the window at the Denver skyline. ''Scott, your mother and I have been over and over this, believe me. We were on the verge of putting him in a hospital last December—three months ago. But Dr. Hopper said it could leave emotional scars for the rest of his life.'' What good was going to a doctor, I asked him, if we didn't follow his advice?

Scott was not convinced. In the end I told him I'd investigate facilities around Denver; I'd asked my assistant Ivonne to start looking into it that very afternoon. And yet . . . we'd committed ourselves to a treatment plan, hadn't we? Shouldn't we give it at least a chance before abandoning it?

About three o'clock John phoned from Newark to say he'd

found my friend's apartment O.K. When it was time to go to the airport, Jo Ann told me she wasn't coming. She was half-sick from crying all day. "If you're going to tell him he can't come home, then I don't want to be there."

I took along all the money I had in the house for John to live on in Denver till he found some kind of work. I also took a plastic jug of antifreeze from the garage. If I knew John, he hadn't put anything in the Volare's leaky radiator since the last time I had.

John was almost the last one off the plane. He looked awful—unshaven, eyes glazed. He said he'd bought a hamburger with some extra cash my New York friend had given him, and eaten a second meal on the plane. We found an unused boarding area and sat down while I lectured him as to why he could not come home. "You've broken every promise you've made to your mother and me. Our part of the agreement was to provide you a home and an allowance while you worked at becoming independent. I don't know what you've been doing these past months, but it hasn't been that, and we've reached the end of our rope."

He looked at me like he couldn't believe his ears. I gave him the $200 I'd found at the house and suggested the YMCA as an inexpensive place to live. He didn't want to live at the "Y."

"Well, it's your decision, John. From here on you're on your own."

I asked him where he'd left his car and of course he'd left it in the parking garage right at the terminal, the most expensive area in the airport. That was the kind of thing that drove me absolutely wild about John: He just didn't *think*. I was right about his radiator, too. I added the antifreeze and got the car running. I told him to stay in touch. Then I watched him drive slowly away down the ramp. . . .

I did not see my son again face to face until we met in Butner Prison.

33

JO ANN:

I did see John a number of times in Evergreen after he got back
from New York. He'd drive the Volare up to the house in the
daytime from the cheap motel where he was staying, always
leaving before Jack got home. Each time he came he'd take a
few phonograph records from his closet. "How can you listen
to them in a motel room?" I asked.

"I'm selling them," he said. "Some of them are worth
money."

Selling his precious Beatles albums? I'd promised Jack I
wouldn't give John money, but I'd clip help-wanted ads from
the classifieds for him and cook him a nourishing meal
whenever he showed up.

I asked John if he didn't want to see Dr. Hopper, but he said
the biofeedback sessions never helped. Dr. Hopper telephoned, wanting to know how John was doing. I didn't know
what to say. After the doctor had put so much of himself into
this case it seemed heartless to tell him it had been wasted
effort. I told him John was fine, living on his own down in
Denver.

But John could never stay in one place for long. He'd been
back in Colorado two weeks when he began talking about
going to California. "California again, John?" I asked in
dismay. "You hated it last time you went." Yes, but he hated
Denver more. "Call tonight when Daddy's here," I pleaded.
"Talk it over with him."

So John phoned that evening. It was March 24. Since Jack
and I were no longer supporting him we really didn't have

anything to say about where he went, except to try to help him not to make foolish decisions. "How do you plan to get there?" Jack asked. There couldn't be anything left from the $200 and his phonograph records surely weren't bringing that much.

He was going to drive.

"I'm not sure I'd trust that old car in the desert," Jack cautioned him.

"Well, that's what I wanted to talk to you about." John proposed that we sell the car and let him have the money to fly out to California and live on there while he looked for work.

"John," his father told him, "that's simply another way of asking us to go on supporting these travels of yours all over creation. East coast, west coast, anything but settle down and earn a living like everyone else."

"But why should I get some lousy job here where it's freezing cold and I don't know anyone, when I can find a lousy job out there—where it's warm and I have friends."

Lynn! I thought, listening on the kitchen phone. Whenever John got this sudden travel fever, it doubtless meant that Lynn was back in the picture. I'd been urging him, since he felt Dr. Hopper hadn't helped, to try a different psychiatrist down in Denver, perhaps the other name Dr. Benjamin had given us. I brought this up again now, but John once more refused to consider it.

We hung up with him sounding undecided about the trip. Next morning after Jack left for work, however, John called to say he *was* going to Los Angeles, and would I drive him to the airport if he brought the Volare up to leave it in the garage. He looked so troubled and forlorn when he arrived that I longed to tell him, of course you can come back home! I was furious at Jack and Dr. Hopper for insisting on this wretched "plan." Furious at myself for ever agreeing to it.

I told John again he was doing the wrong thing, but he refused to discuss it. We made the long drive down to Stapleton in absolute silence. I was in such turmoil that staying on the road was difficult. I was berating myself for giving him $100 against Jack's instructions, trying not to let John see how upset I was. Above all, I was frightened—frightened that he would do something to hurt himself.

He got out at the curbside in front of the terminal and reached into the backseat for his suitcase. I couldn't even look at him. "I want to thank you, Mom, for everything you've ever done for me, all these years."

The fear climbed up into my throat. "You're very welcome," I managed to get out. I drove away, blinking so hard I could hardly see the road. That was the kind of thing a person said when they might never see you again. . . .

I was fighting tears again now, in that high-ceilinged hotel room in Washington, D.C., unable to meet Dr. Steinbach's probing look, the concerned faces of the four lawyers. I fumbled in my purse for a Kleenex.

"The rest you know," I said.

"You know a lot more than we do," said Jack. "Who were these friends of John's out in California?"

Vince Fuller shook his head. "We really don't have time to get into that now, Jack, with you leaving Washington in a few minutes." The point of this Sunday morning meeting, he reminded us, was to ask Dr. Steinbach to recommend doctors who could make independent psychiatric evaluations of John. Several names had in fact occurred to him as we talked, Dr. Steinbach said.

"But, hearing what you have this morning, Doctor," Jack said, "you must have some opinion right now. What would make a person do what John did?"

Dr. Steinbach shook his head. "The mind is endlessly complex, Mr. Hinckley. Even we so-called experts don't always agree on a diagnosis. Certainly I wouldn't venture one without knowing more than we do now."

"But *we* don't know anything, my wife and I!" Jack turned to the lawyers. "We've answered your questions for two days now. Told you everything you asked, no matter how personal, or how dimwitted it makes us look. Can't you at least answer a few of ours? Did John really go to California when Jo Ann left him at the airport? And if so, how did he end up here in Washington?"

The FBI was apparently satisfied that he'd gone to Los Angeles, Greg Craig answered courteously. There was even some question as to whether he'd had the Washington trip in mind at all at that point. At any rate, the day after he arrived on the west coast, John had boarded a cross-country bus for the four-day trip across the continent.

"Look, Jack," Vince Fuller broke in, "it's better for right now if you and Jo Ann *don't* know all this." The government was going to want to question us, he said. And if the case should ever go to trial, we'd have to take the stand. "It'll make your job and ours a whole lot easier if you're only concerned with what you yourselves saw and heard, and don't have to filter out all the things you didn't learn until later."

"But we don't want to be kept in the dark for weeks," Jack objected, "while everyone else is digging into our affairs."

Vince smiled ruefully. "We're all in the dark on this case, Jack. And it's not going to be weeks. It may be months even before we know what all the charges against John will be. The country's up in arms about assassinations and the government may make this a test case."

A dizzy feeling swept over me. President Kennedy . . . Robert Kennedy . . . Martin Luther King . . . Governor Wallace. Jack and I had been as loud as anyone insisting that the assailants be punished. "But surely," I pleaded, "just looking at John—I mean, what possible reason could he have to want to kill the President?"

That's what everyone was trying to discover, Vince Fuller said. "But your role, Jo Ann, and Jack, is extremely simple." We were to tell the truth. Whatever we were asked, by whomever we were asked it. To the four of them, to the government investigators, to a jury if it came to a trial, we were to tell exactly what happened, as accurately as we could remember, no matter how irrelevant or how damaging it might seem.

That was why he didn't want us overly involved with the facts investigators were currently turning up, lest we get confused as to what we ourselves knew on a particular date. Above all, he didn't want us trying to judge the effect of this or that piece of testimony. "In 25 years as a defense lawyer, I've discovered that the unvarnished truth is the only defense worth going for."

There was a rap on the hallway door. The Colorado security men stepped into the room, carrying their coats and bags. We were all scheduled to leave Washington on early afternoon flights. Dale and the Governor's aides returning to Denver, Jack and I bound for a few days with Diane and Steve in Texas.

Getting out of the Jefferson without being followed, however, posed a problem now that camera crews were staking out the hotel. Rose Narva, the efficient manager, had told us to phone her half an hour before we were ready to leave. While Jack placed the call I handed Vince the four letters I'd labored over so hard. "Jack thought you'd know how to see that they get to the President and the others."

Mr. Fuller read them over, then passed them to Greg Craig, who in turn asked Lon Babby and Judith Miller to look at them. The four lawyers went into a huddle, then: "I know you mean every word that's here, Mrs. Hinckley," Judy said, "but we feel that the letters ought to be more—spontaneous sounding. I mean, some of these phrases are exactly the same in each one. If people got hold of all four, they might accuse you of writing them as a ploy for sympathy."

My heart sank right into my shoes. I didn't *know* any other words: It had taken me hours to find these! I always felt awkward trying to express myself on paper—and now I had to do it four different ways! Shattered, I took back the letters and packed them away in my suitcase.

We thanked Dr. Steinbach for giving up his Sunday to help us, then said goodbye to the four lawyers. Vince, energetic and positive. Greg Craig who could put me at my ease with a smile. Bright Lon and Judy—the ages of our own children. We'd grown so close to them all that it was hard to believe we'd met for the first time just two days before. We'd poured out our hearts and lives to them. Things I never thought I'd share with any human being I'd told these strangers . . . and they were strangers no more.

34

JACK:

The lawyers had scarcely left when there was a knock at the door and Rose Narva motioned us to follow her. I grabbed Jo Ann's suitcase along with my own and hurried past the police detail in the corridor to the waiting elevator.

The elevator car didn't stop at the lobby level but took us straight to the hotel basement. Mrs. Narva led the five of us past the furnace room, down a narrow passageway, through the hotel pantry and then up a narrow flight of concrete stairs to an alleyway at the rear of the building. Waiting there in the gentle spring drizzle were two unmarked cars driven by plainclothes police officers.

At Dulles airport we said a grateful goodbye to Dale and the two Colorado security aides. Then the police drove Jo Ann and me far out onto a runway for our flight to Texas. Once more we were the first to board the aircraft. We made our way almost automatically to the last row where "Mr. and Mrs. Smith's" seats were reserved. The flight's first stop was Dallas, but that's not where we were meeting the kids. Their house offered no more immunity from inquisitive strangers than ours in Evergreen, so Steve and Diane had driven down to a lake called Horseshoe Bay and rented a condo for three nights. "Just register us all under 'Sims,'" I'd suggested over the phone. "Any name but Hinckley."

We got off the plane in Austin, and there they were—Diane with a big bouquet of flowers for her mother. Best of all, there wasn't a reporter or a camera in sight. No one even glanced our way—except for the smiles that always followed Steve and

Diane. They had left Chris and little Stephanie with Steve's folks in Mexia so that we could talk and walk to our hearts' content.

And cry. . . .

It was six days, that Sunday afternoon at Horseshoe Bay, since the news had come over Arnie Bjork's radio in the Vanderbilt office. Six days when I'd had to appear strong and in control of things for Jo Ann, for our investors, for strangers. There in that rented condominium in Texas I broke down and cried for the first time. Cried uncontrollably for John in a concrete cell in North Carolina. Cried for the people he'd hurt. Maybe I permitted myself to do it because Steve and Diane were there to give Jo Ann the support she needed. For whatever reason, it was wonderful, just for a while, not to be wise, not to be in charge.

At Horseshoe Bay for the first time, too, Jo Ann and I saw the story in print. Gradually over the next three days, we began to learn the things the rest of the country already knew. . . .

When his cross-country bus arrived in Washington from California, John had checked in at the Park Central Hotel. He'd stayed there just one night, according to the FBI, apparently intending to continue on to New Haven next day. He'd told them that it was catching sight, purely by chance, of the President's schedule in a Washington newspaper that had drawn him to the sidewalk outside the Hilton Hotel.

That he'd gone to the Hilton intending to commit murder there seemed no doubt. Nor was there much doubt that he'd expected to be caught, and perhaps killed, in the process. It was all spelled out in a letter he'd left behind in his hotel room, addressed to an eighteen-year-old movie actress called Jodie Foster—whose name we'd heard for the first time on Monday. I knew Vince Fuller didn't want Jo Ann and me confusing our own recollections with facts we hadn't known—but how could we help finding them out? The letter to Miss Foster was reproduced in every article we picked up:

Dear Jodie,

There is a definite possibility that I will be killed in my attempt to get Reagan. It is for this very reason that I am writing you this letter now.

As you well know by now, I love you very much. The

past seven months I have left you dozens of poems, letters and messages in the faint hope you would develop an interest in me.

Although we talked on the phone a couple of times, I never had the nerve to simply approach you and introduce myself. Besides my shyness, I honestly did not wish to bother you. I know the many messages left at your door and in your mail-box were a nuisance, but I felt it was the most painless way for me to express my love to you.

I feel very good about the fact that you at least know my name and how I feel about you. And by hanging around your dormitory I've come to realize that I'm the topic of more than a little conversation, however full of ridicule it may be. At least you know that I'll always love you.

Jodie, I would abandon this idea of getting Reagan in a second if I could only win your heart and live out the rest of my life with you, whether it be in total obscurity or whatever. I will admit to you that the reason I'm going ahead with this attempt now is because I just cannot wait any longer to impress you. I've got to do something now to make you understand in no uncertain terms that I am doing all of this for your sake. By sacrificing my freedom and possibly my life I hope to change your mind about me. This letter is being written an hour before I leave for the Hilton Hotel.

Jodie, I'm asking you to please look into your heart and at least give me the chance with this historical deed to gain your respect and love.

> I love you forever.
> (signed) John Hinckley

Jo Ann and I read it through, then read it again, and once again. Far from helping us understand the events of a week ago, the letter left us more mystified than ever. It was obvious from the contents that John and Miss Foster weren't even acquaintances. When the FBI had gone to New Haven to interrogate Miss Foster, the newspaper accounts continued, the Yale coed insisted that John was a total stranger.

Yale!

Those "writing seminars," whose ad I could never find.

Those trips back and forth to the east coast. I skimmed John's letter. There it was in the fourth paragraph: *by hanging around your dormitory*. . . .

"You were right about one thing," I said to Jo Ann. "There *was* a girl behind the Yale idea. Only it wasn't Lynn Collins, it was this Jodie Foster." I wondered whether Lynn had known about his infatuation with this other young actress. She certainly knew now.

According to the papers, John's attraction to Jodie Foster had come about through seeing her in a film called *Taxi Driver*. It was a violent story, from the accounts, in which the movie's hero stalks a presidential candidate with a gun in order to get a girl friend's attention. But—that was make-believe, a story on celluloid. John knew the difference between fiction and real life . . . didn't he?

The letter was only one of the bizarre and baffling things the FBI had turned up in John's room at the Park Central. There was a post card of President and Mrs. Reagan on which John had written that he and Jodie Foster would someday occupy the White House. There was an illustration torn from an art book of "Napoleon on the Bridge at Arcole." Beneath the picture John had written:

Napoleon and Josephine
John and Jodie

Some of the findings brought those newfound tears to my eyes, not because they were strange, but because they were so very familiar: throat lozenges, cold remedies, a package of Digel, bottles of Surmontil and Valium, Cystex tablets, Drixoral, Tylenol.

There were cassette tapes, too. . . . "Listen to this!" Steve picked up one of the news accounts and read aloud: " 'One of the tapes was recorded on New Year's Eve, according to investigators who inventoried the contents of Hinckley's hotel room, and contained a *New Year's Message* to the world.' "

"New Year's Eve," Jo Ann echoed. "Don't you remember, Jack, how he wouldn't join us in front of the fire, stayed in his room all evening?"

"Does it say what the 'message' was?" I asked Steve.

"Let's see. They just give a little of it:

Anything that I might do in 1981 would be solely for Jodie Foster's sake. I want to tell the world in some way that I worship and idolize her."

We gazed at one another in bewilderment. I remembered that night so well—how John had declined to drink a champagne toast with his mother and me, sitting alone in his room with a bottle of—"what was that drink he got you to buy for him, Jo Ann?"

"Peach brandy."

"John?" Diane asked in astonishment. "I've never even seen him finish a beer."

I buried my head in my hands. The strain of trying to fit together two portraits of John was getting to me. They just wouldn't mesh. Why, the day after he made that tape he'd started the biofeedback program we had such hopes for. All that next month John and Jo Ann and I worked on the "plan." A job by the end of February, the three of us had agreed, his own living arrangements by the end of March. It sounded so realistic.

It never touched John's reality at all.

Here—on that New Year's Eve tape—was where real life had been for John. A strange, warped devotion to some girl I'd never heard of and he himself had never met. . . .

Diane was thumbing through another paper. "Have you come to the Band-aid box yet?" she asked. That was another of the discoveries at the Park Central. Inside the small tin box Federal agents had found a note printed in capital letters—a seeming parody of all the airplane hijackings ever reported:

THIS PLANE HAS BEEN HIJACKED! I HAVE A BOMB WITH ME, PLUS FLAMMABLE LIQUIDS AND A KNIFE. A COMPANION IS ALSO ON THE PLANE WITH A FIREARM. ACT NATURALLY AND LEAD THE WAY TO THE CABIN. STAY CALM!

Just a bizarre piece of play acting. And yet . . . the notion of John waiting with a loaded gun for the President to appear was equally bizarre. . . .

"Let's go for a walk!" I said, jumping up. I had to get away

145

from these horrible reports, endlessly repeating facts that made no sense. We walked for an hour, then went to our separate bedrooms to write letters to John, assuring him we loved him. Whatever the bafflement, whatever the ugliness, you do not stop loving your child.

But somehow love had not been enough. Not the tough love I thought was needed, nor the tender love Jo Ann gave. Both of us had been reacting to behavior, never suspecting that behind what we could observe, a tortured private scenario was unfolding. What could have lifted the curtain for us?

Wednesday the four of us reluctantly left our hideaway and drove to Steve's parents' home in Mexia, picked up Chris and Stephanie, and continued on to the Dallas airport. It was my first glimpse of our new granddaughter. Jo Ann cuddled her in her lap for the entire two-hour drive, handing her back to Diane only when our flight to Denver was called.

Scott met us at Stapleton Airport. I guess we looked as drained as we felt because he confined the conversation to business as he drove us up to Evergreen. No good prospects had appeared for the company positions that were open; there hadn't even been any candidates since the man I'd been lunching with at the time of the shooting, nine days and a lifetime ago.

Brookline Road was a sleepy suburban street once more, no camera trucks, no police cars. Jo Ann and I were both by nature very private people, but I'd never fully appreciated the privilege of anonymity.

Indoors, too, the phone was no longer ringing off the wall. The Sells had seen to getting our number changed to an unlisted one while we were gone. Sue Sells brought over a casserole. "For real, this time," she said with a chuckle at the decoy meal which had been part of our elaborate getaway.

Bill Sells had arranged for the post office to hold our mail. It was too late Wednesday to pick it up, so Thursday morning we drove over to our little branch office and Jo Ann ran up the steps while I kept the motor running. In a few minutes she reappeared in the post office door. "Jack, I can't carry it!"

Incredulous, I went inside. Two large grocery cartons overflowed with the accumulation of a week. I lugged them into the house and emptied them onto the dining room table. Hundreds and hundreds of letters. . . . We sifted through them, pulling out those from people we knew and the bills that had to be handled. The rest were from strangers, from all over the country and beyond. On the top of the pile was an envelope addressed simply to: The Hinckleys, Colorado. Further down one with English stamps read: The Hinckleys, U.S.A., and another from South Africa was for: The Parents of the Man Who Shot the President, U.S.A.

Jo Ann and I sat down at opposite ends of the table and began to open them. Most of the letters were sympathetic. An astonishing number echoed the lady who'd telephoned last week to say she'd feared it was *her* son.

"We thought at first it was our Robert."

"I cried with relief when they gave the name."

"But for the grace of God it could have been Richie."

Were there so many anxious parents across the nation? How ironic, Jo Ann and I kept saying, that we—for whom the widespread nightmare had become a reality—had never had such fears.

On and on the letters went. Some enclosed novena cards, religious tracts, printed sermons. Other people sent books, tapes, magazine subscriptions. We didn't get a tenth of them even opened on Thursday, and on Friday there was another big batch at the post office. Saturday and Monday, more still.

We took out a permanent post office number. A curiosity seeker had simply walked off with our rural mailbox up on the road—and anyhow there was no way it could hold so much. Only a very occasional letter was abusive or threatening. Some took us to task for loosing a monster on society: "You should have known he was a killer when he bought so many guns." Others reproached us for our supposed wealth: It was never just "money," but always "oil money," as though there were something sinister about this means of earning a living.

But the negative letters were dwarfed by the avalanche of compassion. Strangers as well as friends wrote offering their own homes as shelters from the press. These past few weeks I'd begun to think of "the public" as an insatiable glutton for details of our private lives; I was overwhelmed to discover how much of this public reacted with distaste at media tactics.

Other generous souls enclosed money, some not even providing an address to which we could return it. The most touching gift was a $5 bill from a lady whose own son was in prison: "When Billy was arrested I didn't have enough money to place a long distance call to him. I'm working now and I'm sending this so you can call your son."

How in the world were we to answer this immense outpouring of concern? All through April and into May the flood of mail continued—Easter cards, Mother's Day cards, thousands and thousands of letters, many of them describing family problems that made ours seem smaller by comparison. That was the second surprise: As many people wrote to seek help as to offer it. Not material help, but guidance, consolation, understanding. That anyone would ask *us* for advice seemed extraordinary to me—we would seem to be the last people on earth with answers. Maybe they felt that, having experienced our own tragedy, we could relate to theirs.

We tried at first to answer every letter, but no matter how late into the night we sat up, we were always further behind the next day. We'd forgotten what it was like to see friends or watch a ball game or do anything over the weekends but answer mail. Finally we worked out a standard reply—one of those form thank-yous that I hated to receive and hated even worse to send—which I had xeroxed at the office, leaving space at the bottom for Jo Ann or me to handwrite a personal note. Still we were never caught up before it would be time to go east again.

And then there was all the other correspondence generated by the situation, reports to skittish investors, letters to attorneys and government officials, to family and friends. I had promised myself while we were in Washington to write personally to each of the police officers who had provided security. I contacted the department for their names and was astonished to discover that there had been 42 men involved in protecting us. I wrote them all.

Jo Ann meanwhile labored for two weeks after our return home, redoing the letters she'd written in Washington, finding a different way to tell each of the four victims that we were praying for the healing of his body and spirit, suffering with him. When she finished them at last after innumerable rewritings and recopyings, we forwarded them to Vince.

"Why can't I simply mail them to the people myself?" Jo Ann wanted to know, but nothing, apparently, could be done simply anymore. We were figures in a federal case and anything that might have a bearing on it had to pass our lawyers' scrutiny.

It was a case whose procedures and timing and even terminology I didn't begin to understand. The first stage in the legal process, Vince explained over the phone, would be a Grand Jury hearing to determine whether the government had enough evidence to bring an indictment against John. It seemed to me that with several million eyewitnesses to the crime there was hardly a need for this, but such a hearing was mandatory, Vince explained. Jo Ann and I would have to testify, so would Scott and Diane, and anyone else the government decided to subpoena—but John would not have to be present.

"And then they bring an indictment?" I asked.

"Not *an* indictment," Vince said. There'd be a number of charges in connection with the shootings. How many, we wouldn't know until the indictments were handed down.

"And when they are?" I asked. "After he's indicted what happens?"

"Then John appears before a judge to be formally arraigned." At which time, Vince went on, he would have to plead either Guilty or Not Guilty.

"I shouldn't think there was any doubt about it."

The phrase *not guilty* was actually a misnomer, Vince said; *not responsible* would be more accurate. There were instances when a defendant's mental condition rendered him Not Guilty in the eyes of the law, even when there was no question that he had committed an unlawful act. What was John's mental condition on March 30? That was the issue that a team of three psychiatrists and a psychologist were trying to determine for the government at Butner. It was also the issue that three psychiatrists and a psychologist retained by us—men recommended by Dr. Steinbach—were attempting independently to assess.

Vince expected to have their preliminary reports on his desk, he said, on our next trip to Washington, the first week in May.

35

JO ANN:

On April 22, President Reagan gave his first press interview since the shooting three weeks before. Back in the White House, though on a restricted schedule and still in pain, he assured reporters he was continuing his rapid recovery. Asked how he felt about John, he answered, "I hope he'll get well, too. He seems to be a very disturbed young man."

We were tremendously touched and grateful for these compassionate words. The next day, however, our lawyers telephoned from Washington. "In view of the President's statement," they felt that the timing was wrong for forwarding my letter to the White House.

"You'll send only the other three?" I asked. No, it wouldn't look right to communicate with the other men and not with Mr. Reagan. They'd hold all four letters "until the right moment."

I hung up the telephone close to tears. Although Thomas Delahanty and Timothy McCarthy had also been discharged from the hospital, they would have slow, painful recoveries ahead. And James Brady, the very day the President was interviewed, had had five hours of additional brain surgery. How could there be a wrong moment to express compassion and grief?

When Jack and I could take a few minutes from the mail, we were continuing to go through the cartons in the garage as the lawyers had requested. Mostly they contained John's old school work—loose-leaf notebooks, spiral pads, exam papers going back to his freshman year at Texas Tech. Strange how tragedy destroyed not only the future but the past: Just seeing his handwriting on a term paper could fill me with grief.

Since getting back to Colorado on April 8, we'd spoken to John on the telephone every Monday and Thursday. The medical team at Butner hadn't wanted even this much "distraction" during his evaluation, but Warden Ingraham and his assistant, Jesse James, understood our need, too, and arranged the twice-weekly contact. John's voice was generally listless, Jack and I making most of the conversation. John told us he was not allowed to watch or hear newscasts, or to receive mail, other than family letters, and "for security reasons" was not permitted outdoors.

The first week after the shooting Jack and I had been unable to watch the news programs or read the papers; now these things were almost a compulsion with both of us, as though we could deaden the pain through repetition. But fresh shocks kept assaulting us, like the night a commentator revealed that then-President Jimmy Carter had been in Nashville the day John was arrested there with guns in his possession. Was *that* the reason John had gone to Nashville?

We had no way of knowing which news reports were accurate, which not. One totally fictitious story was circulated by a leader of the American Nazi Party, who claimed to have met John at a Party rally in St. Louis in 1978. Wearing a storm trooper uniform, the man told reporters, John had urged his fellow Nazis to resort to violence. "Subsequently," newspapers quoted the man as saying, "a Nazi leader in Texas conducted a character assessment of Hinckley" after which his Nazi membership card was supposedly revoked.

John never had such a membership card, according to the FBI, never joined the party, wore a uniform or attended a Nazi meeting. The whole made-up story stemmed, apparently, from that photograph of another man resembling John circulated by the Associated Press, and the Nazis' seeing the chance for some favorable free publicity.

The picture I hated most, though, was one of John himself. It was an ID photo taken at a time when he weighed over 200 pounds. It had caught him, as photo machines will, with his eyes half shut: He not only looked bloated, but malevolent. It was the media's favorite. Everywhere I turned that hideous picture would glare at me. It lay in wait on the tabloids at the grocery check-out counter; it glowered from the corner of the TV screen every time there was a scrap of news.

It was on TV that we learned that John had been taken "under heavy guard" to Duke University Hospital near Butner, for CATscans and other tests of his brain functions. I couldn't sleep that night, remembering how in February he'd asked to have his head X-rayed.

We'd been granted permission for a second visit at Butner on May 6, a month after our first trip there. We wondered if the hospital tests meant our trip would be postponed, but on Tuesday, May 5, "Mr. and Mrs. John Scott" flew on schedule from Denver to North Carolina. It was a relief to file through the boarding ramp with the other passengers and take seats forward of the "No Smoking" signs. At Raleigh-Durham Airport we picked up the rented car reserved in the "Scotts'" name. The last time we'd been here, Charlie had driven us, and we'd scarcely glanced out the window at the gentle green countryside, so different from our towering western landscape.

We checked into a motel, arrived at Butner next morning to find the entrance free of reporters. Once again we were led through that series of locked doors and down an outside walkway to that separate eight-cell unit.

The relief, the strange calm, which Jack and I had both noticed in John on our first visit, was gone. He was uptight, fidgety. The doctors engaged by Vince had been down a number of times to talk to him, as well as the government's experts. Day after day, he said, he'd answered the same questions about school, jobs, friends, until he dreaded the sight of a clipboard.

John looked pale to me, though maybe it was only the orange of that prison jumpsuit. We talked about the family, the lameness in Titter's hind legs. When Jack brought up the subject of the Grand Jury hearings scheduled in Washington later that month, John grew so morose that we steered the conversation back to neutral areas.

Too soon the allotted visiting time was over. "He seems tenser than he did last time," Jack said as we got back into the car. The almost-euphoria we'd noticed last month was gone. It was as though, immediately after the shooting, he'd been expecting something exhilarating and wonderful to happen.

He'd seemed to be almost holding his breath, like a child on Christmas Eve. Whatever it was, it had evidently not happened; some light of expectancy had gone from his eyes.

36

JACK:

At Washington's National airport, again marvelously, no reporters, no police. We took a taxi to the Jefferson where Rose Narva greeted us like returning family. She saw personally to our registration, once more under an assumed name, of course. We'd read somewhere that Attorney General William French Smith lived at the Jefferson. It was a strange feeling, knowing we were under the same roof as the man whose job it was to prosecute our son.

We went to a nearby restaurant for dinner, feeling like released prisoners ourselves, now that we could come and go from the hotel. Next morning for the first time we went to the law office of Williams & Connolly. It was only a four-block walk from the Jefferson: around a couple of corners and across a small park where a bronze statue of Admiral Farragut stood beside a coil of bronze rope. On the sixth floor of the building, Vince Fuller's secretary was all but invisible behind a mountain of paperwork. His desk was even worse: an unbelievable clutter of documents, notes, law books and court transcripts, with *No Smoking* signs balanced precariously among the piles.

But though his desk looked unorganized, we soon learned that Vince could put his hand in an instant on anything he wanted. Greg Craig, Lon Babby and Judy Miller joined us for a discussion of the legal situation.

All were agreed that the Grand Jury hearings, in this case, were a mere formality. John would be charged with an unknown number of offenses, to which he would have to enter a formal plea of Guilty or Not Guilty. The doctors retained by Vince had now seen John, and their preliminary reports, totally independent of each other, all indicated acute mental illness and probable psychosis. The word psychosis meant little to me, except that it sounded terrifying, but according to Vince it opened the possibility of an NGRI defense.

"A what?" Jo Ann and I asked together.

"Not Guilty by Reason of Insanity."

The room fell so silent I could hear the pigeons on the windowsill. *Insanity?* People locked away in attic rooms, hearing voices in their heads? John was a severely troubled person, obviously, or he would never have pulled that trigger. But *insane?* We'd just been with him. He was perfectly coherent, rational—knew who he was and where he was.

"That's impossible," I said.

"And how could he be 'Not Guilty,'" Jo Ann objected, "when we all know he did it?"

Vince explained to her, as he had earlier to me, that Guilty in the legal sense implied the ability "to appreciate the wrongfulness of his conduct." Not *Responsible* by Reason of Insanity, Vince said, was the term preferred by many authorities, but the statute books retained the old wording, Not Guilty. For centuries courts in every civilized country had tried to separate willful wrongdoings from the actions of individuals in the grip of overpowering mental illness—approaching them as sick people rather than criminals.

Back in Denver I began putting in longer days at the office, knowing we'd soon have to return to Washington for our Grand Jury testimony. Vince guessed that Jo Ann and I would be called on May 27 or 28, during the second week of hearings. We were pleased about the timing in one way because it meant we could get down again to Butner for John's birthday on May 29. But it meant phoning World Vision in California and backing out of a big meeting they'd scheduled then. I'd already canceled the Guatemala trip at the time of the shooting, and a second trip to Africa in mid-April. What great schemes I'd had for helping all mankind; I hadn't even been able to help my own family. . . .

Scott and Diane had been subpoenaed for the hearings, too, as Vince predicted. They were to appear before the Grand Jury on Thursday, May 21, a week before Jo Ann and me. To our gratitude their request to be allowed to see John down in North Carolina the following day had been granted by the Butner authorities.

In our twice-weekly phone conversations, John sounded a little better. They'd permitted him to have a second-hand guitar which Greg Craig had brought to the prison but had to leave with the security officer. John had sold his old guitar, along with his phonograph records, for money to live on those last frantic weeks in March at the Golden Hours Motel.

Then on May 13, a month and a half after John's attack on President Reagan, a gunman in Saint Peter's Square, Rome, fired at Pope John Paul II. Amid the sickeningly familiar scenes of police cordons and interviews with stunned eyewitnesses, a cry went up from an outraged world to "stop the carnage." There could scarcely have been two more different individuals than John and the Papal assailant, Mehmet Ali Agca, or two more different motives, but the act of firing a gun at a world leader was the same. Even as we prayed and agonized for that courageous man in Rome, we dreaded the fallout on John's situation.

Vince phoned from Washington as distressed as we were: In the present climate he believed Youthful Offender status would be next to impossible to achieve.

And John's own past actions continued to add up against him—and to appear condemningly in the newspapers. That final month he'd lived here in Evergreen, we read with dismay one morning, he'd been systematically checking out books on violence from the local library. I remembered how pleased Jo Ann and I had been that he was starting to get out of the house. . . .

How was such government information constantly getting to the press, I wondered. And why were we even considering an NGRI plea when John was being tried and found guilty on every TV news show?

37

JO ANN:

Scott and Diane phoned us from Washington on Thursday evening, May 21. The Grand Jury hearing had been scary. Steve had made the trip east with Diane but had not been allowed into the Grand Jury room with her. Each witness had to go in alone to face a panel of twenty jurors and a court recorder taking down every word. The U.S. Attorneys—Mr. Ruff and Mr. Adelman, whom we'd met in Vince's office—were the questioners, but as Vince had forewarned us, our own lawyers had not been permitted to be present. Scott, Diane and Steve were all looking forward to their trip to see John the next day.

Scott got back to Denver Friday night with a report on their visit in North Carolina. He was tremendously glad to have seen his brother but was afraid the reunion had been hard on John. It was the first time our three children had been together in the nearly two months since the shooting, and we gathered the meeting had been strained. I could so well imagine it—that bare little room with those straight-backed fiberglass chairs, the prison guards looking on. It hadn't been too bad, Scott said, until the hour was up and they had to leave. "Somehow the fact that we could walk away and he couldn't—it made the whole thing real."

Jack and I flew to Washington four days later for our turn before the Grand Jury, again using a pseudonym to board the airplane. It was hot and muggy in Washington, the lovely spring of three weeks before already past. To save money we took the bus in from Dulles and walked several blocks to the Jefferson, Jack lugging our baggage in the heat. Rose Narva was off that day. We were given a noisy corner room but felt too dispirited to ask for a quieter one. Just as we were leaving Evergreen, Vince had telephoned to say that our bid to plead guilty under the Youthful Offender Act had been turned down, as he anticipated.

Vince himself had flown to Butner immediately after phoning us. He rang us that night at the Jefferson to tell us John had taken the news pretty hard.

Next morning we met at Williams & Connolly to discuss our Grand Jury testimony. "They'll want to know about John's contacts in Lubbock and Los Angeles," Vince said, explaining that the FBI had still not ruled out a possible conspiracy.

"Lynn Collins can give them a lot more information on Los Angeles than we can," Jack said.

As on previous occasions when Lynn's name was mentioned, I saw an embarrassed look pass among the lawyers. I had the feeling she'd testified already—perhaps hadn't been too cooperative. Well, if she'd been hurt by John's strange attraction to some girl he'd seen only on a movie screen, I couldn't blame her.

"Before you go into the Grand Jury room, Jack and Jo Ann," Vince said, "you ought to know one thing." He lined up the *No Smoking* sign with the edge of his desk as though steeling himself for the shock he knew would follow. "There is no Lynn Collins."

In the silent room I could hear the hum of traffic on 16th Street.

"What do you mean?" I managed to get out at last.

"I mean there is no such person. The FBI is satisfied on that point."

"But—the things they did in California! The time she came to Lubbock!"

"I'm afraid none of that happened, Jo Ann."

"But look here!" Jack objected. "Christmas—the one before last. If John wasn't in New York with Lynn, where was he? He didn't come home."

"The FBI believes he never left Lubbock." Greg Craig's voice was gentle. "They believe he spent Christmas alone in his room."

157

I remembered the rest of the family gathered in Evergreen, missing John to pass out the gifts beneath the tree, waiting for his call. Then . . . he was *not* making the rounds of New York publishers? Not having that stimulating time with Lynn's actor friends. He was sitting by himself in a solitary room near a deserted campus. . . .

"What about Tom?" Jack asked. "Tom Perry. Is he—imaginary too?"

Federal investigators, Vince said, had apparently located someone by that name at Tech. "But he scarcely knew John. Certainly he never went into business with him."

I was drifting, afloat in a world that had no moorings. What about LISTALOT, then? Had there really been such a company? What about John's novel? And the record company contacts?

Vince went on to describe the preliminary deposition Jack and I would be asked to make at the courthouse that afternoon. I wasn't listening. I needed time to adjust to the revelation about Lynn. She'd been part of our lives for so long it was like the loss of a personal friend. The meeting in the laundromat . . . the weekend at Malibu . . . meals at her apartment . . . the wonderful week in Lubbock: going "under protest" to the disco, eating an ice cream cone while she shopped . . . the prospect of living together in California, against which I'd argued so strenuously. Jack and I had lived every minute of it, accepted every up and down of that hot-and-cold relationship just as John described it.

Why . . . without Lynn, all that was left was John alone. Terribly, terrifyingly alone. No Tom Perry as a business partner, no book agent in New York, *no one at all* with whom I knew for sure that John had had a relationship in years and years.

This afternoon, Vince was saying, two of the lawyers could come with us to the courthouse; tomorrow—at the actual hearing—Jack and I would go alone. We had a sandwich lunch in the office, then took a taxi, Vince, Lon Babby, Jack and I, to the immense, severely modern United States Courthouse.

If I could have foreseen the number of trips we'd be making to that building, I don't think my legs would have carried me inside. Near the door I saw some reporters, but the Grand Jury hearings were public information anyway; by tomorrow anyone who cared would know Jack and I were here. Two months had passed since the shooting; the police believed there was no longer the same risk of personal danger to us.

Jack was called first into the conference room where Mr. Ruff, Mr. Adelman and representatives of the FBI were already assembled. Vince and Lon went in with him, leaving me alone in an outer office to wait my turn. I had plenty of time to get nervous. I kept repeating to myself what Vince had said about Attorney Ruff, that he had children of his own. Once, the door opened and Mr. Ruff himself wheeled his chair out just to see how I was holding up and assure me it wouldn't be much longer.

Ten minutes later he came out again. Instead of speaking to me, he spun himself rapidly across the room and disappeared through another door. A couple of men followed him from the conference room. Mr. Ruff reappeared and went back inside, still without a word. A minute or so later Jack came out, a puzzled expression on his face.

"Something's going on," he told me, "and I'm the only one who doesn't know what it is."

I looked up to see Vince standing in the conference doorway. "Jack, Jo Ann, I need to talk to you. In private."

I gripped Jack's arm as we followed Vince into an adjacent room. "Sit down," Vince urged me. There'd been a call from Butner, he said. "John has tried to take his life."

Apparently he'd swallowed a large number of Valium and Tylenol tablets. "We're trying now to find out how bad it is—at this point we believe he is still alive."

The room was going dark. I was trying to stay upright in the chair. I heard Jack saying, "Oh God, help John, oh God, help John," over and over.

Vince wanted to get back to his office where he could keep a phone line open to Butner. "You've been excused from further questioning," he said. "I suggest you return to the hotel—I'll call you as soon as we have anything definite."

Somehow we got out of the building and into a cab. It stopped at Williams & Connolly first and Vince and Lon sprang out. Vince's face was so anguished that my heart went out to him, even in my own terror. I'd known he was committed professionally to John's case; till that moment I hadn't realized how much he cared personally.

The Jefferson was an older hotel with window air conditioners. We turned the fan up as high as it would go against the street noise and sat on the bed waiting for Vince's call. We couldn't talk. I saw myself going downstairs in Evergreen, slipping into John's room to count the pills in his Valium bottle. How could he have gotten hold of an overdose in prison?

"The kids!" Jack said suddenly. "And your folks. We ought to call them before they hear it on the news."

I couldn't, so Jack placed the calls. If I heard Daddy's voice I knew I'd start bawling.

It was more than an hour before Vince called to say John was alive and the first crisis was past. "They're pretty sure there's no brain damage." The problem was the liver, "but they have him on a new drug."

Jack then placed a call to Warden Ingraham, who confirmed that John was going to survive, though still extremely sick. He was semi-conscious, responding to voice signals. Later the warden called back to say he'd arranged the phone hookup to the prison infirmary that Jack had requested so that we could speak to John ourselves. A minute later John's voice came faintly over the line. He was too groggy to hold a conversation, but seemed to know who we were.

Now that the worst was behind us, I started shaking. I kept thinking of the birthday gifts in my suitcase. His twenty-sixth birthday was two days away, and he almost hadn't lived to see it.

Jack turned on the evening news where we learned to our astonishment that "government officials" questioned whether it had been a serious suicide attempt. The warden himself had told us only minutes ago that John had almost died. Jack got so upset listening to the inferences that it was all a plea for public sympathy that he had to get out of the room and walk off steam. I didn't want him to be alone in his present mood so I went with him. We walked a long way in the bright spring twilight, then Jack suggested we get some food in our stomachs. I didn't think I could hold anything down, but I swallowed a little soup while he picked at a salad.

I couldn't walk any farther. Jack walked me back to the hotel entrance and kept going while I went up to our room alone. In the washbasin I lost the little food I'd gotten down. The carpeting in the bathroom was bright cherry-red—odd the things you remember. I lay down on that splash of color and sobbed.

And there alone, as was happening more and more often, I seemed to hear God. . . . hear Him say that Jack was carrying more than his share of burdens, and that I must not be another one. When I heard Jack's key in the door I scrambled up, splashed water on my face and hurried out to the bedroom. There'd been no calls from Vince or from Butner, I told him, which was good news.

We got into bed, but as soon as Jack was asleep I went back into the bathroom and was sick again. I curled up on that red rug and lay for hours crying and praying and crying some more.

38

JACK:

Thursday morning we got another call through to the prison infirmary. John sounded more alert, though the extent of damage to his liver was still not known. We walked to Williams & Connolly. Vince looked awful, circles of sleeplessness under his eyes.

I'd picked up some newspapers on our way over; all made light of "the incident." It made me so angry I wanted to write blistering letters to the editors, but Vince reminded me that they were only reporting what they'd been told. The government, he pointed out, was hardly going to admit publicly that a prisoner had been able day after day to fake taking his medicine until he'd squirreled away a life-threatening dose somewhere in a tiny cell.

The Attorney General's office had phoned, Vince said, to

tell us we could postpone today's Grand Jury appearance till a later date, but we refused to do anything to slow this already drawn-out legal process. Getting psychiatric help for John was now our number-one priority. Psychotherapy was available at Butner, we'd been told, but only for men serving sentences, not those, like John, undergoing pre-trial evaluation. "We'll go ahead with the Grand Jury," I told Vince. "Get this case moving."

That afternoon Jo Ann and I alone took a cab to the courthouse. Jo Ann was wearing dark glasses because she'd been crying. Sure enough a cluster of photographers was waiting on the steps. "Maintain an absolutely neutral expression," one letter writer had cautioned us from personal experience. "If you smile, you're heartless, indifferent to the victims. If you frown, you're mean and hostile."

Again, I was summoned to testify first. I was relieved at this for Jo Ann's sake; she thought I didn't know she'd been up sick all night. The Grand Jury room was a formal, imposing place with twenty men and women of all ages, mostly black, sitting on three tiers of benches. U.S. Attorneys Ruff and Adelman and others on the prosecuting team were present, along with court recorders. No one from the defense.

For two hours I answered questions, again with the eerie conviction that the questioners had more of the answers than I did. As Vince had told us, the idea of accomplices was still being explored. Six bullets had been fired at the Presidential party and at first it was questioned whether all of them had come from the same direction. Soon police discovered that two of the bullets had simply ricocheted off the sides of the President's bullet-proof limousine. But conspiracy theories continued to abound—fueled partly by John's allusions, in letters home, to a mysterious political group in Lubbock. According to Vince, investigators could discover no evidence that such an organization ever existed. It appeared now that, like Lynn, like Tom Perry, this group had been only another of John's imaginary contacts with the world. However, the government had to pursue even unlikely leads, to make certain that a conspiracy myth would not continue to haunt this case as it still did President Kennedy's.

I came out of the Grand Jury room exhausted, praying they would not submit Jo Ann to the same long interrogation. The indictment was such a foregone conclusion I couldn't understand the reason for our being there in the first place. Mercifully, she emerged in only half an hour to report that Adelman had been considerate and easygoing.

Early next morning—John's twenty-sixth birthday—we flew to North Carolina. Warden Ingraham and Jesse James met us at Butner to express their sincere regret about the overdose. They should have been doubly alert, they acknowledged, because of the Youthful Offender turndown.

We were subjected to an even more rigorous search than previously before being admitted to the prison proper; most of the birthday gifts had to be left behind. Only his cards and two packages that contained books were allowed in with us. John had been returned from the infirmary to the building where we'd met before. This time on the steel outer door was a printed sign:

Inmate Is Suicidal

He looked suicidal as he was led into the visiting cell between two guards, his eyes scarcely leaving the floor. "Happy Birthday" seemed a cruel phrase in these circumstances. We handed him the cards and the books—the security officer had removed the ribbons from the packages. Anything he might use to injure himself had been taken from his cell, the guards told us. His guitar (long strings). His electric shaver (the cord). Even all pencils over two inches long. For the first time I realized the significance of the short-sleeved, beltless jumpsuit, the laceless slippers in place of shoes.

How do you talk to someone so down he can't even meet your eye? In a dozen ways his mother and I tried to convince John that when he hurt, we hurt. But he had withdrawn into some dark distance, deep inside.

Afterward we asked to meet with the Butner psychiatrist, Dr. Sally Johnson, to see if some kind of medication or therapy couldn't be arranged. She was a very young woman, only two years older than John, small, pregnant, articulate and well-educated, brown hair drawn back in a no-nonsense bun. She doubted that treatment would be permitted while John was undergoing various examinations. Nor could she be the therapist. She was the government's chief psychiatric expert in the case, charged with making the evaluation on which they would proceed. In the circumstances, we realized, she could hardly act as his counselor.

"What about at least getting outdoors occasionally?" Jo Ann pleaded. Couldn't Dr. Johnson put in a request on the basis of mental health?

Dr. Johnson was sympathetic, but not very hopeful because of possible danger from other inmates.

It was prison policy, Warden Ingraham had explained, when someone was accused of a publicized crime, to segregate him from the rest of the population. I knew every organization had its rules, but in this case, I thought bleakly as Jo Ann and I headed back to the airport, the one who wanted to hurt John most was John himself.

39

JO ANN:

Our lives were like a pendulum, swinging between Colorado and the East Coast. This time we were home only two weeks—two weeks to tackle the continuing flood of mail and throw our clothes in the washing machine. I packed a small suitcase with toilet things, nightgown, a change of blouses, ready for instant departure. *Inmate Is Suicidal* . . . that black-lettered sign haunted my sleep.

Our neighbors were wonderful. Phoning, bringing meals, dragging me out of the house when I could so easily have crawled into a shell. I especially appreciated the food; for some reason grocery shopping had become the worst chore of all. Cooking had been a way to express love for my family. I couldn't look at the diet-food section where I'd searched for appetizing things for John, couldn't even walk past the shelves of fruit juice. When he was home, I'd always kept apple juice in the refrigerator. I'd make long detours with my cart to avoid that aisle.

We went through more cartons in the garage, though we didn't really know what we were supposed to be looking for. Jack would haul a box upstairs and set it on the coffee table in the living room—the dining room table was buried beneath the mail. I'd sit on a cushion on the raised hearth, Jack in his brown armchair, and we'd go through lapful after lapful of papers in John's handwriting. Among school assignments and classroom notes we'd come across poems. On a sheet of loose-leaf notebook paper he'd written:

> *Pretend*
> *Pretend you are a virgin on fire*
> *An outcast in the midst of madness*
> *The scion of something unthinkable*
> *Satan's long lost illegitimate son*
> *A solitary weed among carnations*
> *The last living shit on earth*
> *Dracula on a crowded beach*
> *A child without a home*
> *The loser of a one-man race*
> *Rare meat thrown to a hungry lion*
> *A faded flag on a windy day*
>
> *Welcome to the truth*
> *Welcome to reality*
> *Welcome to my world*

In a spiral pad we found:

> *Regardless*
> *Regardless of your lovely life*
> *I am still here writhing in pain*
> *I am still reeling from the truth*
> *Regardless of the outside sun*
> *I remain the far side of crazy*
> *I remain the mortal enemy of Man*
> *Regardless of a million smiles*

I can't escape this torture chamber
I can't begin to be happy
Regardless of your dream come true
I continue to grovel for normalcy
I continue to scream inside
Regardless of everyone's friends
I plot revenge in the dark
I plot escape from this asylum
Regardless of Disneyland
I follow the example of perverts
I follow the long lost swine
Regardless of Miss America's attitude
I stagger from day to day
I stagger toward the future
Regardless of the laughter of children
I cannot continue to pretend
I cannot continue to live

Such despair, such self-despising. . . . When had he developed this terrible, terrible hatred for himself? And why hadn't we seen it? A poem in that same spiral binder had obviously been written at the time he was seeing Dr. Hopper here in Evergreen; with bitter sarcasm it noted how we were all failing to perceive the seriousness of the problem:

But Not Really
I'm feeling better now but not really
An attack of something has crippled me.
Hey doctor, there is a small problem
That I seem to have with communicating.
Shut up, and listen to my life story
Although I don't want to tell it.
I was born, I grew up and now
I've come to you for some guidance.
I'll call you a counselor instead of a shrink
The word psychiatrist scares people
Especially my neighborly parents.
Can you counsel me and tell me
That everything will be fine and dandy
Because you will help me to help myself?
Oh Boy! Now I have confidence
In myself.

Here I come world,
Ready or not I can do anything now
Because my attitude has been turned around.
Didn't you say my attitude was everything?
Hey doctor, how can I thank you?
I'm feeling better now but not really.

My neighborly parents . . . I remembered, in fact, worrying about what the neighbors would think if they saw our car parked at Dr. Hopper's.

Jack was turning the pages in another school notebook. He looked up, eyes anguished: "Do you remember the 'Elephant Man'?"

I thought I remembered a movie with that name.

Yes, there'd been a movie, Jack said, but it was based on an actual person, a tragically deformed man whose skin progressively thickened like an elephant's hide, in spite of everything doctors could do. "Read this," he said, springing up from his chair and thrusting the notebook at me. It still embarrassed Jack to cry.

The Elephant Man and I
Perhaps the Elephant Man would understand my
dilemma
We seem to have so many precious things in
common
It's all a question of face to face communication
The Elephant Man and I shy away from such
encounters
We are both doomed creatures and destined for
early deaths
A heart of gold may as well be tarnished in our
case
The risk of giving ourselves away is also the
problem
But we are aching for contact with the human race
To simply caress a loved one could be a miracle
cure
The Elephant Man and I would kill for someone
to love
For the time being though we will continue to
suffer

167

*Let's watch the people stare at us in horror and
   run away
I do believe my friend we are involved in a lost
   cause
Take my hand Mr. Elephant Man so we can
   disappear together.*

40

JACK:

My desk at Vanderbilt was beginning to look like Vince's—
except that he knew where everything was. Mine was piled
high with reports I hadn't read, phone messages I hadn't
returned. I'd sit down determined to clear it up and an hour
later discover I'd been remembering some piece of paper we'd
pulled from a cardboard carton the night before.

I'd wrench my attention back to Vanderbilt. Problems at the
office seemed to be multiplying. The day we testified before the
Grand Jury in Washington, in fact, the day after John's suicide
attempt, another of our most important men had quit. "He just
came in and said he was leaving," Scott reported. "Nothing I
could say would change his mind."

But John's problems crowded out my other worries. Greg
Craig from Vince's office flew out to help us sort through the
material we were uncovering in those boxes. One of the things
we'd found was the draft of a letter John had started to Jo Ann
and me but never mailed. We came across it along with some
lecture notes on ruled notebook paper. It had taken a while to
read beneath scratched-out lines.

There was no date on it, but it had to have been written in

November 1979, just before the Christmas John spent in New York with Lynn. No, I corrected myself, the time he *hadn't* gone to New York. The Christmas he spent alone in his room in Lubbock. I still had trouble letting go of what we'd believed was happening.

But since the un-sent letter mentioned a stock certificate, it had to have been then. In October 1979, when business was going great, Vanderbilt had announced a stock split. Through an office error John's new certificate was mailed to him at Tech instead of coming to me to put in his safe deposit box. I'd asked him over the phone to mail it back. John never argued on the telephone—or in person, for that matter. His thoughts came out more readily in writing.

"Enclosed is the stock certificate plus my history paper," he'd written on the top line of the ruled page. That sentence was crossed out. Beneath it he'd started again:

Enclosed is my history paper. I plan to go and talk to my professor tomorrow. The reason I didn't enclose the stock certificate is because I would like to discuss this situation with you now.

I get tired of constantly having to ask you for money every few weeks. And I'm sure you're pretty tired dol-ing it out. Why wouldn't it be a good idea to let me cash in at least part of the stock and thereby relieve me of my constant money worries? I just don't see how my cashing in some Vanderbilt stock would hurt the com-pany, since hundreds of thousands of shares are spewed out.

The last three uncomplimentary words were x'd out: "have been issued" he wrote instead.

I realize that I wouldn't have the stock in the first place without your generosity, but I'm forever out of money! It's my understanding that you want me to wait until I have a wife and suburban home before putting my hand in the till. Well, Father and Mother, ("Father and Mother" crossed out) the way things are going now, it will be years and years and years before this prodigal son settles down to your idea of maturity; and/or the way things are going

169

now, I may never get out of this college alive. It's literally driving me to the funny farm. But there's nothing funny about it.

Some of the next lines were scratched out, the handwriting becoming harder to read, but Jo Ann and I deciphered it word by word.

I'm so depressed it's all I can do to get out of bed every morning and go to class. . . . The proposed graduation date of June, 1980, looks shaky now. I'm failing half my classes now (Spanish and Geology) and I almost don't even care.

Another crossed-out line followed: "Go ahead and scream because I deserve it." The letter draft, the cry for help he'd never mailed continued:

I can't explain it, except to say that I feel that there is something wrong with me mentally as well as physically. Go ahead and faint but I've been giving some consideration to going to the school psychologist for help. My thoughts are not normal and neither is my life.
    A great deal of my anguish revolves around the fact that I'm being held up. . . .

An illegible word followed and here the letter draft ended abruptly. A couple of lines below it he'd scrawled the beginnings of a poem:

Your hair is what attracts me, long and straight and wavy in the right parts.

Your eyes are what attract me round and brown and revealing the naked brow.

Your face is what attracts me sweet and cute and capable of melting hearts.

And so on, all in an amorous vein. We handed the page to Greg Craig. Greg finished reading and looked up: "And he never sent the finished letter to you?"

"Never. The stock certificate simply arrived in the mail, no comment."

If only he had! Or if he'd spoken over the telephone about his abnormal thought-life. . . .

The day after Greg's trip to Evergreen, Jo Ann and I flew again to North Carolina. It was two weeks since the bleak birthday celebration when John was still sick from the overdose. He seemed physically recovered, though Jo Ann and I both noticed how nervous he'd become, biting his nails, constantly twirling a loose thread in his jumpsuit sleeve. Since the overdose he was no longer being issued Valium; for the first time we realized what a difference that medication had made.

We'd been so pleased this trip east, to be permitted three consecutive days to visit. But I wondered as we drove to our motel that first afternoon, whether he or we could survive two more sessions like this one.

That first get-together, as it turned out, was the easiest one. . . . We arrived at Butner next morning, Sunday, at nine and were allowed to stay past noon. For three hours the only thing John would talk about was getting out of that solitary cell block, away from 24-hour surveillance by the guards. Becoming an ordinary prisoner subjected to ordinary prison routine looked from where he sat like a huge improvement—no matter how long a term he might be given. He was ready to chuck all efforts to get at the "why" of his behavior, just to have the process over and done with.

"John," I reproached him, "that's been your problem all along. You're concerned with the immediate goal, not the long term consequences." I looked over at Jo Ann for support, but she sat stiffly in that blue molded-fiberglass chair, eyes on her lap.

I pointed out to John that even if there were no defense effort at all, he'd still be going through the same mandatory evaluation by government doctors, still have to wait here in Butner until he was indicted and sentenced.

But he wouldn't have to wait in Butner, he told me. If I would just post bail for him, he could walk out now. That was his right, wasn't it? Until a person was found guilty, he couldn't be kept in prison month after month, could he?

I stared at him in disbelief. "John, do you have the slightest notion how angry people in this country are? Do you know that your mother and I still receive threatening letters—just for being your parents? And even if you could be hidden away somewhere, do you think any judge is going to trust you on your own, after you tried to commit suicide?''

Obviously he hadn't thought of any of this, nor would he now. He asked over and over why I wouldn't put up his bail: "I should think you'd be willing to part with some of your precious money for one of your own children.''

"It isn't the money, John, you know that." We'd already spent more on lawyers and doctors than all three college educations had cost, and we hadn't even started. "It's your safety, your welfare.''

He wasn't listening. "You'd get your money back, anyway,'' he said. "I'm not going to run off to Mexico or anything.''

"John, for the last time, it isn't money!'' I heard my voice rising and was aware of the listening guards. "There's not a judge in this land who would turn you loose now, no matter how much money we put up. *You shot the President.*''

It was the first time I had spoken to him in so many words of his crime.

Somehow the basic *damage* he'd done had even now failed to register with him—the irreversible fact of having fired bullets into other human beings, one of whom was lying right this minute in a hospital bed with permanent brain damage. A real person, really in pain. It was as though John had signed up for a course that didn't turn out the way he expected, and wanted now to drop it. . . .

Most of the morning passed that way, my trying to get John to face reality, John hanging on to the pipedream of bail, with the money a test of my love for him, and Jo Ann no help at all. "We're only trying to do what's best for you,'' she'd say to John. Or to me: "John didn't mean it that way." As though he and I were unable to communicate without her as interpreter.

John said one thing that I felt was probably accurate. I told him, trying to impress the mood of the country on him, that there was talk of legislating a mandatory death sentence for anyone attempting to assassinate the President. "That wouldn't have stopped me,'' he said, absolutely matter-of-fact.

I stared at him, realizing it was true. "What would have stopped you?'' I asked.

He thought a moment. "Maybe if I'd had to wait awhile to buy a gun. Had to fill out forms, or get a permit first, or sign in with the police, or anything complicated. I probably wouldn't have done it."

41

JO ANN:

Monday morning, guards placed a fourth chair in the visiting cell. Dr. Sally Johnson arrived with John, to my secret relief. I'd been torn apart yesterday watching Jack and John at odds with each other, each looking to me to back him up. Of course Jack was right about the bail—Jack was always right. I just wished he wouldn't hammer his points home so hard.

John handed Jack a note on a folded piece of paper, which he asked his father not to read till he got to the airport. It was our last few hours together before we flew on to Washington; after Dr. Johnson left we kept the conversation on the kind of safe and superficial subject matter we were learning to choose. We prayed together before we left. At least Jack and I prayed and John bowed his head. We left him a copy of *Born Again* by Chuck Colson, hoping the prison part would be a point of contact.

Then Jack and I sped back to the airport to return our rental car before the three-day rate expired. For all Jack's trying to assure John that money was not an issue, I knew he was worried about mounting expenses. We'd found a Day's Inn Motel near Butner where we'd paid only $71 total for three nights' lodging.

We found seats in the boarding area and Jack unfolded his

note from John. He didn't speak for so long that my stomach began to churn, fearing more unreasonable demands from John. At last he passed the note to me. It was a message for Father's Day, a few days off, telling Jack how much he hoped that someday, somehow, he could make his father proud of him. As always, John had been able to express his real feelings on paper. . . . Jack's delight and gratitude were touching to see. He loved John so—why was there such conflict between them?

The Jefferson was the only hotel we knew in Washington. It felt almost homelike by this fourth visit, "but next time," Jack told me, "we'll look for a cheaper place."

We spent the next two days in psychiatrists' offices. Dr. Steinbach had recommended three, of whom two were in the area. Dr. Thomas Goldman had a large local practice there in Washington, and Dr. William Carpenter was head of the psychiatry department at the University of Maryland in nearby Baltimore. Just from the questions the two doctors asked about John, we were beginning to comprehend what a complex field psychiatry is—and how naive we'd been to think that a psychologist in a couple of sessions could identify "John's problem" as we'd asked Dr. Benjamin to do. Or that we could just take John to the nearest psychiatrist, as we'd done with Dr. Hopper, without knowing a thing in the world about the different methods of diagnosis and treatment.

Meanwhile, at Williams & Connolly's office on Farragut Square, we discussed the practical aspect of the insanity defense. We didn't know, of course, what the various doctors' eventual conclusions would be, whether they would find John well or ill. Greg Craig, who'd spent more time with John personally than the other three lawyers, was increasingly convinced that John was in the grip of an overpowering delusion. "He really, truly did it because he thought in some way it was supposed to form a bond with Jodie Foster. Don't ask me how. I just know it was *his* reason." In fact Greg believed that Miss Foster continued to dominate John's mental landscape, remained more real to him than President Reagan or James Brady—"or inquisitive lawyers," he added with the smile that so often lit up these distressful sessions.

Vince did not argue this, nor that the insanity defense might be appropriate in this instance. He simply felt it would be very difficult to win, especially with the kind of publicity the case was receiving. He showed us a copy of the *New York Post* featuring still another set of photos of some young man in a Nazi uniform, this time brandishing a gun, with captions identifying the unknown Nazi as John. In the accompanying article the paper acknowledged that the FBI had ascertained that the man in the photographs was *not* John—yet the *Post* had gone ahead and printed them anyway. I'd never seen Jack so irate. He wanted Vince to sue the writer, the photographer, the publisher and everyone else he could think of. It took all four lawyers to calm him down and persuade him that suing would only prolong the negative publicity.

But I saw what Vince meant about the difficulties of the insanity defense. Publicity like this made John out to be a political terrorist. How would we ever find twelve jurors who didn't remember these photos, at least subconsciously? We'd have less than a one-in-ten chance of winning in court, Vince believed, no matter how solid the medical case.

Plus, he reminded us, NGRI meant a trial and expenses would be enormous. Above all a trial would take time. Vince knew how anxious we were to get John out of his present stalemated situation, with neither medication nor counseling to help him get through his tormented hours.

He was coming to feel that the best thing for John—if they could work out a plea bargain with the government—would be to plead Guilty, avoid the trauma of a trial, and request that the agreed-upon sentence be served in Butner where John could receive therapy. Certainly it was what John wanted. What we ourselves wanted.

"But," Jack said, "I thought we'd tried to plea bargain and been turned down flat."

"Our first proposal was turned down," Vince admitted. "The Youthful Offender statute. But we can make other proposals."

John would be charged with a still-unknown number of separate felonies. In a new plea bargain John would plead Guilty to some of the charges in exchange for having others dismissed. With fewer marks against him, he would be eligible sooner for parole—maybe even, Vince thought, as early as ten years.

As our taxi inched through rush-hour traffic toward Dulles

airport, I tried to picture John, age 36, emerging from ten years in a federal penitentiary into a world he had not been able to cope with in the first place. And that was the best possibility. If this second attempt to plea bargain was also rejected—my mind refused to form that picture at all.

42

JACK:

Back in Denver I found nothing but headaches waiting for me at the office. A well in North Dakota in which Vanderbilt had sunk a great deal of money was running into problems at the 12,000-foot level. Far worse, the entire oil and gas industry was in trouble, with market demand and prices falling, and a growing glut of natural gas. It was my gut feeling that small energy companies were in for tough times, if not bankruptcy. At last Scott and I came to the reluctant conclusion that the best thing for our stockholders would be either to sell or merge Vanderbilt with a larger firm. It was a bitter decision, the end of my lifelong dream of starting my own business and seeing a son of mine carry it on.

Nor was selling going to be easy in the current market. Scott wasn't going to get much sleep that summer: With our inability to fill key positions, too much responsibility was falling on him too fast.

I wouldn't be able to help him much, either, while John's situation was so up in the air. "It could be another six weeks—the end of July—before we know whether the government will accept a plea bargain," I told Scott. "And if not, and we have to go to trial, I imagine that could stretch out—oh, all the way through October."

How little I knew.

On the way home from work one night in June I stopped at a bookstore to pick up a copy of *The Fan*. This was another of those disclosures in the press that made Jo Ann and me fearful of opening a newspaper: A copy of this book, in which a deranged killer menaces an actress, was among previously unreported items turned up by the FBI in John's Washington hotel room. Before going to bed that night I read about half of it: If John could seriously relate to that twisted character, he was far, far sicker than I had ever dreamed.

Our house continued to be an object of curiosity. We'd see sightseers up on the street, snapping pictures from their car windows. When the doorbell rang, we learned to look through the peephole first; more than once Jo Ann had discovered a total stranger standing on the doorstep, camera in hand. We couldn't have stuck it out without our neighbors who discouraged questioners, refused information.

Each day we expected the indictments to be handed down: The Grand Jury hearings had been completed four weeks ago. As soon as that happened, according to the steps Vince had outlined, John would be brought up from Butner to be arraigned in federal court. In order for the new plea bargain to have a chance, Vince reminded me, John at that time would have to plead Not Guilty. If he answered Guilty to all charges the lawyers would have no position from which to propose that some counts be dropped.

I understood. I also understood that the decision in the last analysis rested with John. The lawyers and we could argue, beg, point out the logic, but John alone when he stood before the judge's bench would have the final word. Slowly, protestingly, I was learning what it was to be powerless. The only thing Jo Ann and I could do was fly to Washington as soon as the arraignment date was announced—surely before the end of June—to be present at the arraignment as moral support for John, whichever way he decided.

Early on June 24, however, there was a call from Vince. "The government's asking for a thirty-day delay before bringing the indictments."

Thirty days? Another month for John in that solitary cell block? We could file a formal protest, Vince said, but it wouldn't speed things up much. "If we cooperate with them, there's a better chance they'll cooperate with us."

I dragged myself down to the office. My back was hurting and I knew it was tension. By the end of the week there was a fresh crisis with John. "He's threatening a hunger strike," Greg Craig phoned to report.

"Not the bail thing again!" I groaned.

"No. This time he wants to speak to Jodie Foster. Says he won't eat until we arrange for him to talk to her on the phone. Of course we're not going to do any such thing."

The more I thought about this bit of blackmail, the madder I got. John was ready to antagonize everyone—lawyers, guards, doctors, prison staff—all for a momentary contact with a young woman who'd made it clear she wanted no part of him. It was a lousy day at the office, the North Dakota well still giving us fits, and the next day was worse—a turndown from a firm I'd thought might be interested in acquiring Vanderbilt.

Jo Ann had gone for a quick visit to her folks in Oklahoma City. When she got home I told her about John's latest attempt to coerce the rest of us into doing what he wanted. "I think we should tell him that if he wants us to go on knocking ourselves out for him, he's got to cut out this ridiculous behavior."

"You mean . . . stop helping him? Jack, how could you even suggest such a thing!"

"Of course we'd never do it, really. But now he just takes it all for granted, never stops to think how many he hurts."

Jo Ann wasn't listening. To her I was a man who would abandon a child in trouble. Soon neither of us was listening, except to his own rapidly rising voice.

The first few weeks after the tragedy in Washington, Jo Ann and I had been closer than in years, drawn together by calamity. Now, three months later, it was not the catastrophe itself which was wearing us down but these small daily crises. I was physically ill that night, unable to find a position where my back didn't kill me, wondering if the marriage itself could survive the months ahead.

I had to get away for a few days, that was all I knew. Away from problems with John, problems with Vanderbilt, away from the swamp of self-pity I was floundering in. I needed time alone, time to sort things out. July 4 was coming up, a long weekend when the business world pretty well shut down anyway. I climbed into the Omega and headed west, into the mountains, I didn't care where.

178

43

JO ANN:

I watched Jack's car pull up the driveway and disappear down Brookline Road, feeling frightened for the first time in my life to be left in my own home alone. I closed the front door and bolted it. What was the matter with me? Jack often had to be away on business; our home had always seemed like an extension of his strength and protection.

I ran up to the bedroom and shut the door. How could he go off now, this weekend, when firecrackers were exploding in the neighborhood, each one bringing back the sound of those gunshots outside the Hilton. Earlier that week someone had thrown firecrackers into our yard. Colorado in the summer was full of visitors; a sheriff's deputy had stopped by the day before to check on us, saying that people were asking local shopkeepers where we lived. Fourth of July events were scheduled at the Club. Jack pictured me having a big social weekend. As if I'd go without him! What would I say when people asked where he was? Make up some kind of story? Or tell the truth: "He didn't want to be around me"? Not even to my closest friends was I willing to admit that Jack and I were having problems.

And what about Diane? She always phoned us on special days. What reason would I give her when Jack didn't come on the line? Never, ever in my life had I seen my own parents argue. I wanted us to be that kind of example for her and Steve.

I was startled awake in the night by a light shining from the street below into the bedroom window. In an instant it was dark again, but I lay shaking, afraid even to get up and look out. "It's the sheriff," I kept telling myself, "just checking on us." But suppose it wasn't the sheriff. . . .

For hours one fear-filled thought triggered another. "Trust God." That's what Jack was always telling me, just as he told John. But how did one do it with the pine trees moaning. Jack didn't trust God. He talked about it, but he worried and worked as though nothing would happen that he himself didn't bring about.

He came home four days later looking better, with no suspicion of the agony I'd been through. Jack needed to be alone when he was hurting as much as I needed people. I bit my lip and said nothing, and afterward I was glad, because all summer the situation at Vanderbilt grew worse.

Vince believed that the postponed indictments would now be handed down on Monday, July 27. By then our three psychiatrists, and the psychologist we had also engaged, should have completed their evaluations so that we would know whether a Not Guilty by Reason of Insanity plea was tenable—even though we now intended to use it only as an arguing point in pressing for a plea bargain.

The government doctors had not announced their findings yet, either, and of course it was possible that *they* would conclude that John was legally insane on March 30. Greg Craig was more and more convinced of it. "He's so out of touch with reality that I have to keep reminding him he's accused of a *crime*," Greg said. In some kind of magical way, he felt, John saw himself as a hero—the hero of an epic unaccountably gone wrong.

On July 23 I went into the kitchen to start breakfast while Jack had his "quiet time." I switched on the radio in time to hear the announcer report that "government doctors have determined that John W. Hinckley, Jr., was mentally responsible at the time he shot President Reagan and three other men in front of the Washington Hilton last March 30."

I raced up the five steps to the bedroom wing. Jack read the news on my face before I said a word. It was a Thursday morning; Jack was delaying his departure for the office until our semi-weekly telephone connection with Butner. We couldn't tell from John's voice whether he'd heard the report from the government psychiatrists or not. He sounded listless and depressed, but that was always true. We talked about how

180

good it would be to see him "in Washington" next week—we couldn't bring ourselves to say "at the arraignment." John asked if we'd gotten his last letter; I said I'd look for it when I went to the post office.

Later that morning there was good news on the radio. Mr. Brady was up walking, with the help of crutches, around his hospital room. I phoned Jack at the office to be sure he'd heard. We worked on the wording of a telegram to send Mr. Brady and his courageous young wife on their eighth wedding anniversary.

Jack came home at five o'clock so we could watch the early-evening news together. It was even worse than we expected: That depraved-looking ID photo scowling from every channel and the words *found responsible* repeated over and over. "It's just the government doctors' opinion," Jack kept reminding me. "Ours may disagree."

John's letter had come in the mail. He was off on the subject of bail again: If we didn't help him arrange it he'd go on a hunger strike. Jack had come home with an aching back and the news that yet another key man—one of their best geologists —had resigned from Vanderbilt that day. I longed to find something cheerful to say, but again it was solitude Jack wanted. He went out the door and walked for a long, long time.

Monday the 27th, the day Vince expected the indictment, came and went with no news. Tuesday still nothing. I kept looking into the refrigerator, trying to decide whether to lay in food for the rest of the week or wait another day. On Wednesday Jack phoned from the office to say he'd had a call from Vince: The indictment had been postponed again, this time indefinitely.

"But why, Jack! How can they keep John sitting there month after month?"

"Vince didn't know. There's a 'new development'—that's all the government would tell him."

181

44

JACK:

It wasn't until the next day during our regular Thursday phone hook-up with John that we understood. Knew what had happened, that is—understand we certainly did not. While John had been in the shower room, observed even there by a guard, other guards had searched his cell and found some penciled notes which "could sound bad."

"What kind of notes, John?" I asked.

Just things he'd written because he was bored.

"But what did the notes *say?*"

"Nothing. It was just stuff I made up."

It was from Vince, who called me at the office later in the day after talking with the FBI, that I learned that the notes described an imaginary conspiracy—either with the political left or the political right, Vince wasn't sure which—to assassinate the President. It was so far-fetched Vince couldn't believe investigators were taking it seriously, yet apparently in this kind of a case even the remotest possibilities had to be checked out. John had sketched rough maps, put down tantalizing initials. Vince feared that the FBI would have to spend days, even weeks, chasing these phony "clues" across the nation.

"But why did he do it, Vince? Why should John make up such nonsense?"

Vince didn't know.

I hung up the phone utterly defeated. It was July 30, four months to the day since I'd heard the news over Arnie Bjork's little radio and I was as baffled by my son as ever.

The next day Vince called with still more bad news. Dr. Sally Johnson had completed her 16-week long evaluation of John: Her report was on Vince's desk. Although she found John to be "schizoid" with a "personality disorder," she concluded that at the time of the shooting he had been mentally responsible, that is, capable of appreciating the nature of his act and desisting from it.

My confusion about the whole realm of mental illness, and the doctors who treat it, redoubled. That same week Williams & Connolly received the reports from our three psychiatrists: All three independently, without knowing one another or discussing the case together, diagnosed John as psychotic—totally out of touch with reality—at the time he fired that gun. Was psychiatry a science, with known laws like other sciences, or an art, or a gigantic hoax? Every one of the authorities hired by the prosecution had found John legally sane; every one hired by us had found him legally insane. Was that what an NGRI defense would amount to—the "experts" contradicting each other?

As Vince predicted, the discovery of the "conspiracy" notes delayed the indictment again, not just days but weeks, while every lead was painstakingly examined and eliminated. John had condemned himself to another month in that solitary cell while his preposterous story was checked out.

Our fear now was that as the time dragged on he'd do himself worse damage still. A change from his present situation, at whatever cost, seemed the only thing on his mind. What if in this desperate mood, in spite of everything we and the lawyers could say, he pled Guilty when the arraignment finally came? We wouldn't know until he actually said the words "not guilty" in front of a judge in a courtroom, whether we had a defense case or not. "We can advise him only," Vince kept reminding us. "The decision is his."

The problem, of course, was that John thought he *was* mentally responsible. To this moment he apparently saw nothing insane in the effort to win the love of one stranger by killing another. Far too late, I was reading everything I could lay my hands on about mental illness, and this was one of the hallmarks: Disturbed people might see *themselves* as perfectly rational.

● ● ●

183

The week following John's "conspiracy" brainstorm, there was fresh tragedy. James Brady had a grand mal seizure along with several smaller ones, later was reported losing spinal fluid through his nose. Our prayers for Mr. Brady, with which we had begun and ended each day since March 31, intensified.

That week too, Vince called to say that it looked now as though there could be as many as ten counts against John in the indictment. District of Columbia charges, he'd learned, were being added to the Federal ones. To me this sounded like a technicality, but apparently it could make a tremendous difference to John's fate if all plea bargain offers were turned down and we decided to go ahead with a trial—and if by some miracle we won. Persons found NGRI on a D.C. charge were committed automatically, Vince said, to St. Elizabeth's Hospital, an ancient institution on a hill in Washington overlooking the Anacostia River. Vince didn't know much about the place but he was going to find out more.

In early August doctors examining John's CATscan, done at Duke University Hospital in May, discovered physical brain abnormalities. They wanted to repeat the tests once John was brought up to the Washington area for arraignment.

Our next regular trip to see him was scheduled for Thursday, August 13. That morning before leaving for the airport we had our scheduled Thursday phone connection with Butner. John was invariably depressed during these talks, but that morning his mood was darker than usual. He didn't want us coming to visit, he said. The only reason we could get out of him was that they were taking him up to Washington the following week to be on hand for the arraignment and he'd rather see us there.

I hung up, confused and frustrated, to begin canceling plane and car reservations. We couldn't force our presence on John: Butner admitted visitors only at the request of the inmate. "He hates Butner so," Jo Ann said, groping for an explanation, "maybe it's just too hard when we come and then leave again."

Maybe. But over the next ten days an anxious thought mounted. John hated confrontation. Could he be planning to plead Guilty at his arraignment, and not want to face us ahead of time with this decision? I thought of all the people working on his behalf, trying to secure treatment for him instead of punishment. John could undo it all in thirty seconds before the judge's bench.

JO ANN:

On Tuesday evening, August 18, television news announced that John had been transferred that day by helicopter to Quantico Marine Base near Washington. A new photograph replaced at last the hideous ID picture which had pursued us since April. The new picture, taken apparently with a telephoto lens, showed him on the helicopter pad surrounded by tall U.S. marshals. Next to them, behind his horn-rimmed glasses, John looked no more than a child. He was wearing slacks and a navy blazer supplied, I supposed, by the government. I wondered if it felt strange to be out of that orange jumpsuit. Beneath his open shirt collar I could see a bulletproof vest. The part of the photograph I could not look at were the handcuffs.

Later that week the financial section of the *Denver Post* carried the news that Vanderbilt Energy Corporation was for sale. Nowadays whenever an item about Vanderbilt appeared, John's name and identity ("loner who shot the President and three others") was sure to be included. Jack worried about the effect on potential buyers, but though he protested repeatedly to the editors that the subjects were totally unrelated, the damaging practice continued.

We couldn't speak to John at Quantico until Wednesday, the day after the transfer. He said he hadn't slept; like the first time he'd been there, right after the shooting, bright lights were kept on all night.

Friday we talked to him again. Literally. Jack and I talked, John answered, if at all, in monosyllables. The indictment was scheduled now for Monday, three days off, with the arraignment to follow four days after that, on Friday, August 28. "We'll be right there in the courtroom with you, John."

No response.

"There's good news from Mr. Brady's doctors," Jack told him. Surgery had corrected the seepage of spinal fluid.

Silence.

When the one-sided phone visit was over I turned to Jack in despair. "He's just sinking lower all the time!" I was getting to the point where I didn't care what we did, so long as John could have medicine and attention from a doctor soon.

Vince was to call Jack on Monday as soon as the indictment was handed down, and Jack was to call me at once from the office. To make the time pass I set up the ironing board to press some things for our trip east at the end of the week. It was five months since that other Monday when I'd been ironing for another trip. . . .

Jack phoned around eleven o'clock. "Thirteen counts," was all he said.

All he needed to say. It was worse than our most pessimistic guess. . . . That night the TV news reported the stiff indictment. On the same program came the news that Mark Chapman, whose shooting of John Lennon last December had plunged John and millions of other fans into mourning, had been sentenced that day to a term of twenty years to life. If anyone ever sounded sick, that young man did—yet he was going to prison.

"The NGRI plea wouldn't stand a chance!" Jack summed up both our reactions as we went up to bed. Our fear was that the government realized this only too well. They'd assume that our stated intention of going to trial was only a bluff, and have no reason to bargain.

At the airport in Washington Thursday night we rented a car, and drove to a motel south of the city, expecting John to be returned to Quantico after the arraignment. There was an awkward moment at the registration desk when Jack couldn't recall which of our assumed identities he'd used to make the reservation. He tried three names before coming up with the right one. I kept thinking of the pride Jack's mother had instilled in him for the name Hinckley, pride all wrapped up with love for the father he had lost so young. Every time he had to deny it at an airline counter or a motel desk, I saw him wince as though at some deep disloyalty.

186

In the morning we drove into the city and picked up Vince en route to the courthouse. Vince was as tense as Jack and I over what John would actually do that morning. Again and again Vince had explained to John that a plea of Not Guilty today did not necessarily mean going to trial, only giving them a basis on which to plea bargain.

The courthouse was the same massive, starkly modern building where we'd come for the Grand Jury hearings three months earlier. Courtroom 19, however, was on an upper floor. In the corridor outside there was an electronic metal detector; beyond this a security guard repeated the check with a hand-held wand.

By nine a.m. we were inside the stately, high-ceilinged room where our son's future would be decided. This would be the same room, Vince said, where a trial would be held—"if it ever comes to that." Rows of wooden benches at the very back of the room provided limited seating for spectators and the press. Vince left us there and took his seat down front at the defense table. To his right was a two-tiered jury box which today, of course, would not be occupied, to his left on a dais, an imposing mahogany desk with a high-backed leather chair —also for the moment unoccupied. The judge, Vince had told us, was always the last person to enter the courtroom.

Around 9:30 reporters began arriving, taking their places across the aisle from us. The first two benches soon filled with "sketchers," artists with large lap boards and mini-binoculars attached to ear pieces which they put on like glasses. To our dismay they turned at once in their seats and began drawing Jack and me.

Just before 10:00 John was brought in through a door to the left of the judge's bench, flanked by four marshals. He was wearing the navy blazer, gray trousers, and a shirt beneath which I saw the bulge of a bulletproof vest. He sat down at the defense table next to Vince.

A moment later a court bailiff ordered all present to stand. A door to the right of the bench opened and Judge Barrington Parker appeared. I caught my breath at the first sight of the man who so largely held John's welfare in his hands. Dignity was the overwhelming first impression. An unsmiling man in his mid-60s, with receding gray hair and a close-cropped mustache, he was black, scholarly looking—and crippled. Self-discipline . . . that was the second impression: an iron self-control that took no notice, and allowed others to take none, of his disability. Step by step, aided by two angled metal crutches, he made his way up the steps of the dais under the eyes of that silent, standing courtroom.

When he was seated at last the rest of us too sat down, except for Vince and John who remained standing, facing the judge, their backs to us. At a nod from Judge Parker the clerk of the court read aloud the indictment:

First count: Attempt to Kill Ronald Reagan, President of the United States

Second count: Assault on Ronald Reagan with Intent to Kill him, while Armed

Third count: Assault on Ronald Reagan with a Dangerous Weapon

Fourth count: Assault on Agent McCarthy, a Federal Officer, while Performing his Official Duties

Fifth count: Assault on McCarthy with Intent to Kill him, while Armed

and so on, for thirteen counts.

"You have heard the charges against you," Judge Parker said to John. "How do you plead?"

The room was so silent I could hear the scratch of a sketcher's pen. I reached out and took Jack's hand. And then. . . .

"Not guilty, Your Honor."

John's voice was so low I barely heard—but it was enough. He had not given up. Or, if he hoped for nothing, at least he was letting us go on hoping for him.

John sat back down while Vince made the routine request for release on bail that was John's legal right; John himself must have been the only one in that courtroom who believed there was even a chance it would be granted.

Then we all stood again while the judge made his labored exit. John was escorted out next. For the first time his eyes searched the room. He spotted us and attempted a smile as the marshals led him away.

The whole process had taken twenty minutes.

46

JACK:

We returned to Williams & Connolly a mighty relieved threesome. The two options, plea bargain or trial, were now really viable possibilities, thanks to John's plea of Not Guilty. With the four lawyers we took a hard look at what might happen now. Suppose, they asked us, their present plea bargain offer, and any subsequent ones, were categorically rejected by the government. Were we really willing, if that happened, to go to trial? Together we looked at the pros and cons.

For trial was the fact that Jo Ann and I, incredulously and belatedly, had become convinced that John really *was* legally insane, isolated in a world of fantasy. I still struggled with the word: to call my own son "insane" seemed to me to call him something hideous, less than human. But if the word meant, as the doctors said, a mind that had lost its anchor in reality, then our son was insane, and to plead Guilty even to one of the charges, in a plea bargain, was simply wrong.

Also *for* trial, if we won, was the prospect of hospitalization for him instead of imprisonment. He would be behind bars in either case; the "criminally insane," at least in the District of Columbia, were held in a maximum security facility that to all appearances resembled a prison. But behind those hospital bars would be therapy, medicine, a staff familiar with his disease.

For trial, again if we won, and if the therapy was successful, was the chance of eventual release into the outside world.

Against trial was the overwhelming probability that we

would lose. Vince had originally estimated our chances of winning at one in ten; with the recent sentencing of Lennon's assailant, Mark Chapman, he felt they were even less.

Against trial was the time it would take: another two months (I naively thought) before it would even start—all of which time John would be confined in isolation under 24-hour surveillance without treatment or medication. We'd watched John retreat further into his unreachable personal hell with each passing week at Butner. Could we in good conscience condemn him to months more of the same?

Against trial was the cost. Not even Williams & Connolly with all their experience could estimate what the total expense of this case would be. I could see two places where the money might come from: sale of our Vanderbilt stock, or a bank loan. It was a bad, bad time to do either, with oil prices dropping and interest rates going through the roof—but like any family in time of illness, you do what you must.

Against trial was the nature of this case. That John had committed the act, he and we and millions of others knew. A trial would focus on his mental condition, force him to sit on public view while the pathetic collapse of his thinking was paraded before the world. Force Jo Ann and me, too, to see our home, our family, our most private selves dissected and found wanting.

Were we willing, the lawyers had asked. I only hoped we'd never have to find out.

At 3:30 Jo Ann and I returned to our motel south of town to be nearer Quantico when our visiting hour was announced. At 4:30 Vince telephoned: John had not been returned to Quantico. He had been transferred to another military base, an army installation known as Fort Meade, ten miles north of Washington. We could see John there at 5:30.

Forty miles away on the opposite side of the city! We jumped into the car and joined the bumper to bumper traffic inching around Washington's beltway in the Friday evening homebound jam.

Fort Meade turned out to be an enormous complex sprawling across the green Maryland countryside. We drove through street after street of unused wooden barracks—which, from their appearance, must have been built during World War II—past newer brick dormitories and blocks of neat brick homes that were probably officers' quarters. On a drill field some soldiers were playing baseball in the warm August evening. I rolled down the window and, hating the question, asked directions to the stockade. We came to a sign announcing "Installation Detention Facility." A few yards beyond this a sentry hut blocked the road.

"We're the Hinckleys," I told the young man on duty. Strange to blurt out the real name.

The soldier spoke over a two-way radio, then instructing us to leave the car there, pointed out a low white building a hundred yards away. We were surprised how small the stockade was, not much larger than the eight-cell unit reserved for John alone at Butner. It was a one-story, concrete block affair dwarfed by an enormous brick smoke stack that rose just behind it. Around it was a ten-foot high heavy chain-link fence topped by a V of barbed wire with additional coils of razor wire looped in the angle.

The gate in that formidable fence was unlocked electronically from somewhere inside and we followed a marshal to an office where for the second time that day we were searched with a hand-held metal detector. On the desk a closed-circuit TV was monitoring one of the cells. We could see a high barred window, a lidless toilet, a straight-backed chair, a narrow metal bed.

On the bed, elbows on his knees, John sat staring at the floor.

We were not allowed into the cell area to visit. Instead we were taken through a locked door and down a short hall to a small room marked "Chapel." "Wait here, please," the marshal said. The room had a simple altar and several rows of wooden pews, with a number of folding chairs and a large floor fan at the back. Small barred windows, high in the wall, like the one we'd seen in John's cell, let in a little of the fading daylight.

From somewhere down the concrete corridor we could hear the nerve-jarring slam of heavy steel doors; for the first time I realized where the term "slammer" as a nickname for prison came from. The stockade, the marshal had explained, was used mostly for short-term drunk-and-disorderly infractions on the base. The marshals, working around the clock in shifts of five or six men at a time, were not part of the regular staff but assigned solely to oversee John.

The door at the back of the chapel opened and a second marshal brought him in. Gone were the blazer and slacks we'd seen in the courtroom that morning: He was wearing a long-sleeved fatigue shirt and baggy olive drab pants, both several sizes too big for him. Since the drawstring had been removed, John had to grip the waistband to keep the trousers from sliding off. My eyes traveled to his feet: laceless cloth slippers similar to the ones he'd worn at Butner. Since his suicide attempt three months ago I appreciated the significance of these seemingly minor details.

John was sunken-eyed, but said he was glad to be out of Quantico, and even gladder to be out of the airless cell in the courthouse basement where he'd spent the previous night. How soon, he asked, would the judge rule on bail?

Afterward Jo Ann and I made the forty-mile drive back to the motel, then forced ourselves to sit up for the late news to see how the networks were treating today's court proceeding. To our relief most coverage consisted of the simple announcement that John had pleaded Not Guilty. Though I felt the courtroom sketches made the two of us look grim-faced and sour, the treatment of John was generally fair. I allowed myself to sink with relief onto the motel bed.

The next moment I was on my feet in agitation as the commentator wondered aloud what John had been doing in Dayton, Ohio, last October on the day when President Jimmy Carter made a campaign speech there. Dayton? John had been in *Dayton* last fall? It was the first Jo Ann and I had heard of that. The newsman pointed out that in that same month three handguns had been found in John's possession in Nashville, Tennessee—on the day Carter was scheduled to speak *there*. Jo Ann and I could only stare at each other in dismay. Would there be no end to these ghastly revelations?

In the morning we checked out of the motel, no sense staying so far from Fort Meade, and arrived at the stockade around 10:30. Again we met with John in the chapel in the presence of two marshals. Vince had instructed us not to query John about Dayton, wanting neither our testimony nor his influenced by discussions after-the-fact. We talked instead about his upcoming trip to Johns Hopkins Hospital in Baltimore for new CATscans of his brain.

Near the base that afternoon we located the motel that was to become our home away from home. Colony 7 Motel on the Baltimore-Washington Parkway was a complex of yellow brick buildings with a Schrafft's restaurant in the front. As I would do countless times over the next months I carried our bags into a ground floor room. We still thought, that Saturday in late August, that by the end of October at the very latest a resolution of some kind would have been reached. I listed them for Jo Ann.

One: John would be sentenced to prison, hopefully Butner, for a limited term under a plea bargain.

Two: He would stand trial, be judged legally insane, and be committed to St. Elizabeth's Hospital for an unknown period.

Three: He would stand trial, be judged legally sane and guilty, and sentenced to prison—perhaps Butner, perhaps somewhere else—for a long term.

Even if the worst happened and the sentence was life imprisonment, we thought that two months from now he would at least know where he stood and be receiving some kind of medication for his bottomless depression. How could we have dreamed that two months, four months, six months, eight months would pass with John still in solitary confinement in a "temporary" cell in Fort Meade's stockade, still under surveillance every moment of every 24 hours, his case unheard, his future unknown.

47

JO ANN:

The pendulum swung now between our home in Evergreen and the Colony 7 Motel. We met John always in that little stockade chapel, with the marshals present. We learned to switch on the floor fan to give our conversations at least an illusion of privacy. Not that we talked about anything very momentous. His nephew, Chris, had started nursery school that fall, a new doctor had diagnosed Grandma Moore's problem as diabetes. As John grew thinner his Army-issue clothes hung ever looser on him and his grip on the waistband became more determined.

As much as we could we avoided controversial subjects. Jack realized, or should have, that John's thinking was not logical, but his orderly engineer's mind could not resist outlining facts. We took to visiting John in turns, Jack for an hour, me for an hour. With me John was more relaxed, and through the doctors we were beginning to understand this phenomenon a little. The world of the mentally ill, they explained, is an endlessly menacing, fear-filled place. Only with beings he saw as non-threatening—a cat, his little nephew—could John let down his guard. Diane and I fit that category; we were both "nurturing" figures, in the doctors' phrase, tending to be protective of him.

Still, it was hard on Jack never to achieve this rapport. He was working so hard to help his son in this calamity, constantly writing letters, making phone calls, eating, breathing and sleeping John's problems—receiving only resentment from John in return.

Nor were the intervals back in Denver any letup for Jack. The harder he worked, the worse things became. By this time many small energy companies the size of Vanderbilt—and even much larger ones—were closing their doors. But Jack felt that he was being blamed in Vanderbilt's case, for what was actually an industry-wide problem. "A director as much as told me today that if I'd been doing a better job, this last drop in the stock price wouldn't have happened."

He would never even consider, though, omitting a trip to see John. Our days at the Colony 7 Motel fell into a routine—and the best part was the first. Ever since that very first morning in the Jefferson Hotel, when Dale Morris had led us in a prayer as we waited to meet our lawyers, we'd followed the same pattern. One of us would read a passage of Scripture aloud and we'd pray for the day ahead. We always asked first for Mr. Brady's recovery and John's, then for guidance for ourselves. The view beyond the motel window wasn't an inspiring one with its rows of Washington-bound tour buses parked end-to-end. But to me that first hour of the day was a bit of heaven, the time Jack and I were closest.

From one visit to the next we watched the decline in John's spirits. In September we'd had to take his beloved Titter to the vet to be put to sleep. The orange cat was 16 years old and unable to swallow without pain. We felt dishonest keeping the news from John, yet he seemed so wretched that each visit we'd put off telling him "until next time."

I was sure that fresh air and exercise would help. Inside the stockade fence was a postage stamp of an exercise yard—just a square of concrete paving in the shadow of that giant smokestack, but there, I thought, John could at least get some sun on his pallid skin. The marshals would not consider it in the daytime, pointing out that a clump of trees overlooking the little compound could conceal a sniper. Occasionally after dark, however, they would let him walk there for a few minutes.

John's deepening depression alarmed us all. Vince filed a motion that would permit John to be institutionalized while awaiting disposition of his case; he argued that since the government was already paying for round-the-clock marshals, they could supervise him just as effectively in a hospital room as a cell. The motion was turned down.

The sicker we realized John to be, paradoxically, the more

195

we were recoiling from the idea of an NGRI defense. The stresses and delays of a trial, in his present condition, could only do more damage. What would we gain after all, even in the unlikely event that we were to win? Commitment to a mental institution none of us had actually seen. St. Elizabeth's would be the goal of a long courtroom battle, but was it a goal worth struggling for? Vince contacted the hospital administration for permission to visit.

48

JACK:

On a rainy fall morning Jo Ann guided me with a map on her lap across the Anacostia River into an area of Washington far off the tourist track. Martin Luther King Jr. Avenue was a congested thoroughfare through a run-down business district. Neon signs with missing letters blinked through the drizzle, buses honked. And suddenly there it was, a tree-studded oasis behind a wrought-iron fence: St. Elizabeth's Hospital. Vince, Greg and Judy Miller were waiting in the parking lot with a doctor who'd been assigned to show the five of us around.

The largest federal mental institution in the nation, St. Elizabeth's consisted of scores of institutional-style red brick buildings, the oldest dating to the 1850s when it was known as the Government Hospital for the Insane. Frequently underfinanced and understaffed, it was caught now, the doctor said, in the current squeeze of federal cutbacks. We encountered no other visitors; people with families or other resources, he explained, did not choose St. Elizabeth's.

The last stop on our tour was the John Howard Pavilion, a U-shaped six-story building set off by itself beyond the graveyard where lay buried those patients whose families had not claimed them even in death. This was the maximum security facility for the criminally insane, the place where John—if he went through a trial and won—would be sent.

We got out of the car and stood in the rain staring up at the row after row of barred windows. It looked more like a prison, I thought, than Butner—and the impression was reinforced when on entering we not only had to pass through the familiar metal-detection gate, but step onto a low platform where the security check was repeated with a hand-held device. An attendant with an enormous ring of keys led the group of us through a maze of corridors, stopping every few steps to unlock a metal door. Even the elevators required a key to operate.

There were about 240 patients in the John Howard Pavilion at any given time, the doctor told us, housed in twelve separate, locked wards. We were shown a typical patient's bedroom: its linoleum floor, tile walls and spartan furnishings again reminding me of a prison cell. We were visiting one of the small cafeterias located on each floor when somewhere nearby an outburst from a patient brought attendants running and we were hurriedly escorted from the building.

Jo Ann and I were silent as we drove back across the river, the slap of the windshield wipers the only sound. The others had gone ahead to hold a table for us all at the Monocle restaurant on Capitol Hill where we were to discuss our reactions. But what was there to say? If we won, we lost. Physically anyhow, modern Butner seemed a far more desirable place than the antique red brick vastness of St. Elizabeth's.

Sitting around a corner table, four out of the five of us, Vince, Judy, Jo Ann and I, agreed that to delay treatment still further for John while we went to trial, in order to gain commitment to St. Elizabeth's, simply made no sense. Only Greg remained silent, pushing his food around his plate in as poor a pretense of eating as Jo Ann and I were making. At last he laid down his fork.

"John is not guilty," he said with quiet firmness. "Not as the law defines guilt. How can we counsel him to tell a judge he acted rationally, when every one of us at this table knows he did not?"

There was a charged silence. Truth has a way of putting an

197

end to discussion, and at that moment I believe each of the five of us knew truth had been spoken.

Then the moment passed and the arguments began again. I agreed with Greg—but what good was standing on principle, I asked, when the lawyers themselves admitted there was almost no chance of winning in court . . . with St. Elizabeth's as the reward if we did?

In the end, the decision was taken out of our hands, in part because of John's own continuing irresponsibility. In spite of the patent failure of his effort to somehow "impress" Jodie Foster by a brutal act, in spite of her repeated denial of any knowledge of or interest in him, some persistent fantasy about her still apparently ruled his actions. Seeing his name and hers linked in print, no matter how negatively, in his mind made their relationship real. No amount of reasoning by us or his lawyers could talk him out of replying to queries from newspapers, hinting at dire consequences to Jodie if she continued to ignore him. *Time* and *Newsweek* sent questionnaires to him, and then printed his answers—the responses of a mind so sick that we wondered if our society didn't have to be sick too, to attach any importance to them.

Each infuriating communique from John was greeted by a fresh outburst of editorials demanding punishment. Each one made it harder for the Attorney General's office—even if it wanted to—to be lenient.

And there were outside events. That October 1981, President Anwar Sadat was murdered in an Egyptian reviewing stand. Distant as that event was in miles, utterly different in motivation, we didn't have to wait for Vince's phone call to know that the death of that distinguished statesman was also the death of any remaining chances for a reduced sentence. For days the media were filled with cries for an end to assassinations. Three world leaders gunned down inside seven months —who could fail to feel outraged and fearful?

Vince spoke with Attorney Ruff who confirmed that Sadat's murder plus John's pronouncements to the press had hurt our case badly. He would still press for a plea bargain, Vince assured us. But he no longer spoke of the possibility of release in ten years. Fifteen years, he thought, with luck, was the best we could hope for now.

49

JO ANN:

In mid-October John was brought to the federal courthouse again for further pre-trial hearings in heavily guarded Courtroom 19. Vince was trying to keep the government from introducing at a possible trial the fictitious "conspiracy papers" taken from John's cell at Butner. Vince contended that since the handwritten notes had been inside a Williams & Connolly envelope, they had constituted confidential attorney-client material illegally removed by the guards. I couldn't understand why it mattered, since the FBI had submitted a 3,000 page memo on their investigation showing the "assassination plot" to be a total fabrication. Vince explained that just raising the specter of a conspiracy before a jury would be damaging.

Once more Jack and I tried to keep our expressions neutral as courtroom sketchers peered at us through binoculars. We were both sick and looked it. Jack's back made the long days on the wooden spectators' bench agony, and he carried a supply of handkerchiefs to daub at an almost constant nosebleed. I'd had a feverish headache for weeks and had spent much of our last trip home in bed. Our doctor friend Em Harvey in Evergreen told us our symptoms were the result of tension, but that didn't make the ailments go away.

With adjournments and postponements the hearings dragged on for two weeks. Vince was also petitioning Judge Parker to exclude statements obtained from John the afternoon of the shooting. Vince argued that the "Miranda ruling" (so called after a famous case) established John's right to remain silent until legal counsel was provided: The police, the FBI and the Secret Service had all interrogated him, Vince maintained, in violation of this right.

During the hearings John was confined in the courthouse basement where we could not visit him. Afterward, at Fort Meade, he was so hopeless and listless that we were all the more convinced he could not hold up through a full-length trial.

There was a new and ominous development, however. Vince's latest plea bargain offer, like all the rest, had been categorically turned down by the government; if subsequent ones continued to be denied, he now feared we could be forced to trial. The only other possibility, a plea of Guilty, was probably no longer an option. Vince believed Judge Parker would not entertain an uncontested Guilty plea in the presence of written opinions from all three of our psychiatrists diagnosing John as psychotic. "He'd insist that we defend him, as the law provides."

Our meetings among the *No Smoking* signs of Vince's cluttered office were increasingly counsels of desperation. "We've got to be ready for trial," Vince would say at the close of each fruitless discussion on reaching an out-of-court resolution. Once more we'd go over the months before the shooting. Occasionally some detail from Jack or me—meaningless to us—would provide a missing fragment for the four attorneys who knew so much more about our son's recent history than we did.

"Tell us again about last New Year's Eve," Vince said one day. The tape John had made that evening down in his bedroom, Vince believed, would be introduced by the government as evidence that John had planned his murderous deed in advance.

And so once more I went over the unremarkable events of that day ten months ago. I told about picking up a bottle of peach brandy for John while I was at the supermarket, coming home and—

"*What* kind of brandy did you say?" Greg Craig demanded. The tall young lawyer was always so calm and courteous that I was startled.

"Peach. John asked if I—"

"I knew it!" Greg was out of his chair, scattering paper in all directions. "Of course! It *had* to be peach brandy!"

I stared at him in amazement, not understanding why it mattered. "That was what Travis Bickle drank!" Greg explained. And when I still looked blank: "In the movie."

Greg was convinced that the movie *Taxi Driver* was the key to all that had happened. Not to John's becoming sick, but to the form the sickness had taken. John had sat through the film probably sixteen times during the months he spent in Los Angeles in 1976. "He became Travis Bickle," Greg said. "He *was* Travis."

The movie was no longer current, five years later, and Jack and I had been unable to find a video tape, though the lawyers kept assuring us it was essential to an understanding of John's inner universe. "The guns John bought were the same guns Travis bought," Greg told us. "He stalked political figures because Travis did. He shot people for Jodie Foster's sake because that's what happened in the film." The movie became John's reality, Greg believed, far more than Lubbock or Evergreen had ever been.

Jack and I still had trouble believing that a movie could have had so much influence on our son. Granted, we hadn't seen it, but how could any picture, no matter how gripping, have that kind of hold on the mind? Clearly, we needed to learn a great deal more about the nature of mental illness. . . .

Much was known, we discovered as we read and queried doctors; much was still unknown. "Process schizophrenia"—the name Dr. Carpenter gave to John's condition—develops gradually but, according to some researchers, has its original roots in an incomplete separation from the mother. Was it my fault, then? I wondered in anguish. Doctors repeatedly assured me it was not. Schizophrenia, they said, struck people from any and every kind of upbringing—one in 100 Americans at some point in their lives. In spite of its prevalence, it remained one of the least understood mental diseases. Debate raged over the part played by genetics, brain chemistry, early experiences, environment, allergies, diet, even infection. All that was known was that somehow, somewhere along the line, a fundamental stage in human development remains incomplete; the schizophrenic individual fails to perceive himself as a separate and distinct entity.

In "a supportive home setting," as doctors termed ours, such children usually do well enough until puberty, when both biology and society pressure them to leave the nest. As internal and external pressures mount—to go to college, to get a job—so does the anguish of the schizophrenic. His efforts to remain in the womb of the family become more desperate. Generalized, hard-to-pin-down physical ailments occur. Pain, very real and often acute, shifts from head to foot and everywhere between, leaving doctors baffled.

It was John. It was our son's last eight years these doctors were describing. Yet they were not speaking of an individual but only of "syndromes," typical patterns of a disease we'd scarcely heard of, yet recognized all too well.

Schizophrenia, to me, conjured up a "split personality," Dr. Jekyll and Mr. Hyde. That condition, doctors explained, was a very different illness—and a far rarer one—known to medicine as "dual-" or even "multi-personality." Schizophrenics, on the contrary, lack enough sense-of-self to piece together even one personality, let alone two or more. For the missing "I, myself" at the core of his being, the schizophrenic typically substitutes identities found in books, movies, fan magazines.

What is "split" in such an individual are his thoughts and his feelings. Without that spontaneous connection, the schizophrenic's emotions are curiously muted, he feels neither joy nor sorrow. I remembered a teenage boy who never lost his temper, never laughed aloud. . . .

The government had set November 12 as the date on which they would announce their final decision on a plea bargain. We planned a trip east to be with John at that time, spent several hours on November 11 trying to prepare him for a probable turn-down and the unavoidability of a trial. It seemed to me he scarcely listened; his hopes were clearly pinned on a resolution of his case being reached the next day.

"But if we have to go to trial, John," Jack told the pale young man twisting his beltless trouser tops between his fingers, "Vince Fuller has great faith in juries. He feels twelve ordinary people can usually be trusted to get at the truth."

And yet how *could* untrained people sift through all this, I wondered. How could twelve citizens chosen at random be asked to judge the intricacies of mental illness, when even the experts disagreed on definitions, causes, cures.

Next morning Jack and I drove into Washington to be at Williams & Connolly when Vince and Greg came back from their meeting at the Attorney General's office. One look at their faces as they walked in told us the answer. "No plea bargain, Jack and Jo Ann. They're determined to try this case, and they want to go for the maximum penalty the law allows."

Vince still believed that Attorney Ruff had been sympathetic to our compromise appeals, "but Ruff's going to be stepping down." I thought of the soft-spoken family man who'd wheeled himself into the waiting room the day of our first visit to the courthouse six months ago, simply to inquire after my welfare. Mr. Ruff was a Carter appointee, Vince explained; the Reagan administration was pledged to "get tough" on criminals—as I'd enthusiastically approved when I went to the polls last November.

I was touched by our lawyers' reactions. For all four of them John's situation had become far more than a case. Vince said it was the first time in 25 years as a defense attorney that he could not leave his work behind him when he left the office. He asked Jack and me to put off our visit to the stockade until evening so that he and Greg could break the news in person to John that afternoon.

The two of them left for Fort Meade, while I tried to fight down the knot of fear in my stomach. As hard as we had tried to talk positively to John about a trial, his heart had been set on things being "over with" today. In his disappointment, there was nothing . . . dangerous he could do, was there? No way he could harm himself?

A prosecuting psychologist arrived and spent two hours questioning Jack and me. Vince and Greg returned from Fort Meade and outlined procedures for the trial beginning next month, December. And all the while I kept trying to thrust aside the thought of John hurting himself. A photograph found by the FBI among John's things, and recently released to the press, haunted me awake and asleep. It had been taken the Christmas John spent alone in his room in Lubbock. With a time-release camera he had snapped himself holding a gun to his own head. While the family in Denver pictured him making the rounds of New York book publishers with Lynn and her friends, he had sat there friendless, day after day, thinking only of suicide. . . .

He had no gun now, of course. What could he do, with the marshals watching not only in person but on the TV monitor. He hadn't been given any medication for months, nothing he could have been accumulating in secret as he had at Butner. He had no belt, no shoelaces, nothing he could—I wouldn't even complete the thought.

At 7:30 we were admitted to the stockade to see John. He was subdued and glum as he entered the chapel, but not more so than usual. We told him we'd rent an apartment in downtown Washington for the duration of the trial. By the time the marshal escorted him back to the cell block, John seemed almost reconciled to the idea. Why didn't the lump of fear go away?

50

JACK:

I can't even remember what Jo Ann and I quarreled about that evening. The specifics were never important; it was just 24 hours of daily togetherness under these pressure cooker conditions. Why couldn't the moment of perspective every morning when I saw God in charge of all our affairs last through the day, I wondered. All my stewing and thrashing about wasn't helping in any case: Here, after months of effort, we were having to go the route we hated most to face.

A trial meant, too, that I'd have to apply for another bank loan when we got back. The value of Vanderbilt stock was continuing to plummet and Scott had called the day before to report more problems with certain wells.

Next day we looked at apartments. We reserved one as of December 1, two weeks off, then drove back up the Baltimore-Washington Parkway for a last visit with John before we returned to Denver that night.

"We found an apartment!" I told him when I'd switched on the fan. "We'll be back the first week in December to start settling in."

John's eyes were on the floor, his voice barely audible. "What for?"

"Why, so we can be near you during the trial."

"It isn't starting in December." I had to ask him to repeat it twice, he spoke so low. "Greg just called."

The news had come while we were apartment hunting: The start of the trial had been put off until January 4. Coming on top of the fact that he'd have to stand trial at all, this new delay had plunged John into the pits. We trotted out every scrap of encouragement we could, though our own supply was perilously low. I kept glancing at my watch, hating to leave him, yet not wanting to miss the flight that our cut-rate fare was based on. We held hands for the prayer with which we always closed our visits, then hugged him goodbye. I spoke in an undertone to the marshal as we left:

"Keep a close watch on him for a few days. He's had a couple of pieces of bad news—he's really in the dumps."

We collected our belongings from the security room, but at the front door Jo Ann stopped. "I want to talk to the marshals, Jack. I'm so afraid he'll try to hurt himself."

"I just talked to them," I said. But we turned back and spoke once more of our concern, then joined the Friday evening rush hour for the long trip to Dulles airport.

It was midnight when we reached Evergreen, snow already on the roads in mid-November. Saturday morning I went down to Vanderbilt. But though I spent all day at my desk I was no nearer a solution to our business woes that evening. The oil industry was in trouble everywhere: No amount of careful management of one small company could stop the decline.

Sunday Jo Ann was ill and stayed in bed. Our scheduled phone conversation with John did nothing to improve things; he sounded moody and miserable. Afterward I fixed breakfast, but neither of us could eat.

We had been driving down to Denver each Sunday we were home to attend Calvary Temple, the church of the man who had telephoned and shown such concern the night of the shooting. I went alone that morning, but the usual uplift did not come. As always at the close of the service, Pastor Blair invited those with special needs to come down to the altar rail. To my horror, when the pastor reached me I burst into uncontrollable sobs, soaking the lapel of his immaculate black suit.

His prayer and concern for me helped for a while. Back home I switched on the football game. But the black mood returned. I put on a coat and took a long walk in the cold mountain air. Walking could generally raise my spirits but not that day. All I could see ahead was disaster: the permanent crippling of James Brady, the ruin of my business, the deterioration of my marriage, and to cap it all, for my son a long, long term in prison—if not his whole lifetime, certainly the rest of mine. For the first time in my life the thought of killing myself entered my mind. Why should I go on battling problems that had no solution?

I returned to find that Jo Ann had gotten up and set out supper on the kitchen table. The corner was no longer green; we were away so much that many of her plants had died. At six p.m. we were sitting down to eat when the telephone rang.

Vince's voice, strained and thin: "I'm afraid it's bad news, Jack. John hanged himself in his cell window."

They'd cut him down, Vince said, and rushed him to the base hospital, but no one knew how long he'd been hanging or whether he would live. Jo Ann had run to the phone in the living room and I heard her sobs as Vince continued. The marshals had discovered him about five o'clock eastern time—three hours ago now. He'd stood on the chair, woven his fatigue jacket through the bars in the window and tied the sleeves around his neck.

"But," I broke in, "a marshal was six feet away in the corridor! Another one watching the monitor!"

But it seemed John had gauged his timing to coincide with the Sunday afternoon football game, counting on the young marshals being absorbed in television. Through my mind flashed what every doctor had stressed about mental illness: "It doesn't mean stupid."

When a marshal had glanced at the monitor at last, there was a wild scramble for the cell. They could not get in. John had jammed the lock on his door with cardboard shredded from a cracker box. The key would not turn. The driver of the ambulance which had been summoned had the presence of mind to smash the heavy glass window from outside and cut the jacket from the bars.

John's unconscious body dropped to the floor. Still the cell door would not yield; for precious minutes guards hammered and pried at it. At last it gave. Marshals burst in, untied the sleeves from the neck of the crumpled figure on the floor, and carried him to the waiting ambulance which rushed him to the base hospital.

Vince had the number there. I dialed it, eventually talked to a man named J. D. Fitz who was the doctor in charge. Dr. Fitz could make no predictions. John was alive, though still unconscious. It was too soon to know whether there was brain damage; the fight now was simply for survival. I hung up with his promise to phone us as soon as there was anything to report.

Two hours passed and no word. Once again we made hurried calls to the family, wanting them to know from us before they heard it on the news. Eight-thirty came—10:30 eastern time—and still no call. Jo Ann had brought her suitcase down to the front hall minutes after Vince's call—the one she'd kept packed since John's suicide attempt at Butner six months before. But we couldn't leave the telephone to go to the airport.

A nine o'clock news spot carried the story. Bill Sells called immediately to tell us that he and Sue were right next door if we needed them. A few minutes later we heard a car pull down our driveway. Thinking it was other friends coming to stand by, I went to the front door. "Do we know anyone with a green Cadillac?" I called to Jo Ann as I squinted through the peep hole. Then I saw two strangers climb out and begin assembling a TV camera.

I opened the door. I don't remember the words I used, but I've never seen a camera packed away so fast. What kind of ghouls, I wondered, would want to interview parents at a time like this?

It was ten p.m. Denver time when Dr. Fitz telephoned at last. John was still in critical condition but the doctor sounded guardedly optimistic. Monday we flew east. It was not three days since we'd made this trip in reverse. One thing about this past weekend: For the first time in my life I understood the despair that could drive a person to suicide. John's depression no longer seemed so unimaginable to me.

I also knew as the plane carried us back across the country that I myself would never even flirt with such a thought again. The pain caused to others was too great. If only John knew how much he was loved, he would not keep repeating these acts of self-destruction. But that of course was the very core of his illness. The single thing, according to doctors, that most distinguished the schizophrenic was his feeling of utter worth-lessness. He might fight it down with grandiose fantasies and superhuman daydreams, but beneath them all was the convic-tion that he could not possibly matter to anyone at all. . . .

We'd expected Fort Meade's medical facility to be a utilitarian Army affair; instead Kimbrough Hospital was a large modern complex built to serve the neighboring area as well as the base. A pleasant young man met us on the third floor and introduced himself as Dr. J.D. Fitz. He cautioned us not to be shocked by what we saw: John was responding to treatment, he assured us.

But no amount of advance warning prepared us for the sight waiting in the Intensive Care Unit. The tiny curtained cubicle was so filled with people—two marshals, a nurse, an orderly, a couple of men apparently representing the Justice Department —that at first we couldn't even see John. The back of his bed had been raised so that he was in a semi-sitting position. Tubes protruded from nose and mouth, needles from both arms. His face was grossly swollen, covered with vivid red blotches where blood vessels were broken beneath the skin. His neck was raw with burn marks. But most terrifying were his wide-open eyes. They were bright scarlet red.

They were so lifeless it was hard to tell how much he was seeing. Dr. Fitz had told us that it was still too early to know if there was brain damage. Only an occasional tear welling into those crimson eyes told of the physical pain he was in.

"God, please—" Jo Ann whispered, and then burst into tears. When it was clear she could not go on, I bowed my head and choked out an anguished prayer. It was awkward, baring our deepest emotions in that tiny alcove crowded with strang-ers, but as I finished, a single hearty "Amen!" rang out. It was Dr. Fitz who had stepped through the curtain behind us.

It was probably Dr. Fitz's experience with trauma cases that had saved John's life. Apparently John had hung from those window bars for twenty minutes or more before being cut down. We could never pin down the length of time after that when he had lain unconscious on the floor while guards battered at the jammed door. Long enough, in any event, for tissue to die and overburden the kidneys. The prosecutors' office had sent a doctor who wanted to rush him at once to the Trauma Center at Johns Hopkins. Dr. Fitz felt that moving him would increase the danger, and assured the government doctor he knew what he was doing.

And so it proved. By Tuesday the chief concern was the poisons in the kidneys and muscle damage to the neck and left arm on which he had fallen and lain so long. But at least it was clear there would be no permanent brain damage—though John could remember nothing of Sunday afternoon. He had no recollection of stuffing the door lock with bits of cardboard, no memory of climbing on the chair and threading his jacket through the window bars. He only knew he'd waked up sometime Monday in a hospital bed. For a long while he believed it was Johns Hopkins and that he was there for a CATscan.

All day Tuesday they forced tremendous quantities of fluids through him to flush out the dead tissue. His eyes remained that ghastly red, his skin mottled and swollen, his pain terrible to see. What we could not understand was the treatment of the hanging by the news media. One wire service reported that John had never lost consciousness, another that he was being held in the hospital merely for observation. We tried to remind ourselves that they were only quoting what "a government spokesman" told them. But to treat John's desperate bid for death as though it were just a publicity stunt made me shake with anger.

Tuesday night at the Colony 7 the message light—as always—was lit on the dresser telephone. The callback number was Vince's home phone: For the first time in many months he had good news. Judge Parker had ruled in our favor on both pretrial motions: John's rights *had* been violated when he was interrogated without counsel the day of the shooting, and prison guards had illegally removed papers from his cell at Butner. Neither issue had any real bearing on the case, but we were clutching at any straw just then.

The following night on our return to the motel room the red light signaled a call from a reporter for the *Baltimore Sun*. I don't know how he'd found out where we were staying (we were registered of course under another name), but I was desperate to tell John's side. It all poured out—our begging the powers-in-charge for antidepressant medication, our warning the marshals as we left last week that John was suicidal, what I saw as a deliberate government coverup of what had happened.

Thursday morning the *Sun* bannered a big story based on that telephone interview. I'd been so eager to counteract the government version that I'd all but forgotten it would mean a fresh flurry of articles. Our name was in the headlines again, and this time I'd put it there. How long before Jo Ann and I could go back to being private people?

51

JO ANN:

Thursday night Jack reluctantly returned to Denver for Vanderbilt's quarterly board meeting the following day, while I stayed on with John. Now that I was at the Colony 7 motel alone, I appreciated all the more the friendliness of the ladies at the front desk. They were aware of what brought us so often to Maryland and always had a kind word, using our real names when other guests were not around.

For ten weeks I'd waited for the right moment to tell John about Titter's death. I dreaded terribly having to do it, yet knew I must, before the trial. Here in the hospital, I decided, with medication available in case he had an agitated reaction, would be the safest place.

As always, John reacted by withdrawing. "I want to be alone," was all he said. For an hour Friday morning I paced the corridor, crushed that John was not able to share his grief even with me, since I'd loved the old cat as much as he had. When I returned to his bedside he'd written me a note asking me to bring a written account of what had happened when I came back that evening. "I can't talk about it," the note said.

I spent most of the afternoon putting on paper Titter's difficult last months, her painless final moments. John put my note to one side when I handed it to him, presumably to read later. Not the following day nor ever again did he bring up the subject of his beloved pet.

To my surprise, as I left the hospital Friday evening, I was told that John was being returned the next day to the stockade. It seemed to me they were rushing this; he was still in great pain from the damaged kidneys. But Saturday afternoon I drove as instructed to the little concrete block building. As I waited in the chapel I heard hammering and realized they must be working to repair his cell.

John was led in by two unfamiliar marshals. He was wearing the usual baggy trousers, but only a short-sleeved T-shirt—no jacket in spite of the late-November chill. One look at his face and I knew there was more bad news. It wasn't only the blood-red eyes and the painful shuffle; something was upsetting him. I waited for the marshals to step aside as they had in the past, so we could talk, but they remained standing just inches away. Clearly new security orders had been passed down.

"I'm in a different cell," John said.

That was only to be expected with the door and the window of the original one broken. John was too tense to say more. At last he asked one of the marshals for a piece of paper and the stump of a pencil which was all he was ever allowed. The new cell, he wrote, was a tiny windowless one with a narrow metal rack which folded down from the wall to form a bed—nothing else at all. There was no pillow on the bed, only a one-inch mattress covered with a paper sheet. He was not to be allowed a chair, his guitar, not even books or writing paper.

I tried to understand the reasoning behind each restriction as he scrawled it out. But to John it seemed that he was being punished for an act he could not even remember. By Monday, after two nights on that hard steel shelf his kidneys were in agony. A light shining on him around the clock kept him from sleeping and he had contracted a bad cold.

Thanksgiving was three days off. Jack and I decided over the phone that I should stay on to be with John. Monday afternoon, at Jack's insistence, Vince filed papers in court requesting a temporary transfer to St. Elizabeth's where they were better equipped to handle suicidal individuals. On Wednesday, the day before Thanksgiving, Judge Parker ruled that John must remain at Fort Meade. After endless long-distance calls from Jack to the marshals and Dr. Fitz, one concession was eventually made when a two-inch mattress replaced the one-inch one on that metal shelf.

The week's good news concerned Mr. Brady: He was managing so well on crutches that he was being released from the hospital in time for Thanksgiving at home.

I had asked the marshals if there was any way I could eat Thanksgiving dinner with John on Thursday. I expected to be turned down, so tense was the atmosphere at the stockade since the hanging. To my delight, however, I was told Wednesday evening to come to the chapel at noon the next day; John would be given his dinner there and a meal brought for me as well. I stepped into the chapel the following noon to find a card table covered by a paper tablecloth decorated with turkeys. Matching paper napkins, elegantly folded, were at each place and two paper cups held an assortment of nuts. The utensils were plastic, of course, the plates paper—John was not allowed anything metal or ceramic—but for a centerpiece someone had provided a Bible.

The marshals brought John in, then inquired as though we were dining out, whether we'd prefer light turkey meat or dark, sweet potatoes or white. The places were set across from each other where I could not avoid seeing John's eyes, still that shocking red, and the ruptured veins in his face, now turning black. But as I read from the Bible and then said the blessing, my heart was filled with thanksgiving indeed, that John was alive, that Mr. Brady was home with his wife and little boy, that people could be kind even here, even where John's behavior had created such a crisis.

We had stuffing and cranberry jelly, pumpkin pie for dessert. I never knew whose idea the Thanksgiving party was—Dr. Fitz, the marshals, the stockade staff, or all of them together. I think the thing I appreciated most of all was that the marshals turned their backs while we ate.

I flew home two days later. John was still in pain when I left, still sleeping poorly in spite of the extra inch of padding beneath him. Jack told me he and Scott had eaten Thanksgiving dinner at Wyatt's Cafeteria.

I had only a week in Evergreen, this time, to get to the dry cleaners and throw out a few more neglected house plants. Jack and I wanted to be back with John on December 8, the anniversary of John Lennon's death. The date could be another of those mood triggers that we were coming to recognize.

It was as tough as we'd feared. We arrived in Washington December 6, stayed three days, with John morose and uncommunicative. His cold had turned into flu. I asked again for warmer clothing for him—I couldn't see how long sleeves could be a danger in a windowless cell. To our great gratitude, Dr. Fitz was continuing to visit John and watch him closely.

We met with our lawyers too, to prepare for the new trial date, less than a month off now. Williams & Connolly had just received the reports of the government psychiatrists, every one of whom concluded that John was ill. It seemed to me that that should settle it, but the lawyers explained that a person could be mentally ill and still legally responsible—in other words, not so mentally or emotionally damaged, that he was out of touch with reality. The *degree* of illness was the issue—and again Jack and I wondered how twelve people no more trained than we were could make such a decision.

While we were east that trip, a *Washington Post* columnist appeared on the "Good Morning America" TV show with the preposterous suggestion that John might have been a member of a Libyan "hit" squad. Our four lawyers had to spend the session that day trying to calm Jack's fury at this irresponsible reporting. Sure enough, no one else in the media took the idea seriously enough to repeat it.

Also on that Washington trip we spent an afternoon with the young man with whom Jack had worked on the water project in Guatemala. Since the day of the shooting, over eight months before, when we'd canceled that trip, Jack and I lived in a kind of isolation chamber, shut off by our personal crisis from the rest of the world. That was another dimension of John's tragedy. Not only private resources, but public ones too, spent on one act of one person. Papers reported that the marshals alone assigned to this case had cost the government to date, $400,000. When we thought of the need around the world for something as basic as water, it seemed a monstrous imbalance.

One thought only cheered us as we swung on our pendulum back to Evergreen. That morning, December 9, thanks to the persistence of Greg Craig and Dr. Fitz, an Army psychiatrist had examined John and prescribed an antidepressant. For the first time since his overdose at Butner six months earlier he would be receiving much-needed medication.

Our next trip to Washington would be at Christmastime. And this would not be just a flying visit with a suitcase each. This time we would be driving with all the supplies for the apartment that we could squeeze into the little Omega. For days I planned and replanned the packing of the car, things for Washington, things we'd need en route. We intended to drive first to my parents' in Oklahoma City, then on to Dallas for an early Christmas with Diane and Steve and the grandchildren. It would be the first Christmas since Scott was born that I would not trim a tree and prepare a holiday meal for my family.

Our neighbors were wonderful, sending us off with gifts and good wishes as though we were bound for a holiday trip instead of a federal trial. Several friends baked Christmas cookies for John; I didn't have the heart to tell them we could take nothing edible into the stockade. We were given so much, in fact, that I had to rethink what I was taking for the apartment. Linens, coat hangers, toaster, iron—I pared my list to a minimum. But at least when we came back to Evergreen next, the nightmare of the trial would be behind us.

52

JACK:

We left Evergreen December 17, drove as far as Dodge City, Kansas, that first day. Last thing before leaving the motel room next morning I put through my routine early call to Vince. "I'm glad you called before coming east, Jack," he said. "There's another delay."

"Vince, we're already on our way. What kind of delay? How long?"

But Vince had no idea. The prosecuting team had appealed Judge Parker's decisions on the Miranda ruling the day of the shooting and on the search of John's cell at Butner. The trial had been postponed until the appeals court could hear their arguments.

"Maybe it won't take very long," Jo Ann and I told each other all the way to Oklahoma City. We got to her folks by lunchtime, drove next day to Dallas for three days with Diane's family. We were there on Monday, December 21, when Vince called to say the appeals hearing had been set for the week of January 25. That meant, Vince believed, that the trial could not be rescheduled before March.

We sat, all of us, in the Sims' cheerful den, asking one another if John could survive two more months in that windowless and chairless cell. And what about this trip, the Omega loaded to the roof with things for a long stay in Washington? Shouldn't we drive back to Evergreen, leave the car and simply fly to Washington for Christmas?

In the end, having come this far, we decided to keep going. We pulled into the Colony 7 around noon on Christmas Eve.

215

The sprawling motel was deserted—not a car in the parking lot, the restaurant shuttered and dark. They told us as we checked in we were the only people staying there over Christmas. As I carried our bags from the car to the room I wondered if they'd kept the motel open just for us. Those who had to work must resent us, I thought. Then I opened the room door and knew that they did not. A Christmas fruit basket sat on the dresser from "The Ladies at the Front Desk."

We spent the afternoon with John. He was more alert and responsive than he'd been in weeks, thanks, we were sure, to the medication. Afterward Jo Ann and I found a seafood restaurant in Laurel, Maryland, and ordered a bottle of wine. It was our 35th wedding anniversary. "Back where we started," I said, remembering that earlier Christmas Eve when we'd set out in a loaded car, headed for a converted mule barn in St. Elmo, Illinois.

Christmas started bleakly. We drove around for an hour before we found a Denny's restaurant open for breakfast. I tried not to think of our living room in Evergreen and the tree Jo Ann would have hung with sentimental ornaments. I'd been after her for years to keep Christmas simple; I'd never imagined how it would come about.

John was in the pits again. Maybe Christmas memories were crowding close on him, too. We gave him a stack of cards from friends and family and the gifts from his brother, sister and grandparents, which along with ours were the only packages permitted him. The ribbons had been removed in the marshals' room and each package opened.

For us John had a letter which as usual he did not want us to read in front of him. Once more a card table had been set up in the chapel for dinner, just as Jo Ann had described it at Thanksgiving. Again unknown individuals had bent regulations to help a family through a stressful time.

Back in the empty motel we opened John's letter. He expressed his dread of yet another wait. "But I'm trying to do what you say, Dad. I'm trying to let God be in charge, not me." He went on to thank us for driving a 4,000 mile round trip to be with him for Christmas. It was so rare for John to express appreciation—or even awareness—of other people's efforts, that both Jo Ann and I had tears in our eyes as we read. Perhaps the medication was giving him some relief from the torment of his mind, allowing the gentle person inside to peer tentatively out at the world.

I sat down at the dresser-desk in the motel room and wrote him back, trying to put on paper what I was discovering about trusting God. "Committing our concerns to Him isn't something we do once and for all. We have to *keep* doing it every time we take something back. Sometimes I have to do it every hour."

The drive back to Colorado after Christmas seemed longer than the trip east. This was the journey that was to have seen it all "behind us." Instead the end was nowhere in sight. If the prosecution did not win a reversal on both counts from the appeals court at the end of January, Vince believed they would carry their appeal all the way to the Supreme Court.

The appeals court hearing was held eventually on February 3. Most on our minds when we met back in Washington at Williams & Connolly the day before was a multi-million dollar claim for damages filed against John by Officer Thomas Delahanty, the policeman John's bullet had struck in the neck. The bullet had been removed surgically from near his spinal column and since we'd been able to learn nothing more since that time, we'd assumed that he had fully recovered. Not, I knew, that anyone could "fully" get over the suffering, both physical and emotional, of such an injury. What I didn't understand was how suing John could help. John's only assets, his shares of Vanderbilt stock, were worth less in the current market than the bank loans I'd taken out against them to pay some of the doctors' and lawyers' fees. How could John in a prison or a mental institution—or even if he was freed someday—earn even a fraction of such a huge claim?

As though the suit were not sufficient crisis for one day, another followed on its heels. "If Mr. Fuller doesn't let Jodie testify," John announced that afternoon in the stockade chapel, "I'm not going to cooperate with any of you."

We stared at him for an astonished moment. "Jodie? You mean Jodie Foster?"

"He won't let her appear as a witness in my trial."

"But—witness to what?" Jo Ann asked, bewildered. "She knew nothing about it."

It was the wrong thing to say. Somehow, unbelievably, in the face of all facts, John was clinging to that romance-that-never-was. For two hours the pitiful argument went on. His imagined relationship with Jodie was the central fact of his life. It held his existence together—by denying it we were denying him.

John was not required to be present at the appeals court next morning, where a panel of three judges heard arguments on both sides. Afterward Vince showed us a list of sixty questions John wanted the lawyers to ask Miss Foster. "He seems to believe that she was his ally in the shooting."

Next week in Evergreen a letter arrived from John demanding again that Jodie Foster appear at the trial. Often, putting things on paper, John was more collected and reasonable than in conversation, but the letter troubled Jo Ann and me more than anything he'd said. Jodie was "in this thing" with him, he wrote. She had a role to play, and "she knows her lines."

Clearly, after eleven months in solitary, John was retreating ever further from reality. Recalling that the lawyers had themselves at one time considered calling Miss Foster as a witness, I urged them over the phone from Colorado at least to contact her—find out what her reaction would be. Maybe meeting the actual person would put an end to the larger-than-life screen character who dominated John's inner world. Vince was hesitant. The young woman had already been victimized enough by John's fixation. At last he and Greg requested a personal interview with Miss Foster at Yale.

The two lawyers traveled up to New Haven on a Sunday. As luck would have it, it was Valentine's Day. John was as excited as a teenager on a first date, Greg told us, at the knowledge that the two lawyers—his representatives—were actually going to meet Miss Foster in person. Jo Ann and I drove down to church at Calvary Temple, then hurried home to wait for Vince's call. The session with Miss Foster and her lawyer had gone smoothly enough, he said: She was very bright and frank. Her lawyer, however, was understandably opposed to her appearing in court in connection with this case.

Afterward I called Greg, who'd had the job of informing John. Strangely, Greg said, the negative report had not appeared to upset him: Just the fact that they'd been with *her*, and had talked to her about *him*—that she therefore had thought about him for several whole minutes—seemed to give him immeasurable satisfaction.

Maybe, Jo Ann and I thought, it would be enough. The

following week, however, John was back on the theme of calling Miss Foster as a witness. Jo Ann and I were exhausted with waiting and worry, and as usual taking it out on each other. Meals once more were eaten in silence. I was drowning in frustration. My back hurt and my sinuses made breathing difficult. After church the Sunday after Valentine's Day, I went for a long drive, then found a downtown motel room where I could spend some time in solitude.

53

JO ANN:

Jack did not come home Sunday night, nor the next night. Again I tried to hide his absence from friends and family, feeling deserted, frightened, bereft of the rock which had been my safety.

At four o'clock Tuesday afternoon Jack phoned from the office. Vince had just called him with the decision of the appeals court. All three judges had ruled in our favor on both counts, reaffirming Judge Parker's position.

Jack came home that night. Together we watched the TV coverage, the first favorable news in eleven months. All the commentators called the ruling a big setback for the prosecution. By Thursday, two days away, the government would have to decide whether to proceed with the trial—with these documents disallowed—or take their appeal further. Above the three-man bench was the full appeals court, with eleven judges sitting. Above that, the Supreme Court itself.

Again, Jack and I could not see the importance to the government's case of this material, either John's statements the afternoon of the shooting, or the papers found in his cell.

The prosecution had conducted hundreds of hours of interviews with him since that time, all of which was admissible in court, and the papers had been proved to be an unfunny hoax. But Vince reiterated to us as we kept in touch by phone through an anxious Wednesday, that the *Miranda* and exclusionary laws were targets of this administration, and that the understandable national rage at John was a made-to-order opportunity to strike them from the books.

Thursday, when there was no word from the prosecution, Judge Parker announced the new date for the trial as March 9—only twelve days off. While Jack started to wind down his business affairs, I began to reassemble household items for Washington.

Late that same afternoon Jack called again from the office: At the request of the government the appeals court had intervened to cancel the March 9 trial date. The prosecution was granted 25 days to submit a new appeal. If the full eleven-man court agreed to hear it, it could be May or June before such a hearing was scheduled, summer's end before the trial could start.

Bad news has a way of coming in batches. The following day, Friday, Vanderbilt's stock dropped to 5⅞, less than half what it had been a year before. In the middle of an operations meeting Jack was called out to the telephone. It was Lon Babby from Williams & Connolly: James Brady had filed a damage suit against John for $46 million.

Monday brought the unkindest letter yet from John. Directed mostly to his father, it told Jack, in effect, to get out of his life. Jack was too devastated to eat dinner that night. I opened my mouth at the table to say something consoling, but instead burst into tears: Whether they were for John or Jack or for us all, I didn't know. We were flying to Washington the next day—back on our old schedule of brief twice-monthly visits. Three days away from the office now would cause more problems for Jack; to receive only hostility from John in return, seemed so unfair.

We found John withdrawn and silent, communicating chiefly through notes. We were sure the current depression was caused by the new trial postponement but the notes harped mainly on the old theme of Jodie Foster appearing at his trial.

At John's request we were visiting in the chapel only once a day instead of twice and even three times as on earlier trips. We

220

didn't understand until he explained, with obvious embarrassment, that ever since the hanging attempt in November he'd been subjected to a strip-search at the close of each visit. In spite of the fact that Jack and I were searched electronically before entering the chapel, John had to remove all clothing and submit to a body check each time we left.

At least by Saturday when Jack and I returned to Denver father and son were once more reconciled, once more able to grasp each other's hands in the circle of prayer with which we always said goodbye. Neither Jack nor John mentioned the date, though I knew both must be thinking of it. It was March 6, 1982, one year from the day Jack had driven alone to Stapleton airport with a jug of antifreeze for John's car and the news that he could not come home. . . .

54

JACK:

All the flight home I silently relived the events of one year ago—the last time I had seen my son outside a prison or a courtroom. I remembered sitting beside him in an empty boarding area at the Denver airport, heard myself say, "You're on your own." *If only* was a useless torture, but *if only* I'd known that the unshaved young man with the glazed eyes was fighting an enemy too big for him, too big for anyone, alone. He wasn't undisciplined or lazy or any of the other everyday words I was using to try to explain my son's behavior to myself. He was battling, by himself, the terrors of insanity . . . and he was losing.

"I don't know what you've been doing with yourself," I'd told him. I knew now: He'd been trailing a girl around a

221

campus in New Haven with a pistol in his pocket. The FBI believed if opportunity had presented itself, Jodie Foster might have been the one he fired at. Doctors agreed: Initially, they felt, back in September, he had traveled to Yale in order to "rescue" her from the degrading life portrayed in *Taxi Driver*. When the realities of her life at Yale stubbornly refused to conform to the movie script, they believed, a new fantasy had replaced it. They would die together, she and he, in a sublime murder-suicide.

Mercifully, external events had not cooperated here either. Hungry, broke and bewildered, he had called his mother and me early that March Friday morning, asking to come home to Evergreen. And I'd said no. . . .

This trip had kept me out of the office only three days, but problems at Vanderbilt had deepened in that short time. Scott met us with the news that one of the company directors had written the others adamantly opposing my selling our family stock in order to pay mounting interest and bank loans. The man couldn't have been half as negative as I was at the prospect: While we were away Vanderbilt stock had continued to drop, to $4.25 per share from over $13.00 just a year earlier. It was a terrible time to sell, but the pressures were killing me.

All month criticism from certain board members mounted. I unloaded my frustration on Ivonne and Scott. I'd been keeping a diary since the shooting, a kind of running dialogue with God about what was happening and the pages as the first-year anniversary approached were filled with the word *why?* It seemed so gratuitous—the oil industry collapse coming almost day and date with our personal crisis, and now this attack from close associates, as though my being at my desk 24 hours a day seven days a week could have made the slightest difference to Vanderbilt's year-end results. Like me, they were alarmed at our falling stock price; understandably they were looking for someone to blame.

As the anniversary date approached, media attention picked up; here, too, we found ourselves the target of criticism. A whole year had passed, editorial writers pointed out indignantly, and justice had still not been done. It must be our "tactics," these articles concluded, that were delaying matters. The very same edition of the paper would sometimes include a news item on the status of the prosecution's latest motion: To me it seemed that it was they, not we, who were causing the delays.

Help! was another word I found myself writing in my diary. "God *help* us!" as I wondered why His answers seemed so slow in coming. "Jo Ann and I are both sick and short-tempered," I wrote one night. "This is hell on earth and there's no end in sight."

A few days later: "Our family has been destroyed spiritually, physically, and financially. Where are You, God? How much worse can it get?"

A lot worse, it turned out. John's frustration, of course, after a year under round-the-clock surveillance, was even more intense than mine. When he reached the cracking point he'd usually announce that he was "firing" his lawyers. I suspected he picked on the lawyers because there's no way you can fire your father; in any case, that month Greg Craig, John's closest ally, was the target. Typically, John couldn't talk about it. All we could glean on our semi-weekly phone hookup was that he and Greg were "through."

From Greg we got the story. One of the new marshals—surprisingly, since all the ones we'd met were genuinely concerned for John's welfare—had informed John that the current issue of a men's magazine carried some photographs of Jodie Foster. The young marshal had even purchased a copy and showed him the pictures through the bars. Of course John was frantic. The marshal, saying that he was "not authorized" to give the magazine to John, told him he would leave it with his lawyer. Which is how poor Greg got involved. Greg, of course, would not pass the offensive publication on to John, fearing it would only feed his sick fantasies. And so in the midst of crises in the office and at home, I had to devote hours on the phone to re-establishing John's relationship with Greg.

We planned our next trip east to be with John on the anniversary of the shooting. As the date grew nearer, recaps and follow-up stories multiplied. A number of reporters phoned the office—our home number remained mercifully unlisted—seeking statements. To the UPI man who reached me first, I said what I repeated to the others, that our son was sick, not evil, and that we believed we could prove this in a trial. "I believe it's the Justice Department who's stalling, denying John his right to a speedy and impartial hearing."

Friday night, March 26, two days before we were to leave

for Washington, Jo Ann and I had an unscheduled phone call from John. Apparently he'd become so agitated that the marshals had kindly arranged the special hook-up. As so often, Jodie Foster was the basis of his mood swing, but this time the change was from despair to frenzied excitement. Greg had just driven out to tell him that Jodie Foster would be coming to Washington the following week to give a deposition in his case. It seemed her lawyer had agreed to her testifying so long as she could do so in a closed session with only the judge and the attorneys present. Her statement would be videotaped to be shown later at the trial.

"But Mom! Dad! I have to be there!" Judge Parker, in signing the order that day for Miss Foster's deposition, had specified that John was to be present. "I have to be in the courtroom when she—you know. . . ." We could hear the swallow over the phone line. "Jodie. When Jodie testifies I'll be right there in the *same room.*"

There was such a mixture of anticipation and panic in his voice that once again Jo Ann and I prayed this was the right decision, to bring Miss Foster into the case at all. But since it meant so much to John—since he'd seen himself all his life as a loser in a world of winners—could it hurt to have this one brief moment when things went his way?

55

JO ANN:

We flew to Washington Sunday night, March 28, on a plane jammed with skiers and their gear. At Fort Meade next morning John was totally preoccupied with Jodie Foster's upcoming deposition—which could occur as early as that afternoon or the following morning. Jack and I spent the afternoon looking again for apartments offering short-term rentals, though without being able to predict the trial dates we could only note addresses.

We got up earlier than usual the next day for our prayer time overlooking the motel parking lot. It was March 30, a year from the day our lives turned inside out. The first item on the screen when Jack finally switched on the TV news a little after seven o'clock was that John Hinckley, Jr., was being sued by Secret Service Agent Timothy McCarthy. The announcer gave the number of millions of dollars involved but such figures had ceased to have meaning to me. Mr. McCarthy was now the third to bring civil charges against John, in addition to the thirteen criminal charges being pressed by the federal government.

"Probably some lawyer talked him into filing before the one-year statute ran out," Jack told me, "just in case the other two suits get somewhere." Jack thought the fantastic exaggerations of our wealth by the media had inspired all three—"they probably think each of our kids has a big trust fund somewhere."

Just before ten Jack phoned the stockade as we always did before leaving the motel to alert the marshals that we were on our way. But John was not at Fort Meade. He had been taken by police escort into the U.S. Courthouse early that morning.

So . . . Jodie Foster was making her deposition right at this minute. How extraordinary, we kept saying to each other, that it should be a year to the day after he'd almost killed four men "for her sake." Neither we nor any other spectators were permitted at the closed session; we could only wait and pray that this face-to-face encounter would bring about the separation in his mind of the real person from the fantasy figure.

To make the time pass we resumed our halfhearted apartment search. A few minutes past noon Jack found a phone booth and called Vince to learn how the court session had gone. He came back to the rental car with a frown on his face.

"Her testimony was harmful?" I guessed.

Jack shook his head: Vince felt the video tape would be helpful when played at the trial. Something had gone wrong, however, at the close of the session and Vince couldn't tell Jack what it was. "The judge ordered him not to discuss it. He says John can tell us about it."

225

But John, when we met in the stockade chapel that afternoon, had little to say about the morning's events. We'd learned from the marshals that he'd been so nervous on the way to the courthouse that he'd been sick in the police car. He seemed calm enough now, only the rapid twitching of his foot giving away some kind of inner battle. His eyes looked to me as though he'd been crying.

He'd pressed for this day so long, and now apparently we were to have no details. When Jack asked him point blank what had gone wrong this morning John would only say, "Ask Greg."

But Greg, when we phoned him later from the motel, was under the same judge's order as Vince. All that the lawyers could tell us was that John had made some kind of scene in the courtroom. "He's a lot sicker than any of us realized," Vince said.

And so we remained in an agony of not knowing. The evening news shows observed the date with video tapes of the shooting a year ago: over and over those awful scenes outside the Hilton. Observing that "Hinckley's lawyers have tried to claim insanity" one commentator stated "the American people will not stand" for a Not Guilty verdict.

To climax the horrible day came the news that Mr. Brady was back in the hospital with a life-threatening blood clot in his leg. After a year of unimaginable suffering was he to lose his courageous battle after all? Jack walked over to the motel dresser and switched off the TV.

"I'm ready to throw in the towel," he said.

It was the first time in this endless year he'd talked of giving up. "When all the doctors agree that John is sick?" I asked. "When Vince just said so again?"

"We know it, and Vince knows it, but all that counts is whether the jury knows it. Do you really think there are twelve impartial people in this country right now?"

Maybe not—but we *couldn't* call the trial off, I reminded him, even if we wanted to. Once even one doctor finds a defendant psychotic (and four had, in John's case), no conscientious judge would be likely to permit a simple Guilty plea.

Since John was the only one who could tell us what had transpired during Jodie Foster's deposition, we pressed him about it again the next day. It took all morning to get from him

226

even the partial picture which was all we ever learned. Jodie, it seemed, had utterly failed to play the role he'd assigned to her in his mental forecasting of the event. I remembered the letter that had come to Evergreen the previous month: "She knows her lines." What she was supposed to do or say we never discovered, just that she had "betrayed" him. When she finally got up to leave the witness stand and he realized that it was all over, that she really *was* leaving without a word on his behalf or a glance in his direction, he grabbed the only thing within reach—it was a ballpoint pen—and hurled it at her. He'd also yelled, "I'll get you, Foster!" before the marshals hauled him hastily from the room.

We sat around Williams & Connolly that afternoon like people at a funeral parlor; once more John had been his own worst enemy. At least we knew, flying home on Saturday at the end of that wretched anniversary week, that the trial must start before much longer. Rather than face further delays, Jack had urged the lawyers to give in on the *Miranda* and exclusionary issues. "What will it matter if we win all the legal fine points and lose our son?" After what they'd seen in the courtroom on Tuesday, the lawyers agreed.

The Monday after we got home, however, a call came from Vince: The Appeals Court had unanimously turned down the prosecution's bid for a rehearing. Furthermore, Vince believed that after three such decisive defeats they would probably not carry their appeal further.

That night over the evening news, though, it was reported that the government would take its case to the Supreme Court. Jack and I went to bed in turmoil. It seemed so wrong to give in on these issues, when three courts now had upheld our position—yet we were absolutely determined not to make John wait in the Fort Meade stockade through the drawn-out process of a high court case.

I was preparing breakfast next morning with the kitchen radio on, Jack listening to the one in the bathroom as he shaved, when over the air came word that a "Justice Department spokesman" had announced that the government would *not* take its appeal higher. We let out cries of relief from opposite sides of the house.

After all the waiting, all the traveling back and forth when nothing ever seemed to be decided, our lives suddenly moved

227

into hectic high gear. The final trial date was set for April 27, just three weeks away. Jack caught a plane to Oklahoma City to try to finalize a merger offer for Vanderbilt.

On the scheduled phone visit with John, while Jack was away, I hoped to find him encouraged by the movement in his case. Instead, incredibly, he was back on the theme of those magazine pictures of Jodie Foster, upset because Greg had hung up on him when he started to talk about it. I understood Greg's impulse to slam down the telephone only too well. With his own ears, last week, John had heard Miss Foster say the two of them were total strangers—how could he hang onto his preposterous delusion?

Because he was sick. I knew it with my mind, I'd read it in the doctors' reports, but each time I came up against his unrealistic thinking the emotional shock was fresh. Surely this was the hardest thing for families of the mentally ill. John wasn't bed-bound or physically handicapped: His illness came out in abnormal and unreasonable behavior that made him hardest to love when he needed it most.

Jack got back to Denver exhausted by the negotiations in Oklahoma City—and I had to involve him in the ridiculous business of those magazine pictures. Next day Vince phoned to say he'd viewed the physical evidence the prosecution planned to present at the trial: bloody clothing, police photographs, the gun they'd taken from John's hand, the bullets removed from his victims. I was sorry these tragic things had to be exhibited at all, since defense and prosecution were agreed on what had been done and who had done it. Vince said the point was their emotional impact on the jury.

Jack flew to Dallas the following day—Good Friday—for an emergency board meeting he'd called to consider the Oklahoma offer. I'd seldom seen him as beat-looking as he did that night when he climbed out of his car in the garage. The board had reluctantly approved the merger, but it had clearly taken all Jack's persuasiveness to push it through.

"Anything new with John?" he asked first thing as he always did. "Are he and Greg back on track again?"

How I longed to tell this exhausted man that things were fine. They weren't: John had been on the phone again, willing to throw anything and everything away to have those photographs. . . .

Saturday morning Scott telephoned his father at home. He

had just seen a new report that seemed to set the value of the other company involved in the merger at far less than Jack and he had been led to believe. Another frantic day of figuring and phoning. Late that afternoon, Jack made the difficult decision to call off the merger. Saturday night, though, came an Easter gift from John, a phone call to say he and Greg were once again communicating. Jack and I had learned, this last year, to receive any scrap of good news with gratitude. The business outlook was back where it had been—hopeless, but we went to bed that night praising God, drove down to Denver next morning for a glorious Easter service at Calvary Temple.

We planned to leave Evergreen by car the Sunday after Easter. Jack spent the intervening week undoing the business deal he'd rushed through the week before, and arranging another addition to our bank loans, while once more I assembled household effects for Washington.

I had another task before we set out: John would need clothes to wear in the courtroom. There were the Navy blazer and slacks that the marshals had provided for his arraignment back in August—but he couldn't appear day after day in those. Here in his closet at home were nothing but T-shirts and bluejeans.

Since John had lost so much weight in prison, I asked one of the marshals to measure his chest, waist and neck. Armed with these figures I drove down to Denver. Each afternoon I'd head for home satisfied with my purchases; next morning I'd go back, exchange everything and start all over. Fit was especially perplexing, since Vince believed John might be required to wear a bulletproof vest and this meant allowing extra room.

Sales people were helpful but uncomprehending. "Just bring the young man in, if you're not sure." Always they'd drape a selection of long ties over the jacket I was considering; my insistence on clip-ons seemed as capricious as my refusal to look at trousers with belt loops.

I finally settled on a three-piece tan suit that I thought he could mix and match with the blue things he already had, a pair of gray slacks for the Navy blazer, dark brown slacks to wear with the tan jacket, and a pair of brown loafers (no laces). Jack couldn't understand why it had required four trips into Denver this week when I had so much else to do, to assemble these few things. I hardly knew myself, except that it gave me an extraordinary sense of fulfillment to do it. It had been so long since I'd been able to do any small motherly thing for John. After the trial . . . I didn't like to think that far, but most likely when he took these "civilian" clothes off, it would be to put on the uniform of a prison somewhere. Perhaps, I kept thinking, this is the last time in my life I will buy clothes for my son.

56

JACK:

For the second time friends and neighbors gave us a royal send off. Bill and Sue Sells again—as so often this past year— undertook to see that our house had a lived-in look. All winter, anytime we were in Washington, Bill had come over each time it snowed, cleared our driveway and made footprints in the yard.

As our car neared Washington on April 20, I could feel the tension tighten in my stomach. The one eventuality we'd wanted to avoid was actually happening: Our son's misery was about to be placed on public view, our family life displayed before the world. With Jo Ann, stress showed up in head colds and by the time we pulled into the Colony 7 she was coughing continuously.

We unpacked just enough things from the car to get by on for a couple of days until we found an apartment. As Jo Ann rummaged for her overnight bag in the overloaded back seat, she dislodged a large bottle of after-shave lotion that had been a last minute goodbye gift to me. It smashed in a hundred green shards on the motel parking lot, the pine scented liquid running in a thin stream beneath the nearby cars. I yelled at her for carelessness; she blamed me for my clumsy packing job.

We were exhausted from days of hard driving, and with worry over the trial our reserves of patience were gone.

We had one of our silent dinners in the motel restaurant and fell into bed to be awakened by a phone call from a reporter who had somehow found out not only where we were staying but in which room. Our allies at the front desk hadn't told him, we were sure of that. Perhaps it was the Colorado plates on our car. Anyhow, I unloaded on him and smashed down the receiver, then couldn't get back to sleep.

In the morning, by the window, I asked God and Jo Ann to forgive my uncontrollable temper. Then we drove to the stockade chapel with John's new clothes. As a one-time concession, the marshals permitted Jo Ann to carry a packet of straight pins into the chapel; that afternoon we found a tailor who did rapid alterations.

We also looked at three apartments. Two required six-month leases, but the third was available by the week. Convenient to bus lines, it looked like the place we'd been looking for—until the superintendent beckoned us to a window. "This guy Hinckley, going on trial next week? That's where he did it. Look, you can see from here—that's the Washington Hilton." The man is probably still wondering why two eager-seeming prospects suddenly left in such a hurry.

Jo Ann's cough was worse that night. We had both fallen asleep at last when around midnight a noisy tour group arrived at the motel. There was little sleep after that. Next day was Thursday. We had to be in an apartment somewhere, clothes unpacked and pressed for the start of the trial next Tuesday morning.

We almost didn't drive in to look at the unfurnished apartment in Chevy Chase, Maryland—there'd never be time to line up furniture. We went anyway and at the sight of the red and yellow tulips outside The Irene's entrance our spirits lifted. The sunny two-bedroom apartment was available on a three-month lease at less than half what we were paying for one motel room, even including furniture rental which the manager, Mrs. Rucker, offered to help us arrange. It could all be in place, she assured us, in 24 hours. We put down a cash deposit so as not to have to give our real name, and hurried off to make our chapel appointment with John.

He was dreading his move, sometime Sunday, to the underground holding cell in the courthouse basement. I remembered how he'd hated the place earlier. But not till that evening when NBC did a special report on the dismal conditions there did Jo Ann and I realize just how grim those courthouse cells were.

By Friday afternoon we'd borrowed linens and a TV set from friends of Dale Morris, arranged for telephone service at The Irene, and hauled everything up in the elevator. The Irene turned out to be a short drive from the last stop on the Metro. Vince had warned us that Judge Parker ran a strict court: Latecomers would not be admitted. Much better to take the subway than get caught in Washington's standstill traffic.

But the thing which let us know that The Irene was really right was when we went down to the manager's office that afternoon to sign the lease. "We'll have to use our real name," I told Jo Ann, "or it won't be legal." I felt embarrassed at not having leveled with Mrs. Rucker right away about who was moving in. "I'll just have to explain to her," I said, "that we've gotten out of the habit of using our own name."

But the explanation, it turned out, was unnecessary. "I was wondering," Mrs. Rucker said as we seated ourselves in her office, "if you'd rather not have your name listed on the building directory, and how you want the switchboard to handle phone calls."

"Then . . . you know who we are?" I asked.

"Yes, Mr. Hinckley. And I want *you* to know that your privacy will be safeguarded here."

Saturday we took a dry run on the subway to learn the route to the courthouse. To be sure of a place to leave the car, we reserved a monthly space in a parking garage near the Metro terminus. Jo Ann got to worrying that John didn't have enough shirts for the trial, insisted we stop at Sears and buy another one. Sears was a madhouse on a Saturday afternoon, with the two of us at the end of our stamina—Jo Ann's cough keeping us both awake at night.

We phoned the stockade and were told to bring the courtroom clothes when we came that evening for our last visit before John's transfer to the courthouse the next day. Then John came on the line. Could we stop on our way and pick up a black sports jacket for him?

I couldn't have stopped and picked up a handkerchief at that point. What was more, neither Jo Ann nor I felt a black coat would be appropriate in the courtroom. It was a trivial thing, but because all three of us were tense, we got upset over it.

Jo Ann cooked our first supper in our new apartment that evening, then we drove to Fort Meade for what would possibly be the last time. It was after dark, but I took the turns through the huge army base automatically; it was eight months since I'd had to ask directions to the stockade.

We carried the clothes into the marshals' room where Jo Ann gave the young man on duty a pep talk on keeping things on their hangers. Only a mother, I thought, would fuss over such a detail. Perhaps she reminded him of his own mother because he promised solemnly to see that the clothes were looked after.

In the chapel we had another ridiculous, unnecessary blow-up with John over the black jacket. Or maybe it *was* necessary. Maybe we needed some such foolish issue to keep us from thinking too much about next week. About ten p.m. we joined hands. Aloud I committed ourselves and the trial and John's future to God, while silently I asked Him to help me mean it—to let me take my own hands off and leave the outcome in His.

57

JO ANN:

The minute Jack pulled up to the curb I knew there were fresh problems. He'd dropped me off to do last-minute errands Monday afternoon. "All the rush for nothing," he said as I got in the car.

"The trial hasn't been postponed again!" I pleaded.

"For you and me it has." Vince had phoned the apartment to say that the prosecution had objected to our being in the courtroom until we'd given our testimony. "And Parker concurred."

"But—that could mean waiting for days!" According to the overview Vince had given us, the trial would begin the next day, Tuesday, April 27, 1982, with jury selection which could take several days. Then would come the opening statements by the two sides; after that, the calling of the first prosecution witnesses, and finally the first defense witnesses—family and other "non-expert" testimony. Only after all that would the expert witnesses for both sides be heard on the issue of John's mental condition.

Vince believed, Jack said, that the first government witnesses would not take long: They were intended to show that a crime had been committed, which we did not contest. This meant, he thought, that Jack and I would be called sometime during the second week of the trial.

"You mean, we have to wait around the apartment until next week?" I asked.

"That's the ruling."

And so, after such a scramble to be ready, another wait. Jury selection was so terribly critical in this case that we'd wanted to be present for it. The lawyers had outlined the process of choosing a jury, a painstaking procedure designed to insure an impartial panel. Judge Parker would start by questioning each individual in a pool of ninety prospective jurors, eliminating those with preconceived positions on the case. Those called back would still be many more than the twelve jurors and six alternates eventually required, and the elimination process would continue with input from lawyers on both sides.

"The jury's *got* to be well-educated," Jack kept saying as we hung helplessly about the apartment on Tuesday. The trial had officially opened that morning, papers calling it "the biggest event since Watergate"—and we felt a million miles away.

Complex medical and legal issues were at stake, Jack went on. Yet John's jury had to be drawn from District of Columbia residents who were largely inner-city people. Two of the questions Vince proposed for potential jurors indicated the problems this posed. Would the person be prejudiced against a

234

defendant from a suburban home? And how would he feel if it were shown that the defendant had "harbored negative attitudes" toward blacks? How could a black not feel angry at John, I wondered. It was a kind of poetic irony, that people John had elected to look down on would now decide his fate.

The hours dragged by. I kept wondering which outfit John was wearing in the courtroom and how his spirits were. We talked to Diane and to Scott, who did not yet know when they would be coming to Washington to testify. Our family doctor, Em Harvey, called to say he was thinking of us: He, too, would have to take the stand, at a yet-unknown point. In mid-afternoon a lovely bouquet arrived for me from friends in Evergreen. Doubtless they were picturing me in the courtroom today and had planned the flowers to welcome us on our return to the apartment.

At five o'clock we switched on both TV sets: We'd also brought our little black and white set from the kitchen at home. For two hours we hurried between the living room and the bedroom, trying to catch as much of the coverage as we could. Apparently the court was still in session, Judge Parker working into the evening in the near-hopeless search for a jury "free of bias." No camera had been allowed in the building, but there were artists' sketches of the courtroom scene. John, I saw with a flush of satisfaction, had worn the new tan suit.

There was much camera coverage of the outside of the courthouse, that severely modern, white building with its tall slit-like windows. Bystanders were interviewed, none of whom believed that John would "get away" with the insanity plea. Neither did the commentators: "Legal observers agree," according to one, "that there is virtually no chance for an acquittal."

"They haven't even chosen the jury," Jack exploded as he paced from set to set, "and the media's already brought in the verdict!"

About eight o'clock Vince phoned. The session had just adjourned and Vince had arranged for Jack and me to visit John that evening in the restricted basement area.

It was raining as we took the car out of the garage beneath The Irene. We drove through the wet streets to Fourth and Pennsylvania. The great federal office blocks were dark and deserted; only the dome of the Capitol glowed through the rain four blocks away. The courthouse that was so modern above ground reminded me of nothing so much as a medieval dungeon below: steep narrow stairways, echoing corridors, barriers where security checks were repeated. We were taken to a windowless iron-barred room where three chairs had been provided. John was brought in wearing crumpled army fatigues with holes at the knees. He was tired after the long day in court; he hadn't slept, he said, since getting to the courthouse on Sunday. But the thirteen months of waiting were over, we kept reminding one another: The trial was underway at last.

We filled the rest of the week as best we could, getting some missing things for the apartment. Our lawyers were under instructions not to discuss anything that happened in the courtroom until after we testified. And so, like the rest of the country, we followed the first week's proceedings on TV and in the newspapers.

Sometimes I wondered why we put ourselves, Jack especially, through the torture. When reporting seemed unfair, I was distressed, but he was in agony. ABC's "20/20" show one night was especially one-sided, calling NGRI a "rich man's defense" and citing instances when criminals had used it to try to deceive juries. They also brought up infamous cases where genuinely mentally ill people had been released after such a verdict—and gone on to kill again, making no mention of how extremely rare such occurrences were.

Jack was livid. We'd read everything we could lay our hands on about the insanity defense since the day in Vince's office when we'd first heard the initials NGRI. We'd learned some surprising facts—that it was a seldom-used defense, for example, raised in less than two percent of felony trials, and successful in less than a quarter of those. The vast majority of those acquitted on grounds of insanity—far from being rich— were extremely poor. Statistically, in fact, an indigent defendant whose insanity plea was supported by a state hospital doctor, was much more likely to be acquitted than a wealthy defendant using testimony from a private doctor. Nor, when released, was he any more likely to commit another crime than a person released after a prison term—except that any new crime, unlike the ex-convict's, tended to be less serious.

"They're sensationalizing everything!" Jack raged as the

program trotted out yet another scare-story. "Why don't they give their viewers the facts?"

I certainly agreed, and yet, curiously, it was a small personal aspect of the week's coverage that upset me most. Each day news reports pointed out that "none of Hinckley's family attended"—almost as though we were deliberately abandoning John in the face of public pressure. John knew the judge's ruling, but I wondered if, sitting on a metal cot in the basement, he remembered why his father and I were never in the courtroom.

58

JACK:

By Friday afternoon the jury selection was still not complete and Judge Parker called an unusual Saturday session to deal with some legal matters, including the all-important issue of whether prosecution or defense had the "burden of proof." If it was the prosecution's burden, Vince explained, the government would have to prove "beyond reasonable doubt" that John had been mentally responsible at the time he fired at the Reagan party. If it lay with the defense, Vince and his team would have to prove that John was legally insane at that moment.

Saturday was the first of May, too lovely a spring day to spend in the apartment awaiting the outcome. Jo Ann and I drove to some nearby Civil War battlefields. We were en route back to Washington when over the car radio came the announcement of Judge Parker's decision. The burden of proof rested with the prosecution.

We were allowed another basement visit with John that evening. Jo Ann brought a pile of shirts and socks back to The Irene to wash before jury selection resumed Monday morning.

Monday both Scott and Diane called to say they'd be coming to Washington the next day. Late that afternoon the final composition of the jury was announced: seven women, five men, including a janitor, a parking lot attendant, a retired night watchman and a hotel banquet worker. Eleven of the twelve, and all six alternates, were black; most had had little formal schooling.

My few remaining hopes were shattered. I took the elevator to the ground floor after hearing the news and went for a walk in the bright May evening. It seemed to me that if the prosecution had hand-picked a jury bound to be unsympathetic with every element of John's case, they could not have chosen better. "Why, God?" I asked over and over.

God didn't tell me why. He never does. But during our quiet time next morning He reminded me of a prayer I'd made ten days before. Sitting at the rented dining room table I startled Jo Ann by letting out a laugh. "I was just thinking," I explained. "I told God I wanted to leave the trial in His hands, beginning with the jury selection. He's obliged by keeping me out of the courtroom for the whole procedure, and ignoring every piece of advice I gave Him."

After lunch I drove to National Airport to pick up Scott. While we waited for Diane and Steve's flight we reviewed the situation at Vanderbilt: no buyers and no hope of any, the stock price now less than a third what it had been just a year before.

Steve and Diane arrived on schedule; they'd left the children with his folks so he could come with her. At the apartment we made up beds for them and Scott. Jo Ann had spent the day resting, trying to throw the stubborn upper-respiratory infection that had plagued her since the drive east. She would be the first witness for the defense, possibly as early as tomorrow morning, and was terrified that she would have a coughing attack on the stand.

At six o'clock the five of us watched the review of the day's court proceedings on TV. The jury had been sworn in that morning, after which Roger Adelman had made the opening statement for the prosecution. As Vince had anticipated, Adelman had stressed John's purchase of not one but a number of guns, the selection of exploding "Devastator" bullets, the choice of the professional "crouch position" from which to fire them. Vince had followed him with his own opening statement, telling the jury the defense did not dispute the facts. What concerned the defense was what motivated John's tragic actions.

Following the opening statements, nine prosecution witnesses had testified, including two of John's victims, police officer Thomas Delahanty and Secret Service agent Timothy McCarthy. Apparently the evidence had been pretty grim: close-up photos of the carnage at the Hilton, clothes still bearing dried blood stains.

Next the jury was shown television footage of Jimmy Carter's visit to Dayton, Ohio, in October 1980, with stop-action shots of John's face in the crowd pressing close to shake the President's hand. An attendant at the Lakewood Rifle Range near Denver testified that John had engaged in target practice there a number of times in December 1980 and January 1981—the first inkling Jo Ann and I had had of this. The last witness of the day had been a neurosurgeon from George Washington University Hospital who described in agonizing detail the path of destruction torn through James Brady's brain by one of John's bullets.

Late that evening we spoke to Vince. He believed the prosecution would rest its opening case some time next morning. Psychiatric arguments on both sides, he reminded us, would come later. He instructed us to be at the courthouse by eleven o'clock in case Jo Ann were called before lunch.

We arrived to find the building cordoned by police and security guards. Marshals motioned Jo Ann, Scott and me through a metal detector on the first floor, then took us upstairs where the electronic check was repeated followed by a hand-bag search. A long line of people stretched down the corridor outside the courtroom: would-be spectators, we were told, waiting for seats to be vacated.

We were led to the Witness Room to wait until we were called. This turned out to be a cheerless setting with six straight-backed wooden chairs in it and absolutely nothing else. No table, no magazines, no TV, just those six chairs and four blank walls. If there ever was a setup designed to turn nervousness into panic, this was it. There wasn't much chance that Scott would be called today—Vince planned to summon Jo Ann first, then me, then Scott and last of all Diane—but Jo Ann and I kept going over our testimony, afraid we'd leave something out or get dates wrong. She was coughing continuously: "What if I can't talk when they call me?"

After an hour and a half, a marshal appeared to say the court was recessing for lunch. He showed us the cafeteria in the basement where, by some unspoken protocol, the court sketchers and media people taking their own lunch break left us alone.

At two o'clock we were back staring at the walls of the Witness Room. The prosecution must be introducing more testimony than our lawyers anticipated. An hour passed. Two hours. At 4:30 young Lon Babby stepped into the room. The court would soon be adjourning for the day. We were to be back here at ten o'clock tomorrow morning.

After the day of waiting, keeping ourselves on the razor-edge of readiness, the let-down was tremendous. A building guard led us to a side door that he believed was less likely to be watched by press people. Sure enough, not a reporter in sight. We'd gone two blocks congratulating ourselves on our escape, when three photographers came running pell-mell behind us. For block after block they stayed with us, snapping hundreds of pictures with their cameras a foot from our faces, until I wanted to take a swing at them.

We got back to the apartment too weary to wait up for the late evening news, left next day too early for the morning programs. So it was as we rode the Metro downtown that we read in the papers about the previous day's events. The gun John used had been identified by a ballistics expert and the bullets retrieved from his victims exhibited, including the flattened hunk of metal recovered inches from the President's heart. The FBI agent who had searched John's Washington hotel room read to the jury the unmailed postcard to Jodie Foster discovered there. I found myself seeing it through the eyes of the jury: "Dear Jodie . . . one day you and I will occupy the White House and the peasants will drool with envy." How would that sit with wage-earning people—especially when the prosecution had informed them, according

240

to the paper, that John was a lazy rich-kid who considered work beneath him?

Sure enough, our picture appeared in the morning editions alongside the articles, Jo Ann, Scott and I walking down the street, my expression pretty tight-lipped, but nothing like as furious as I'd felt.

Having experienced the Witness Room, Scott had elected to stay behind with Diane and Steve that morning. And so Jo Ann and I alone followed for the first time the route we were to take so often in the days ahead. Little did we guess that the trial, already in its ninth day, would stretch on for an interminable six-and-a-half weeks more, that the second half of June would come and we would still be making this daily trip. It was a three-block walk from the nearest Metro station to the side door of the courthouse. The broad plaza adjacent to the building was being refurbished: cement mixers and men with jackhammers made that last block an obstacle course—and a favored ambush for the media as we picked our way across it.

That second morning, we were seated in the Witness Room by 9:30. Vince expected the prosecution to rest its opening case as soon as court reconvened at ten o'clock. But another half hour passed. Then an hour, while Jo Ann's racking cough echoed from those four bare walls. At ten minutes after eleven Lon Babby stuck his head in the door. "Jo Ann? They're ready for you."

59

JO ANN:

I'd worn a suit with pockets, each crammed with lozenges for my cough. My hand tightened around them as I stepped through the tall double doors. The courtroom was larger than I remembered from nine months ago when we'd come here for John's arraignment. It seemed a long, long walk down the aisle between the spectator rows, through the gate in the low partition, past the prosecutors' table.

John was sitting at the defense table, in the navy blazer, Vince and Greg beside him, four marshals seated close by. A court officer was waiting at the entrance to the witness stand holding out a Bible. "Do you swear to tell the truth, the whole truth. . . ." The sketchers with their binoculars, Judge Parker peering down from his raised platform, the court stenographer with fingers flying over his odd-shaped keyboard—it all seemed unreal. Only the Bible under my hand was solid, an anchor.

The twelve jurors stared at me without expression as I took the witness seat. In front of the two-tiered jury box, six more men and women, who I guessed were the alternates, occupied straight-backed chairs. To my relief Vince got up at once from the defense table and walked over to where I sat. Concentrate on Vince, I told myself, as he asked my name, my address, my relationship to John, queries probably meant to calm frightened witnesses as much as give information.

Guided by Vince's questions I went back over John's childhood and high school years, his first semesters at Texas

Tech. It was strange to see John's letters from college stamped with large black numbers identifying them as exhibits. Because of a legal technicality I did not understand, I was not allowed to read them aloud but had to paraphrase them. I was feeling flustered and anxious about this when at 12:30, to my vast relief, Judge Parker announced the lunch recess. Everyone stood while the judge left the room, the thump of his crutches the only sound.

Jack was waiting in the spartan little Witness Room but, of course, I was instructed to tell him nothing of what had happened inside. We had lunch together in the cafeteria, then I returned to the witness box from 1:30 until the court adjourned at 5:00—all on what is called "direct examination," that is, Vince questioning me as a defense witness.

The "cross-examination" by the other side, which was the part I dreaded most, wouldn't even begin until the following morning. Already I felt drained. Answering questions about "Lynn" had been dreadful: trying to go back mentally to the time in question, feeling again my happiness for her and John mingled with worry about how he would support her. Knowing now that there never was a Lynn. That I'd written my letters of motherly advice to a lonely young man in a room where no visitor, boy or girl, ever came.

Worse still were questions about the missing coins from Jack's study. "I believe there were between four and eight, originally," I told Vince, glad for someone to look at other than John who sat staring at the table top in front of him. In all the months awaiting trial he had continued to deny taking those coins—which I told the jury, too, wanting so much for John's statement to be true. But Jack and I had come up with no other explanation for how every coin, one by one, had disappeared —or any other way to explain how John had paid for the frenetic travels of those last months.

Just tell what happened, exactly as it occurred, changing nothing, leaving nothing out. Over and over I repeated to myself these very first instructions Vince had ever given us. It was the foundation of his defense philosophy, and, I was discovering, the most reassuring guideline a witness could have, sitting exposed before the world in that chair. Just describe what happened. That principle got me through the long, long day—that, and something else.

It was about mid-afternoon when, reaching into a pocket, I encountered the little hoard of lozenges. I'd forgotten they were there. Though I'd been answering questions for two hours since lunch, my throat was not sore, my voice not hoarse. I had not coughed a single time, in fact, since I entered the witness stand that morning. Many people had told me they would be praying today: Those untouched coughdrops assured me they had not forgotten.

Jack, Scott and Diane were all sitting in the Witness Room when I joined them just after five o'clock. A bigger-than-ever crowd of reporters and cameramen followed us all the way to the Metro station. Because their turns were still to come I could not tell the others anything that had been said today; they learned what they could, as always, on the evening news. I was too tired even to watch—and I wondered if the jurors weren't just as weary of anything to do with courtrooms. Our lawyers had not requested that the jury be sequestered, reasoning that if they were separated from their families for days on end it would only increase resentment toward John. So they were going home each night, under orders not to read or watch anything concerning the case. I realized that evening how welcome such instructions would be.

I hardly slept that night, wondering how I would handle hostile questioning from the prosecution. But Assistant U.S. Attorney Robert Chapman was considerate of me. The point of his questions, it was clear at once, was that John couldn't really have been sick, or his father and I would have known it. *How I wish we had!* I wanted to cry. *An hour never passes that I don't wish that!* But, of course, in a courtroom you must answer only the specific question you are asked.

A difficult one was why, if I was concerned about John before the shooting, as I had testified yesterday, I had told Dr. Hopper that "things were fine." In this packed and solemn courtroom my reason sounded ridiculous. But because it was true I answered that I had told Dr. Hopper "things are fine" to spare his feelings. To terminate the relationship without seeming critical. To be nice.

In my habitual eagerness to keep the peace, I wondered wretchedly, had I done my son incalculable hurt?

At last, by late Friday morning, the ordeal in the witness stand was behind me. A court officer led me back to a seat in the second row of spectators' benches where, now that my own testimony was completed, I was free to observe the rest of the trial. There'd been a change in the original sequence of defense witnesses. Because three medical doctors in the case—all men with busy practices—had now arrived in Washington, it had been decided to let them testify after me, with Dr. Hopper to appear Monday, the other three family members only after that.

Our Evergreen friend and physician, Em Harvey, was walking down the long aisle now. Dear Em, how I sympathized with him. Greg Craig conducted Em's direct examination, drawing out details of John's physical problems, asking about medications he had prescribed.

It was during Em's cross-examination that the prosecution's approach became clear. Had John ever reported becoming unconscious, Mr. Adelman wanted to know. Had he had difficulty walking?

But, I wanted to object, *no one ever claimed he did!*

Em was considering the question. "He said he was dizzy, but he didn't mention any coordination problems."

"He said he was dizzy? Was he dizzy in your office?"

"No."

That afternoon with the two other doctors the inferences continued. Dr. Robert Von Rueden described the tests he had conducted in Denver after Em's examination turned up nothing, agreeing, when asked, that John had neither become unconscious nor seemed disoriented during his office visit. Then Dr. Rosen, from Lubbock, took the stand. Referring frequently to his medical records, Dr. Rosen described the complaints John had brought to him month after month at Texas Tech. How familiar they sounded. "Diffuse pain in the right lower abdomen." "Pain in the left forearm." "Dizzy spells and palpitations." There was one surprise:

"The physical examination at that time," Dr. Rosen testified, "essentially showed a flat affect, where the patient does not respond to emotional stimuli in a normal fashion."

Flat affect . . . the phrase Jack and I had heard for the first time in the Jefferson Hotel after the shooting. Nearly a year earlier Dr. Rosen had entered the words in an office file. . . .

He had diagnosed this as a "depressive reaction," Dr. Rosen went on, for which he had prescribed the drug Sur-

245

montil. Then came another piece of news. In July 1980, after John had returned repeatedly to his office complaining of "lethargic" feelings:

"I requested him to consider undergoing a psychiatric evaluation."

John had resisted the idea however and Dr. Rosen had renewed the Surmontil prescription. *Why, John? Why did you resist?* I thought of the letter he had written us and never mailed, eight months before that visit to Dr. Rosen, when he himself wanted to see a psychologist. ("You can scream if you want to. . . .") Was that the reason? Was he afraid we would "scream"?

John had returned the following week, Dr. Rosen continued, requesting a tranquilizer for his "anxiety problem." Once again the doctor asked him to consider a psychological evaluation. Once again, John declined.

At any rate, I thought, here was one medical doctor who, even in the course of a physical exam, had spotted psychological problems. The effect, however, was immediately undercut by Dr. Rosen's cross-examination. Mr. Marc Tucker was another of the attorneys on the prosecution team.

"Mr. Hinckley didn't evidence any delusions or hallucinations in his conversations with you?"

"No."

"And he seemed coherent when he spoke to you, and his memory seemed intact?"

"Correct."

The implication was clear: John had not been babbling or frothing at the mouth in Dr. Rosen's office. Therefore he could not have been mentally ill. The prosecution, it seemed to me, was evoking the most simplistic stereotype of insanity.

How recently it had been *my* stereotype . . . How smugly I had supposed that the mentally ill acted in obvious ways. . . .

When court adjourned for the weekend we learned that John would be helicoptered that evening to Fort Meade for some fresh air after nightfall. To think that that patch of concrete behind its loops of barbed wire should come to seem like wide open spaces. Saturday we drove up there. All five of us— Scott, Diane and Steve, Jack and I were permitted into the stockade chapel at the same time, a special kindness by the marshals.

My heart glowed to watch Scott and Diane support and encourage their brother, as they had from the start. Never once had I heard either of them complain of the embarrassment or disruption caused by his illness to their own lives.

The last time the whole family had been together this way was Christmas 1980, a year and a half before, when John had been so depressed over John Lennon's death. At least that was the reason we'd given ourselves. How could we have guessed that downstairs in John's bedroom that Christmas morning were handguns—handguns which he had already considered turning on Jodie Foster and President Carter, in a confused version of a motion picture that was somehow more real to him than the group chatting and laughing around the Christmas tree.

Monday morning, again I was the only one of the family admitted to the courtroom. John was all but hidden by the four husky marshals who led him in from a door to the left of the judge's bench, and then took their own seats nearby. The jacket of John's tan suit hung from his shoulders, sizes too big. He had not, after all, had to wear the bullet-proof vest.

The press section, across the aisle from me, was jammed: Dr. Hopper's testimony was what everyone was waiting for. We all stood for Judge Parker's entrance. He paused for a moment before seating himself in his high-backed leather chair, surveying the room. Something behind me caught his eye. "Who has brought a newspaper into this courtroom!" he thundered. Two officers leaped in the direction of the offending party.

As Dr. Hopper walked down the aisle from the back of the room my heart went out to him. He'd liked John, truly believed he could help him. He'd been generous with his time for Jack and me, too, seeing us for emergency evening sessions, always available on the phone. Just . . . he'd made the wrong diagnosis. John wasn't an unmotivated kid who needed behavioral therapy. He was severely ill. *You'll make a mental cripple of him,* I heard Dr. Hopper say when we told him we wanted to put our son in a hospital. But John's mind *was crippled. . . .*

How ha. ' such diagnoses must be, I thought, as Greg began the direct examination. I remembered how long it had taken to

247

discover Mother's diabetes—and physical symptoms were doubtless easier to read than mental ones. John must have seemed to Dr. Hopper like other suburban young people he'd treated: irresponsible, lacking clear-cut goals. Doubtless he'd seen many such patients helped by biofeedback, or adopting a "plan" for their lives.

An autobiography John had written at Dr. Hopper's request back in November 1980, five months before the shooting, was introduced as evidence. I hadn't known of its existence; as excerpts were read aloud in the courtroom I was stunned at the extent of John's self-knowledge. He described his failure to become involved with student life at Texas Tech: "I stayed by myself in my apartment and dreamed of future glory in some undefined field."

The trips back and forth to New Haven he called "a month of unparalleled emotional exhaustion. My mind was on the breaking point the whole time. A relationship I had dreamed about went absolutely nowhere. I gave up on myself and came back to Colorado and this is when I began the treatment with you."

My mind was on the breaking point the whole time. . . . He knew! John knew! A year earlier he had tried to write the same thing to Jack and me, but lost his courage. Now at last he had not only put it on paper, but showed it to another human being.

And Dr. Hopper failed to take it seriously. The person he saw in his office, he testified, seemed unrelated to the distraught and desperate individual described on paper. Face-to-face, John had obviously been as bland and uncommunicative with the doctor as he was at home. Had John ever told him, Greg asked, about traveling to Washington in November, after therapy was underway, to stalk President-elect Reagan? About sending a note to the FBI threatening to kidnap Jodie Foster, and traveling to New Haven on December 15, between appointments in Hopper's office, to attempt again to see her?

Of course John had told the doctor none of this. Nor, till that moment in the courtroom, had I known these things either. . . .

"Did Mr. Hinckley ever tell you that, while under your care and going through biofeedback treatment in Evergreen, he purchased a .38 caliber handgun in Denver on January 21?" Had John told him that, with that gun, he'd gone to New York on February 14, intending to commit suicide in the doorway where John Lennon was shot?

February 1981 . . . so that was the purpose behind John's sudden disappearance while I was in Dallas. That's what he'd gone to do, when he turned up on the doorstep that evening, ten days later, without a word of explanation. . . .

His Valentine's Day suicide, Greg explained, was to be a love-offering to Jodie Foster. For a long time on February 14, he had stood in the entryway to John Lennon's apartment building on the very square foot where his idol had died two months earlier, his hand clenching the loaded pistol in his pocket, trying to force together the fragmented images in his mind.

John had told Dr. Hopper nothing, as he had told us nothing. Yet it seemed to me that in the autobiography he had been trying, however tentatively, to communicate. In the final paragraph, written before most of these things had happened, John had confided to a sheet of paper words that seared themselves on my heart: "Because I have remained so inactive and reclusive over the past five years I have managed to remove myself from the real world. . . . I have two obsessions in life now: writing and the person we discussed on November 4. I care about nothing else!"

The person they had discussed, Dr. Hopper acknowledged, was Jodie Foster. Tragically, unaccountably, the doctor had probed no further.

His ordeal on the witness stand had just begun. The cross-examination lasted all afternoon and continued the following day with re-direct questioning by Greg, re-cross-examination by Mr. Adelman. Dr. Hopper's original impression of John as spoiled and lazy rather than really sick, the government contended, had been correct. John had invented the writing school at Yale, Mr. Adelman suggested, not because of any obsession with a young woman student there, but simply to extract money from his father.

It was late Tuesday morning when Dr. Hopper was excused from the stand at last. Scott followed him into the witness box, solemn and handsome in the beige suit he'd put on each morning for a week, expecting every day to be called. In answer to Greg's questions Scott described John as "a very emotionless person," recalling that he'd never seen his younger brother angry, nor, at the other end of the scale, known him to burst out laughing.

After John's disappointment in the writing school as the family believed, Scott grew really concerned about his brother. "John was becoming more depressed, more dependent—just less and less able to cope with the realities of the world."

The first week in March, three weeks before the shooting, Scott had visited his sister and brother-in-law in Dallas, where for hours the conversation had centered on John. "Was there a meeting of the minds among the three of you," Greg asked, "as to what should be done about John?"

"Yes. It was our conclusion that John should be hospitalized."

The government, of course, cross-examining Scott, implied that since his father and I had rejected this recommendation, the symptoms could not have been all that alarming. "Mr. Hinckley, isn't it a fact that you have never seen your brother in a frantic state? Isn't that correct, sir?"

But he just said, I wanted to cry out, *that he never saw any kind of emotion in John.*

"No sir, I have not seen my brother in a frantic state."

"And isn't it a fact, Mr. Hinckley, that he has always been coherent when you have seen him, sir? You had no problem understanding what he said to you?"

By lunch time Scott was finished. Jack and Diane met us in the corridor for a hurried goodbye. Scott had been away from the crisis at Vanderbilt for a week, and was rushing back on the afternoon flight. I embraced him, trying to tell him how proud I'd been of him in the courtroom, watching him hold his own against the stiff prosecution questioning.

Lunch in the courthouse cafeteria, after he'd gone, was a pretty silent affair, Diane and Jack tense with their upcoming testimony. Diane was summoned as soon as the court reconvened. My heart filled with pride, as it had for Scott, as she walked that long aisle, spun-gold hair hanging loose and straight below her shoulders. She looked tiny in the big wood-enclosed witness stand, but her voice was steady, the smile she gave John warm and loving. Greg drew from her a summary of John's almost friendless existence in Highland Park High School. She described his comings and goings,

250

later, to her home in Dallas, his attachment to her infant son, who, as far as she knew, was the only friend John had. She, too, recalled the conversation with Scott in March, 1981: "John was so extremely withdrawn that he could not seem to cope with what was going on around him. We felt a psychiatrist at an institution could help."

Mr. Chapman conducted Diane's cross-examination. His questions brought out that John had experienced no difficulty in traveling to Dallas from Lubbock, finding jobs and apartments in Dallas over the years. Diane had hoped the cross-examination would go swiftly, so that she and Steve could return to their children that night, but the afternoon passed and she was still in the witness chair.

60

JACK:

It was lonely in the witness room Tuesday afternoon with Scott on his way back to Denver, Diane on the witness stand. Not that the three of us had talked much; the blank walls and upright chairs somehow dampened conversation. For five endless days now I'd sat in this claustrophobic place— sometimes it seemed to me I'd never done anything but count the speckles on that ceiling.

Just before five o'clock Diane came in, looking exhausted. "Daddy, I'm not through! They're making me come back tomorrow."

Jo Ann joined us soon afterward; she could tell me only that both kids had been "wonderful" on the stand. At eight that evening she and I returned downtown for a basement visit with

John. He was dejected and silent, cross with us because we'd forgotten to bring some magazines he'd asked for. If the trial was a strain for the rest of us, I could only imagine what it was for him, hearing his brother and sister, this past session, air his failures before the world.

Diane was called from the witness room as soon as the court reconvened the next morning, and I settled down to wait once more. In less than twenty minutes she was back. "Goodbye, Daddy! I love you!"

"You're through? They kept you over for just this long?" But with a hug and the promise that she and Steve would be praying for me, she was gone, and the officer was standing in the doorway to escort me to the stand.

After the long, long wait the moment had somehow come unexpectedly. I hadn't realized how crowded the courtroom would be. I spotted Jo Ann to the left of the aisle in the second row of the spectators' section. She flashed me an encouraging smile as I took the witness chair below the judge's bench. John was sitting at a long table fifteen feet away. He did not look up. Vince asked my name, my business, my relationship to John.

"My first question to you, sir, is whether there came a time when you observed behavior in your son which differed from your other children's?"

There had, of course. I went over John's life up through the California trips, the meetings with Hopper to work out the "plan," John's repeated taking off. Then that despairing early morning phone call from New York, and my driving down to Denver next evening to meet his plane.

"Can you tell the jury," Vince asked, "what observation you made at that time regarding your son's appearance or mental condition?"

"He was in very bad shape," I recalled. "He needed a shave. He was just really dragging. His mother couldn't go to the airport with me. She couldn't bring herself to do it."

I described taking John to an unused boarding area. "I told him how disappointed I was in him, that he had left us no choice but not to take him back to the house again."

We'd gone to his car, I said. "I suggested that he go to the YMCA and he said no, he didn't want to do that. And so I said, 'O.K., you are on your own. Do whatever you want to.'"

I saw us standing in that drafty airport parking garage, heard myself saying those words. "In looking back on that," I said,

252

though I hadn't intended to, "I'm sure that was the greatest mistake of my life."

It was as though I was seeing that March evening thirteen months earlier—really seeing it—for the first time. Perhaps it was John sitting so silent a few feet away, eyes never leaving the table, but at that moment there in the witness box I knew that a year ago I had turned a totally helpless human being out into the world.

"I am the cause of John's tragedy," I blurted out to the crowded courtroom. "I forced him out at a time when he simply couldn't cope. I wish to God that I could trade places with him right now."

Horrifyingly, unexpectedly, I was crying. In front of the judge, lawyers, onlookers, in front of the press and Jo Ann. Jo Ann was crying too; officers escorted her swiftly from the room. "Ladies and gentlemen," Judge Parker said to the jury, "follow the marshal."

As I fumbled for a handkerchief I heard the jury file hurriedly out of the courtroom. There was a whispered conversation between Vince and the judge. "This would be a good time," Judge Parker decided, "to adjourn for lunch."

"Thank you, your Honor," Vince said.

Court personnel joined them at the bench to discuss setting up TV consoles around the courtroom; the video tape of Jodie Foster's deposition, I gathered, was to be shown this afternoon at the close of my cross-examination. I wiped my eyes, struggling for control. I, who'd always been so *in* control, bawling like a kid in front of all these people. In the first press row the sketchers' pencils were flying, binoculars trained on me. Of all the faces I could see, John's alone registered no reaction whatever. . . .

I was calmer after lunch, determined that Adelman, at least, would provoke no feelings from me. It was hard to keep my cool though as I perceived the nature of the prosecution's case: If someone wasn't raving mad, they seemed to be saying, he must be sane. On the day in question I had instructed John to phone us from Newark airport, hadn't I? Adelman asked. And hadn't John remembered to do so? "You never saw him have a seizure of any sort, is that right? No hallucinations, seeing things or hearing voices?"

My cross-examination lasted only an hour or so, but by the time I stepped from that box and joined Jo Ann in the second row I was feeling deeply discouraged about the direction of the trial.

Adelman and Chapman, Vince and Greg were huddled at the bench once more in a long discussion with the judge over some technical point. I kept looking at the men and women in the jury box, wondering how after two-and-a-half weeks of such legal jockeying they were able to keep their attention on the issues at all.

During the conference at the bench, technicians had set up TV sets at several locations in the courtroom. The judge addressed the jury: "Ladies and gentlemen, at this point in time you will see a video tape rendition of a deposition of the witness Jodie Foster. You are to view the video tape just as though the witness was testifying in open court under oath."

For the first time since I'd entered the courtroom that morning I saw John look up, shoulders straightening from their habitual slump. Onto the screen came the image of a sweet-faced blonde girl, looking even younger than her nineteen years. In answer to Greg's disembodied questions she explained that she had entered Yale University in the fall of 1980, a fact reported in *People* magazine.

"Did there come a time shortly after you started school at Yale when you received certain written communications from John W. Hinckley, Jr.?"

"Yes, that is correct."

A number of notes and poems had come from John in September, she testified, with a "second batch" in October or November, and a third early in March 1981. None had been mailed: They had been either hand-delivered underneath the door to Miss Foster's dormitory room, or left in an incoming-mail box on the ground floor.

"Did you ever see the person who delivered the communications to your mailbox or beneath your door?"

"No, I did not."

"Did any of your roommates to your knowledge ever see the person?"

"No, I don't think so."

The first two batches, she testified, were "love-type letters," fan mail such as she often received, and which she had thrown out. "The third batch was a different type of letter so I gave it to the dean of my college." These later letters were more "distressed-sounding" she recalled. Meanwhile, too, the

FBI had informed her of a kidnap threat received by them and instructed her not to throw out future notes.

"Jodie," began one of this third batch, "after tonight John Lennon and I will have a lot in common. It's all for you, Foster."

Another note bore a date and an hour: March 6, 1:00 a.m. "Jodie Foster, love, just wait. I will rescue you very soon. Please cooperate. J.W.H."

"Have you ever seen a message like that before?" Greg asked her.

"Yes, in the movie *'Taxie Driver'* the character Travis Bickle sends the character Iris a rescue letter."

"And were you in that film, Miss Foster?"

"Yes, I was."

"And what character did you play?"

"I played the character Iris."

In the spectator section I was recalling for the second time that day the phone call that had awakened Jo Ann and me in Evergreen at 4:30 a.m. on March 6. It would have been 6:30 a.m. Eastern time, five-and-a-half hours after he wrote that note and slipped it beneath Jodie Foster's door.

"Now, with respect to the individual, John W. Hinckley," Greg's recorded voice was asking Miss Foster, "looking at him today in the courtroom, do you ever recall seeing him in person before today?"

"No."

"Did you ever respond to his letters?"

"No, I did not."

"Did you ever do anything to invite his approaches?"

"No."

"How would you describe your relationship with John Hinckley?"

"I don't have any relationship with John Hinckley."

My attention was jerked from the TV screen by a sudden scraping of chairs at the front of the courtroom. John was on his feet, one arm thrust out as though to ward off those words emanating from the video screen. The four marshals sprang up. The next instant John bolted through the door at the back of the room, the marshals racing after him.

Miss Foster's recorded face and voice continued speaking. The rest of us sat paralyzed, all eyes on Judge Parker. Such an unheard-of breach of trial decorum to happen in his courtroom of all places. His stern eye swept jury and spectators, permitting no murmur of amazement at what we had just witnessed. But . . . I thought, what could have caused John such distress that he would literally run away? A young woman stating the simple truth that there was no connection between the two of them? Could he possibly, to this minute, be refusing to accept the obvious facts?

The video tape rolled on in the stunned and silent courtroom, while I wondered how badly John's case had been hurt this disastrous day. First his father breaks down and sobs then John himself dashes out of the courtroom. At least, to my enormous gratitude, the pen-throwing episode, at the time the tape was made, had either been edited out or had occurred after the cameras were turned off.

John was led back into the courtroom at the close of the tape showing, pale and haggard looking, to face a stern reprimand from Judge Parker. I could not help contrasting John's reaction to Miss Foster's matter-of-fact statement, with the detached, even indifferent way he had sat through my breaking down that morning. It was as though the relationship with his family was the imaginary one, the one with Jodie Foster still his reality. . . .

61

JO ANN:

Next morning in the courtroom we listened to the tapes found in John's Washington hotel room. He had recorded two phone conversations with Miss Foster at her dorm. We heard the voice of a roommate answering the telephone, then Jodie's voice, puzzled, obviously trying to get rid of this unwanted caller without being rude: "I can't carry on these conversations with people I don't know."

It was John's voice that struck me. It was . . . young! Like an adolescent venturing his first shy boy-girl conversation. I remembered Dr. Hopper saying that at 25 John had the maturity of a fourteen-year-old. . . .

They lasted less than five minutes, the two phone calls together, and were followed on the tape by recordings of himself playing the guitar and singing. Jack and I leaned forward on our courtroom bench, scarcely breathing. In the fifteen years since he'd taken up the guitar, the countless hours practicing behind a closed door, this was the first time we had heard him perform.

Once more the feeling swept over me that I was listening to a young boy. Tentative and timid-sounding even in front of his cassette recorder, his singing voice was soft, but . . . high, clear and true. I looked at Jack. He, too, was smiling in unexpected pleasure. At the mid-morning recess one of the media people came over to me, Tim O'Brien of ABC: "He's good, Mrs. Hinckley! Really good."

That, in a way, made the account that Dr. Carpenter now began to give more tragic still. We'd glimpsed human potential that morning; as the first defense expert-witness the doctor documented what illness had done to it.

Tall, gaunt, bearded, gray hair flowing to his coat collar, Dr. Carpenter identified himself as director of the Maryland Psychiatric Research Center, a professor at the University of Maryland School of Medicine and a specialist in schizophrenia. He had never before testified in a court case. Over the past year he had spent 45 hours with John.

"Process schizophrenia," he explained to the jury as he had to us, developed slowly. The very gradualness, the unspectacular nature of each small change, made it frustratingly hard for families—and even doctors—to detect. One symptom was an ever-increasing inability to separate the real from the unreal. I watched the jurors' faces as Dr. Carpenter described John's antipathy toward a black roommate, his freshman year in college, and his effort to justify it by "reading the literature of bigotry." From such reading he concocted an imaginary white-supremacist organization which he at first knew was fictitious but slowly came to believe in.

Lynn Collins, too, had originally been a knowing invention,

257

who later became unshakably real. He probably created her in the first place simply to have something good to write home from his rented room in California—and because Travis Bickle wrote *his* parents about a rich and beautiful girl friend.

With no actual friends or even an acquaintance in all of Los Angeles, John went to a lot of movies. In one of them there appeared before his fascinated gaze a character as friendless, depressed and despairing as himself, a New York City taxi driver named Travis Bickle, living alone, like John, in the heart of a teeming and indifferent city. Schizophrenics, Dr. Carpenter told the jury, lack conviction about their own identity. In this terrifying predicament, they snatch fragments of personality from books and films. John sat through *Taxi Driver* sixteen times, gradually "becoming" Travis Bickle. He began to wear the kind of clothes Travis wore, ate the junk food Travis lived on, bought the same kind of guns Travis bought. I thought of the answer John had given when *Newsweek* asked why he had bought so many guns: "I bought so many handguns because Travis bought so many handguns. Ask him. Not me."

Like Travis, John engaged in target practice at a rifle range. Like Travis he went to New York's Times Square looking for a child prostitute to save from degradation as Travis had saved the character played by Jodie Foster—the first I had known this part of his New York experience. Like Travis, John stalked presidential figures. He had been pursuing President Carter in Washington in December 1980, Dr. Carpenter revealed: John Lennon's murder up in New York had possibly prevented an assassination attempt at that time.

Lennon's death compounded the chaos in John's brain. As he had plunked on his guitar in solitude over the years he had *been* Lennon. Now in characteristic schizophrenic fashion, he also became Lennon's assailant.

Inside this mind of mine I commit first page murder

Dr. Carpenter quoted from a poem John wrote after Lennon's death. Abandoning for the moment his Travis role John had come home to mope about the house through that miserable Christmas. He continued to see Dr. Hopper, but could not be open with him, in Carpenter's opinion, in part because Jack

258

and I were seeing Dr. Hopper too—not only in family sessions, but also when John was not present. John had thus seen Dr. Hopper not as an ally but as just another part of the threatening adult world arrayed against him.

The tape John had made on New Year's Eve was introduced as evidence. As it was played for the hushed courtroom I recalled how Jack and I had sat upstairs that evening, an unopened bottle of champagne in the refrigerator.

"I'm sitting here alone like I do every New Year's Eve. I'm drinking peach brandy. Tastes pretty good. I just want to say goodbye to the old year which was nothing, total misery, total death. John Lennon is dead, the world is over.

"Here comes 1981," the expressionless monotone continued. "It's going to be insanity, even if I make it through the first few days. Anything that I might do in 1981 would be solely for Jodie Foster's sake. I want to tell the world in some way that I worship and idolize her. One of my idols was murdered and now Jodie's the only one left."

His fantasy world now began to occupy him completely, according to Dr. Carpenter. He read and re-read the book on which the film *Taxi Driver* was based. He bought the soundtrack of the movie and played it constantly.

When we refused to let him come home, early in March, his last link with the real world was severed. At a motel he signed the guest register "J. Travis." In the film, Travis is never able to get close enough to the presidential candidate to fire at him. Instead, he goes to the dingy hotel where the twelve-year-old prostitute brings her customers, shoots her pimp, the hotel manager, and her current client, and frees the child from her sordid environment. When John caught that cross-country bus in Los Angeles, Dr. Carpenter believed, he was on his way to New Haven; Washington was only a stopover en route to Yale and one more attempt to "rescue" Jodie, as the movie script demanded. "Dictates from his inner world were guiding him. He felt like he was on a roller coaster. He couldn't control the pace or the direction of the ride, but was caught up in it."

The roller coaster hurtled into its final curve. In Washington John noticed in a newspaper the schedule for the President's activities the following day. As Travis and he had so often done, he haunted the fringes of the crowd where the famous man was to appear. Security, of course, would be too tight to get close. He took a few more steps. Incredibly, no one stopped him. Nobody even glanced his way. Once more the plot was going wrong. And then suddenly, there was the President waving . . . giving the signal . . . telling him, "Now is the time."

62

JACK:

Dr. Carpenter was in the witness chair three days, his cross-examination resuming after the weekend recess. Did John "appreciate" the wrongfulness of his act—that was the central issue on which the trial revolved.

Intellectually, yes, Dr. Carpenter concluded. Emotionally, no. To his diseased mind the victims were "bit players," not actual people existing in their own right. Carter would have served the inner scenario as well as Reagan. I scanned the jurors' faces at this. To call the President of the United States a "bit player" might be accurate in terms of John's delusion, but I wondered if people might not take offense at it.

Carpenter was followed on the stand by the second expert witness for the defense, Dr. David Bear, a psychiatrist on the faculty of Harvard Medical School. Spectacles flashing beneath his mop of wavy dark hair, young Dr. Bear was a striking contrast to the gray-haired psychiatrist from Maryland. His diagnosis of John, however, arrived at without reference to the other man, was in all essentials the same. Dr. Bear found the poems John had scrawled in school notebooks over the years especially revealing. Never intended to be seen by anyone else, they were portrayals of a private universe. "Fantasies become reality in my world," John had written years earlier, with painful self-perception.

"This is the psychotic patient," Dr. Bear testified, "slipping deeper and deeper into unreal thoughts." One of these unreal thoughts was that he could somehow win the love of Jodie Foster, which Dr. Bear termed a "pathetic delusion."

Whether it was those particular words, or the accumulated misery of hearing himself described day after day as psychotic, mentally ill and deluded, John got to his feet at this and once more fled the courtroom, pursued by the marshals.

Judge Parker maintained the iron discipline over his own expression that he demanded of others, instructing the jury not to react "with either sympathy for, or prejudice against, Mr. Hinckley." The marshals led John back into the courtroom and up to the bench where the judge warned him against a repeat of this behavior.

Jo Ann and I were admitted for a visit in the basement that evening. He'd left the courtroom, John told us, because he'd felt "faint" and had an upset stomach—which I could well believe. One of the problems with the insanity defense was that a defendant would have to be strong to survive it.

Bear's cross-examination lasted until the noon break on Thursday after which Dr. Ernst Prelinger, a Yale psychologist and specialist in testing, took the stand for two days, finishing on Monday of the trial's fifth week. Why psychological tests had not been performed on John either by Dr. Benjamin or by Dr. Hopper simply added to the confusion in my layman's mind over how the mental health field operated. Such tests had been widely used for decades according to Prelinger. On all but one, John scored in the pathological range, almost going "over the top of the sheet" on some. In one series of tests known as the Minnesota Multiphasic Personality Inventory, John got 117 out of a possible 120 points measuring depression, 109 for schizophrenia. Only one in a million non-schizophrenics, Dr. Prelinger testified, would score over 100 on that particular scale.

"Here is a person who hates himself," in Prelinger's analysis, "who has no motivation of his own."

On the "CBS Evening News" one night during Prelinger's testimony, the commentator referred to John's as the "one-

261

million-dollar trial"—including what the government had spent on security and investigation, in addition to lawyers and doctors on both sides—calling it the most expensive trial of its kind in the history of the world. I was staggered. I had been aware of our own astronomical costs, of course—nearly $10,000 one month for xeroxing expenses alone. Several times during the trial I'd had to call my banker in Denver to ask for yet another loan increase at 18% interest and up. But never had I dreamed we were setting some kind of hideous record.

Whether it was those statistics or simple fatigue, the whole trial suddenly looked preposterous and hopeless. The thing had lasted more than a month already, with Dr. Goldman, the third defense psychiatrist, still to testify before the prosecution's expert-testimony could even begin.

Perhaps we'd only kidded ourselves that we ever had a chance; at any rate it was clear to me that we had none now. I continued to watch the jury, wondering where Vince got the idea he was constantly reiterating: that a cross-section of ordinary citizens made up a far wiser and subtler forum than I imagined. It seemed to me that—understandably enough—several people's attention wandered during Bear's discussion of "paradoxical thinking" and Prelinger's description of statistical theory, and picked up only when the prosecution, in cross-examination, reverted to the "hard facts" on which their case was built. John had taken a shower the morning of the shooting. He'd eaten breakfast at a McDonald's, then taken a taxi to the Hilton. Concrete events that a jury could picture and remember. Didn't such behavior, the prosecution asked, demonstrate a mind functioning perfectly well? Forgotten, it seemed to me, was the point our specialists had made: that mentally ill people could act normally much of the time. I cringed as I saw at least one juror dozing during the re-direct examination that attempted to re-establish this point.

Why go on? I found myself wondering. Why continue the torture on John and the immense outlay of money for a losing battle?

Other people kept us going. Jo Ann's family in Oklahoma City wrote us and John continually. Friends seemed to phone whenever we needed them most. Calvary Temple mounted a 24-hour-a-day prayer vigil until the trial's end, and we were told of other chains of prayer on our behalf. Church congregations all over Washington astonished us with their caring. The Reverend Glenn Knecht in particular, pastor of a Presbyterian church in nearby Silver Spring, Maryland, took us under his wing, having us to dinner in his home, coming to see us.

On Monday of the trial's sixth week, our final expert-witness took the stand. Dr. Thomas Goldman, a psychiatrist in private practice in Washington, was the only one of our authorities who had testified in a court case before. He gave the most thorough and frightening account yet of John's obsession with Jodie Foster. "He not only loved her, he hated her" for not returning that love. Six months before he shot the President, according to Goldman, John had trailed the freshman girl around the Yale campus with a loaded pistol in his pocket and the notion that a murder/suicide would link them in death. An alternate idea was to kidnap her at gunpoint from the "corrupt" life of New Haven, then hijack an airplane, demanding for its release that the two of them be installed in the White House.

I listened absorbed as pieces of the story we had heard only in fragments came together. I had known that John resented, at times even hated me. Only now did I discover that this constituted a "classic Oedipus complex," that when he aimed at the President he was also aiming at me. The President, according to Goldman, was the ultimate father figure, symbol of the authoritative male who was keeping John from possessing the "idealized mother figure" whom he saw in Jodie Foster. I didn't understand how this could be, since she was so young—nor how she could be both love-object and mother-figure—but apparently the subconscious knew no such logical barriers.

Fantasies about Miss Foster, said Goldman who had conducted the most recent psychiatric interviews with John, were still tragically intact. John became furious, Goldman testified, at any suggestion that there existed no bond between them. "What he cannot countenance is the fact that he does not have a relationship with her, that he does not matter to her."

Indeed, John was becoming increasingly restless as Goldman's testimony continued, shaking his head, drumming his fingers on the table. Judge Parker was watching John, too, frowning down at him from the bench. Apparently anticipating some new disturbance, Tuesday afternoon the judge abruptly adjourned the session. When we were admitted to John's cell that evening we found him tense and shaky, upset at the word "pathetic," which Dr. Goldman had used a number of times to describe his deluded thinking.

When, next morning, his agitation at the defense table was worse, Judge Parker instructed the marshals to escort him out of the courtroom. A delay followed while a closed circuit TV camera was rigged up, at the judge's orders, so that John could follow the proceedings, as the law required, but from another room.

Adelman's cross-examination of Dr. Goldman was devastating. John, he implied repeatedly, had exaggerated or even made up much of what he told the doctor. Goldman confirmed from his notes that John had first told him about the hijacking idea in December 1981, *eight months,* Adelman emphasized, after the shooting.

Throughout the trial I'd scribbled notes to hand Vince at the close of each session. "The hijack note found in John's hotel room," I wrote indignantly now, "had to have been written *before* the shooting."

Adelman made a lot of the three visits Goldman had had with John here in his cell in the courthouse. Desperate, last-minute efforts, the inference was, to concoct an insanity defense. Goldman, like the other defense doctors, made use of John's writing, quoting a poem about maggots and lice destroying his brain. The prosecution dismissed any and all such evidence. They were nothing but John's words, made up to create a false impression.

Made up to create a false impression years before he committed any crime? I wondered. Was it believable that a college student would fill notebooks with despairing poems year after year and pack them away in boxes in a garage, so that one day he could invent an insanity defense?

But all that mattered, in the end, was what the jury thought. "Schizotypal personality disorder with psychosis," Dr. Goldman's ultimate diagnosis of John's illness, seemed to me dull stuff compared with Adelman's astonished question: "He waited *eight months* to tell you?"

Jo Ann and I rode the Metro home in discouragement too deep for words. The telephone was ringing as we let ourselves into the apartment. It was Vince. Vince, whose almost superhuman energy could always recharge my drooping spirits. Whose boundless enthusiasm for this case stemmed from his conviction that truth was on our side and that juries responded to truth.

"They've heard all of our witnesses now," he said, voice hollow with fatigue. "And I'm afraid the jury's not convinced."

I was too stunned to respond. We'd never had much of a chance, I knew, but somehow Vince's confident attitude had made me believe in spite of myself. Now . . . "We'll go down fighting," Vince assured me. I spent a sleepless night over this change in Vince's attitude. He was going to bring a motion next day to permit introduction of John's CATscan test results—material the prosecution had so far successfully prevented from being admitted as evidence.

We spent all that following day listening to four X-ray specialists argue pro and con. The government's experts maintained that brain scans, even when they showed abnormalities, could not be used to prove or disprove schizophrenia in an individual case. Our defense experts agreed, but claimed that the atrophy showing up in John's X-rays was significant as part of a larger picture.

At the end of the long day of arguments, Judge Parker ruled that in view of their non-determinative character, the X-rays could not be introduced. A piece of evidence Vince considered even more crucial, the showing for the jury of the movie *Taxi Driver*, was also opposed by the prosecution, the objection upheld by the judge.

And so, with this double defeat, Vince rested our case.

The turn of the prosecution had come.

63

JO ANN:

As we entered the courtroom next morning technicians were once more stringing cords to TV sets around the room; in a surprise reversal of his previous decision, Judge Parker had ruled that the jury could watch *Taxi Driver* after all. For a hopeful moment Jack and I took this as good news. Vince shook his head. "The prosecution thinks we've lost too," he said. "That's the only reason they've withdrawn their objection."

I could hardly believe that at last Jack and I were going to see the film we'd talked so much about. John was back in his seat at the defense table. From the opening moment I understood the movie's grip on his emotions. . . .

Eyes were the first thing you saw, the eyes of a lonely young man looking out at a world of strangers. You were behind those eyes, inside that man, viewing his alien, friendless universe. I looked at John half-turned in his chair to see the TV set, lips parted in enthralled attention though he must know every line, every gesture that was coming.

On the screen Travis Bickle, a New York taxi driver, is struggling to break out of his isolation: "I don't think someone should spend all his time in morbid self-examination. I think someone should become a person like other people." But his efforts to form a relationship are rejected by a beautiful girl from a good family. "Lynn!" I almost said aloud when she walked onto the screen, she was so exactly as I'd pictured John's imaginary friend.

Over and over I recognized John in the movie, or was it the

movie in John? Travis suffers from headaches and worries about his health. He sends his parents glowing accounts of the successful life he is living only in his head. "I've been dating a girl for seven months," he writes from his solitary room, "I know you'd be proud if you could see her."

Travis hates blacks, muttering the racist slurs that had distressed me so when John repeated them. He drags through his meaningless days on a diet of cereal topped with sugar and peach brandy. I understood now why Greg had been so fascinated by John's choice of drink on New Year's Eve. Travis worries about his mind: "I've got some really bad ideas in my head."

Then he buys an arsenal of guns and life comes into focus. He takes target practice at a shooting range and begins to stalk the tall, handsome, charismatic presidential candidate for whom "Lynn" works as a star-struck volunteer. Travis' aimless existence has direction now. I bit my lip as one by one I recognized the accessories of his newly militant life—the sunglasses, the olive-drab field jacket, even the boots—the black ankle-high pull-on boots that John and I had looked for all over Denver one September day. . . .

I wasn't following the plot too well, so absorbed was I in watching John. Body rigid, fists clenched, he was staring at the drama open-mouthed. Only twice did he take his eyes from the screen. When "Lynn" turns Travis down for a date, John snatched off his glasses and turned his head aside. That was a mild reaction, however, compared with the second one. By now Jodie Foster had entered the story as a twelve-year-old prostitute named Iris. I was surprised to discover that it was a fairly small part in the film, but obviously the one where the interest centered for John. He leaned forward, tense with excitement.

Until the moment, that is, when the obnoxious pimp who controls and exploits Iris slips an arm around her. Far from pulling away, Iris snuggles close; it is clear that the victimized girl loves and depends on this hateful man. As the two embraced, John buried his head in his hands and shrank away from the images on the screen. For John to show emotion was such a rarity that I could only stare from him to the film, then back to him, thinking that real life had never drawn such a response.

The end of the movie was as loathsome as it was bewildering. Guns drawn, Travis storms the pimp's stronghold. I closed my eyes on the closeup of the carnage, opened them to see Travis holding a blood-drenched finger to his temple in a pantomime of a man blowing his own brains out. Strangely, though, it is a gesture of triumph. . . .

Suddenly and without any warning, the film ceases to be a realistic if brutal portrait of a disintegrating mind, and becomes a magic fantasy. With the shooting of the pimp, Travis is marvelously transformed from a nobody to an important personage. Iris' grateful parents shower him with thanks for rescuing their daughter, lovely ''Lynn'' is eager to be with him. One frantic burst of gunfire has changed Travis from pathetic failure to hero—loved and applauded by all.

The movie had taken up most of the morning. With the switching-off of the TV screens—John sank back into his accustomed slump—while Vince once more told the court ''the defense rests.''

64

JACK:

Saturday was May 29, John's 27th birthday. The court was recessed for the three-day Memorial Day weekend. We'd hoped John might be taken back up to Fort Meade, but he was not. His face was pallid from weeks in the windowless basement and courtroom, his weight loss alarming. He was wearing a torn old undershirt, while with one hand he held up a pair of threadbare khaki pants with large holes in the knees. The marshals had thoughtfully provided a small cake so the three of us could ''celebrate'' in his basement cell, but John's depression, seemingly worse since the showing of the film, made it hard even to pretend that it was a party.

I kept thinking of his last birthday, in the cell at Butner, when he was so groggy and sick from the attempt at suicide with a drug overdose. A year had passed, a year of solitary cells and round-the-clock surveillance—and for what? How much better to have spared him all this, to have pleaded Guilty in the first place as he had wanted to. He still could not admit he was ill, could not forgive us and the doctors for calling his great romance a delusion.

As Jo Ann and I stood up to leave, though, it turned into a celebration visit after all, at least for me. John may not even have realized what he was doing, but as the marshal unlocked the cell door John stood up and patted me on the shoulder. He had never done such a thing in all his 27 years, and I climbed those basement stairs with my feet barely touching.

When the court reconvened on Tuesday, June 1, we expected the government to take the stand. Instead, Judge Parker announced that, after all, he *was* going to admit the CATscan evidence—so long as it could be produced before court adjourned that same day. As surprised as we, our lawyers dashed out to telephone the radiologist and arrange for her to fly immediately from Boston. Once more Jo Ann and I tried to read this as a favorable development. More likely, I feared, Parker now considered the verdict such a foregone conclusion that he wanted to leave no loophole for an appeal.

Dr. Marjorie LeMay hadn't had much time to prepare when she arrived in the courtroom at four o'clock that afternoon, and looked understandably rushed and nervous as she took the stand. She identified herself as an Associate Professor at Harvard Medical School and pointed out various features of John's CATscan X-rays projected onto a large screen in the courtroom. The pictures were more complicated than ordinary X-rays, revealing "sulci"—folds or creases—on the surface of the brain far wider than normal at John's age, from which she concluded that John's physical brain mass had shrunk.

This "degeneration of brain substance," she agreed on cross-examination, had no "provable" direct relationship to a person's conduct. Adelman, of course, made light of the abnormalities: was Dr. LeMay aware, he asked, that 15% of all people showed atrophied brains in CATscans?

Not at John's age, she corrected him: Only 1% of all people in their twenties exhibited such atrophy.

Next day, Dr. Daniel Weinberger amplified. Director of the clinical neuro-psychiatry unit of the National Institute of Health, he was an authority on the statistical relation between brain scan results and schizophrenia. X-ray results like John's, he informed the jury, showed up in only 2% of the general population, but in over 30% of schizophrenics.

Dr. Weinberger stepped down and for the third time Vince rested the defense case.

The prosecution's first witnesses were the detective who had booked John after his arrest and the surgeon who had been called that afternoon to examine him. Both men testified that John seemed "normal" immediately after the shooting, calm and emotionless—though what could be less normal at such a time I could not imagine.

That night we talked to Scott on his 32nd birthday, he avoiding Vanderbilt news to keep from depressing us, we avoiding specifics of the trial for the same reason.

The following day the prosecution pressed their point with a series of witnesses. All testified that John had behaved normally following his arrest, therefore he must have been sane. I couldn't see what it proved—the government's own publications stated that "severely mentally ill persons may look and act normal much of the time"—but the prosecution was apparently appealing once more to a stereotype of "raving" madness.

Next they produced CATscan experts who contradicted our experts. One doctor offered as an analogy to widened sulci in a young man's brain, the fact that some young men are bald, though baldness is more common in older men. It was hardly a subject for humor, I felt, but this drew a laugh from the media people and I saw several jotting it down.

Friday Dr. Park Dietz took the stand, the first of the prosecution's expert-witnesses called to refute our psychiatrists' findings. This bright young doctor, just a year older than Scott, headed the government team of three psychiatrists and a psychologist, and spoke with the authority of all four. Like Dr. Bear, Dr. Dietz was on the faculty of the Harvard Medical School; unlike Bear he'd made a specialty of forensic psychiatry, testifying in over 100 criminal cases.

His expertise on the witness stand was immediately apparent as he made his points in a forceful, unforgettable manner. John was a spoiled-rotten rich kid, growing up in "luxurious surroundings" which made him scorn the idea of working like other people. He basked in "notions of achieving success and fame in a way that would not require a great deal of effort." Concluding that some sensational crime would be the easiest method of gaining attention, he then "thought about a variety of potential crimes and how much publicity each would attract." From John's voluminous reading on the subject of famous murders, he realized "that no crime carries as much publicity as the assassination of the President of the United States."

Dietz conceded that John had a number of mental disorders, but called them "minor" and "common" and insisted that he had never been out of touch with reality—the hallmark of psychosis. John had planned his crime in a deliberate manner and carried it out as a matter of conscious choice. Dietz had a very great deal to say about the gun—the way it was put together and the manner of loading it—all of which seemed to me irrelevant since no one contested what John had done.

Dr. Dietz' testimony stretched over several days. The idea of feigning insanity, he maintained, had been suggested to John by a book found in his Washington hotel room, in which a clever criminal escapes punishment in this manner. John never had an "obsession" for Jodie Foster, Dietz told the jury, but only the kind of infatuation anyone might feel for a beautiful young starlet. He had exaggerated his feelings for her expressly in order to appear crazy, helped unwittingly by the defense psychiatrists' questioning. Because these doctors had had no experience with accused criminals, they had unknowingly suggested to John the symptoms that he later faked to fool them.

As for his supposedly "becoming" Travis Bickle, *that* idea had come to John from newspaper stories *after* the shooting. "The notion of being influenced by *Taxi Driver* seems to be one that Mr. Hinckley picked up from the media following the assassination attempt."

As Dietz' testimony continued through most of the trial's sixth week, I found it harder each day to sit still. I scribbled note after note to Vince, listing what I felt were inaccuracies and half-truths for him to expose in his cross-examination. I

271

pointed out that John had begun dressing like Travis Bickle way back in 1976, and that all of our doctors had been hyper-aware of the possibility that John might try to deceive them.

Vince used none of my well-thought-out arguments. "Give the jury credit for catching these things," he'd say.

But the jury, understandably enough, seemed numbed by the length and complexity of the trial. A number of times Judge Parker instructed them to stand and stretch as he, too, noticed eyes closing, heads nodding.

The difference in the approach of the opposing sides kept striking me. Our lawyers and doctors seemed to have concentrated on John himself, while the government relied on other people's often fleeting observations. Before Dietz and the other government doctors had their first interview with John (on the day after the shooting), they talked with a dozen FBI and Secret Service agents in "preliminary interviews" which it seemed to me had to affect the way they assessed John. Furthermore, they had all interviewed him together—almost assuring, I felt, that they would reach the same conclusion. Indeed, the 628-page report which they had eventually submitted had been prepared jointly, while our four authorities had evaluated John independently of each other.

Our doctors had attached special significance to the stories and poems John had written during seven years of isolation. Dietz dismissed them as "fiction" and therefore unimportant, saying, "A writer's writings are not that useful in determining the mental state of the writer."

Instead, Dietz had traveled around the country, visiting motels where John had stayed and interviewing any stranger, it seemed to me, who might have had a casual conversation with him. "What does the position of the dresser in a hotel room have to do with John's mental condition?" I scrawled angrily to Vince.

"Take it easy, Jack," he wrote back.

But I *couldn't* take it easy. All my resolves about turning it over, letting go and letting God, went to the four winds as I sat through a succession of "eye-witnesses" to John's supposed normalcy. I reminded Vince of the two Evergreen real estate men who had sworn to the Grand Jury a year ago that John had inquired about buying property through them. And the bartender who'd testified to John's nightly pool playing.

Investigation had obviously disproved both these stories, as nothing was heard of them at the trial—and yet the government continued to rely on this kind of hearsay. One witness, summoned to corroborate Dietz' portrayal of John as a functioning member of society, described the job John had held in a Lakewood music store. Again, they'd flown the individual here from Colorado, but hadn't bothered to check with the store where they'd never laid eyes on John. Vince refused to share my agitation. Any sensational, highly publicized case, he assured me, attracted mistaken "witnesses" who were otherwise responsible citizens, and probably believed their own stories.

On and on the damning portrait went. John was a lazy young man who'd manipulated his elderly grandparents for money. ("All of $20 at Christmas one year!" I dashed off another indignant memo to Vince.) A competent young man capable of founding and managing a successful mail order business. ("Total income, $59, total outgo, $57.")

For me, the most bewildering part was the role of psychiatry in the insanity defense. Jo Ann and I kept asking God to let some crumb of good, however small, come out of all this. Maybe, we'd believed, it would be an increased awareness in our country of the prevalence of mental illness so that other families like ours would handle it better. But here the nation was being treated to the spectacle of experts in the field voicing contradictory opinions, depending on which side had hired them, all the while claiming to be making unbiased scientific diagnoses.

Dr. Bear, with the prestige of Harvard Medical School behind him, had concluded, "It is a psychiatric fact that Mr. Hinckley was psychotic." Dr. Dietz, equally of Harvard Medical School, testified, "Mr. Hinckley has not been psychotic at any time." Dr. Prelinger had discovered that John "hates himself." Dr. Dietz described him as "in love with himself." Dr. Carpenter found John suffering from "delusions," a technical term meaning, he explained, holding onto a belief even when it is proved to be false. Dr. Dietz said John had never been delusional. So it went, on every point, confusing not only the jury, I was sure, but everyone else. Far from making the field of mental health understandable to people like me, was our tragedy only going to add to the public's bewilderment?

65

JO ANN:

Young Dr. Sally Johnson followed Dr. Dietz on the stand. We hadn't seen her since John was transferred from Butner in August when she was well along in her pregnancy. She had the infant with her, I'd been told, since she was nursing. I longed to see her baby, but though she and we had worked together to improve conditions for John at Butner, I was painfully conscious now that we were on opposite sides of this court battle.

Inevitably, perhaps, her diagnosis was the same as the other four government doctors. John "functioned too well," she testified, to be mentally ill. Shooting the President had been a rational decision. "John wanted to prove to himself that he could do something of this magnitude and, in a way, get back at all those people who let him down." Those people, she elaborated, included Jack and me for shutting him out of the house. Either motive—proving something to yourself or getting even with your parents by shooting an innocent third party—seemed to me as insane as anything the defense had put forward. Dr. Johnson, however, concluded that John had only a relatively mild "personality disorder."

One effect of this disorder, she testified, rendered John incapable of "feeling remorse or sorrow or sympathy for the victims of the crime." Once again, this seemed to me like a sign of terrible sickness.

Again and again, I felt, her own observations defied her conclusions. She described John during the five months in Butner as listless, withdrawn and lacking interests, but maintained he was "not depressed," even at the time of his

274

attempted suicide. His extremely high reading for depression on the MMPI psychological test she administered (the same test given by Dr. Prelinger, with the same result) came about, she explained, because he was probably feeling panicky during the testing. She said John expressed his thoughts better on paper than face-to-face, but she attached no importance to his writing.

To allow Dr. Johnson to take her baby home as quickly as possible, Judge Parker kept the court in session all day Saturday. I felt so sorry for one young juror who'd planned to get married this week; as the trial stretched on she'd asked to be excused from jury duty, and at last had postponed her wedding. How many lives had been twisted out of shape?

The eighth week of the trial saw Dr. Johnson on the witness stand again, all day Monday, all day Tuesday. Tuesday afternoon, as she was repeating the government's assertion that John had not fired at the President out of love for Jodie Foster, I was startled to hear John's own voice.

"You're wrong!"

It was only a muttered remark, but unmistakably from John, and of course, an unpardonable breach of courtroom discipline. Once more he was summoned to the bench for a lecture. With all his erratic comings and goings, this was the first time he'd made an audible remark and the judge was incensed.

Not until the next day's papers came out did we read that in addition John had silently mouthed some vulgar words at Dr. Johnson. We only knew that a recess was called after which Dr. Johnson did not return to the stand.

Instead, Mr. Adelman stood up. "Your Honor, the prosecution rests."

I couldn't have heard him right.

Judge Parker looked startled too. "What did you say?" he asked.

"We feel we are in the position to rest our case," Mr. Adelman, repeated, "and we will do so."

Jack and I looked at each other in astonishment. They were finished—after only two expert-witnesses? Our side had called four. In the row in front of us government officials were turning to each other, nodding, smiling, the reactions of the people who had won—and knew it.

We had a hurried consultation at the back of the courtroom with Vince and Greg, who'd been caught as much off guard as we. Suddenly, except for the closing arguments, it was all over. Both sides would now make their summations, Vince told us, first the prosecution, then the defense, then the prosecution again, who by custom had the final word. After that the judge would "instruct" the jury—which meant, he explained, defining the law concerning the insanity plea and the jury's responsibility under the law. And then the jury would start deliberating, probably Thursday or Friday. The verdict could come at once or, if there was any disagreement, it could take several days.

Before the closing arguments, Jack wanted to call Dr. Carpenter back to the stand. "Sally Johnson's had something like two years as a practicing psychiatrist, Dietz only four or five. Carpenter alone has had three times that much. The jury ought to know this."

"Jack," Vince sighed, "I'm aware of that."

At last, reluctantly, Vince requested this rare "surrebuttal." Even more reluctantly, it seemed to me, Judge Parker granted it. And, as Vince had predicted, it was a wasted effort. Dr. Carpenter took the stand Wednesday morning, but was allowed to testify on only a couple of specific points.

At lunch in the courthouse cafeteria Jack scribbled seven full pages of points for Vince to cover in his summation. That had always been Jack's way: If one effort failed, try again, work harder, throw more of yourself into it. I added a few items to the list, though it was clear to me that Vince was handling the case his own way, and our well-meant contributions would not influence him.

At mid-afternoon Wednesday the court session adjourned, the closing statements to be made Thursday, the judge's instructions to the jury on Friday morning. The marshals had a bundle of John's laundry ready for me, but I was sure there must be more shirts in the basement. "What does it matter?" Jack asked impatiently. John had two clean shirts now and I could wash the two in the bundle tonight. "Tomorrow and Friday—and then he appears for the verdict. He can't possibly use more than three shirts."

Jack refused to wait while I collected any more. Something as small as this could get me upset these days. I knew, logically, that Jack was right about the shirts, but what did logic have to do with it! After this week I might never again do a washing for my son.

66

JACK:

I spent the rest of Wednesday afternoon and evening drafting and redrafting a statement to hand the press after the Guilty verdict. Fred Graham of CBS-TV had warned me as we left the courtroom that afternoon that we'd be mobbed when the verdict came in: "There's no way they're going to let you get away without some kind of comment." Better write it out than try to talk at a moment like that.

Adelman's summation was as devastating as I feared. Striding up and down in front of the jury box with the actual gun John had used gripped in his hand, he made sure the fact of the shooting was foremost in the jury's minds. Here was the very weapon with which "this man shot down in the street James Brady, a bullet in his brain!"

Adelman reviewed John's cold-blooded stalking of two presidents, his methodical training at a target range, his cool demeanor following the shooting. He jumped on Dr. Carpenter's phrase *bit players:* "That's an outrageous thought—that the President of the United States and a man shot in the brain are bit players."

John was simply "a bored young man with a lot of money" whose psychological problems were no more serious than "a sniffle and a head cold."

Vince made our closing statement that afternoon. He summarized the psychiatric testimony in his usual lucid way—though I waited in vain to hear my seven pages of points. Vince asked the jurors to "put aside some of the horror" all of us felt at what had happened and consider instead John's deluded inner world. The strangest delusion, he said, was that a relationship existed between himself and a person he had watched on a movie screen.

As Vince continued I saw Judge Parker looking down at John. "It was delusional thinking, pure and simple," Vince insisted. "It's pathetic."

Then I saw it, too. John was crying. Covering his face with both hands he bent forward, shoulders shaking.

Parker hastily recessed the court, sending the jury out of the room. Lawyers on both sides conferred at his bench. In the second row of the spectators' section, Jo Ann and I sat motionless. We had not seen our son cry since he was a child of seven.

Because it was nearly five o'clock, Parker decided to adjourn, postponing the rest of Vince's summation and Adelman's final rebuttal till next morning, Friday. For the first time since the trial began he ordered the jury sequestered. This was an added ordeal for them, meaning a night at a secret location somewhere with guards posted outside their doors, transportation to and from the courthouse in vans with taped windows. One unscrupulous newsman, it appeared, had been following the jurors home, trying to learn their names and addresses—risking a mistrial after so much human and material expenditure.

Washington police offered to help Jo Ann and me escape from the courthouse in a patrol car after the verdict came in—possibly as early as Friday night. The best news was that Scott was flying in from Denver to be with us.

Friday morning Vince completed his summation asking the jury to concentrate on John's "internal frenzy . . . when his father told him, *you can't come home.*" There in the Denver airport, Vince concluded, John's "last anchor to reality was severed" and the fantasy world took over.

Adelman had the last word. His tall lean figure a dramatic contrast to Vince's bulldog build, he returned to the theme that money, not madness, was John's motive. "The anchor that broke away was a green anchor—dollars, cents, money." Facing the jury, his voice rose to a shout, "How dare he say to you to forget the evidence, to forget the Devastator bullets? How dare he say to Jim Brady to forget the Devastator bullets? I defy him, I defy anybody, to go up to the families of these victims and say 'Forget those Devastator bullets!' "

Jo Ann and I ate a silent lunch, returned to hear Judge Parker's specific and complex instructions to the jury. For nearly two hours he outlined the law as it applied in this case, directing the jury to "consider the evidence with respect to insanity separately as to each offense."

By four p.m. he had completed his instructions. The jury filed out of the court to begin their deliberations. The eight-week trial was over.

Over.

It had been more traumatic than I ever imagined, and we had lost, but it was finished. In another week we would be private citizens again.

It was good to have Scott at the apartment that evening. We talked about anything and everything, mostly Vanderbilt business, to keep our minds off what was going on in the jury room. By nine o'clock we knew there would be no verdict Friday night. The judge had ordered the jury sequestered until one was reached, which meant they'd be loaded into vans again and returned to wherever they were staying.

Saturday morning it was the same, trying to pretend we were not waiting every moment for the phone to ring. We hoped the judge would give us 45 minutes—the fastest we could possibly make it downtown—after the jury reached its decision, before he convened the court. This meant, though, that we could not leave the apartment even for an instant, though there was almost nothing in the cupboards for lunch.

I read my press release to Jo Ann and Scott, penciling in their suggestions:

> Obviously, we are terribly disappointed by the Guilty verdict for our troubled son, John, whom we love very much. We are thankful, however, that we live in a country where the right to a fair and orderly trial still exists.
>
> Our family knew from the start that we had two strikes against us because of the extraordinary media coverage of the shooting, and unfavorable past precedents in insanity cases. We and our attorneys did everything in our power to defend John against overwhelming odds. We believe now more than ever that he is seriously ill and was not responsible for his acts on March 30, 1981.
>
> An experienced, highly-respected team of four doctors

who specialize in the diagnosis of mental illness all testified that John has suffered from serious mental diseases for several years. We are convinced that these longstanding illnesses were the cause of tragic events of last year, and that John would never have committed such acts unless he were terribly ill.

We are greatly relieved that the trial is finally over. We freely accept the verdict as God's will for our lives. Our prayers and deep concern continue for the victims and their families.

When there was no word from the jury by afternoon, we decided to go down to the courthouse anyhow; the decision would have to come any minute. We were stunned at the crowd of cameramen, reporters and onlookers, waiting outside the courthouse in the broiling late-June sun. More than ever I felt relieved that a police car would spirit us away from a garage beneath the building when the moment came.

The three of us were admitted briefly to the basement to visit John. He looked awful, eyes sunken in their sockets, eyelids puffy. Even his brother's presence could not jar him from his moody silence, and I berated myself again for ever subjecting him to the long torture of a trial.

Afterward Jo Ann, Scott and I were taken upstairs to a small waiting room, un-airconditioned since it was the weekend, to sit through the sweltering afternoon. Once again the jury adjourned for the day without a verdict. For the third night they were escorted back to their motel—supposedly an unknown location but now reported by the indefatigable press to be a Ramada Inn outside of town.

What could be taking them so long? Maybe, Jo Ann suggested hopefully, they didn't go along with all the charges. The fewer Guilty convictions, of course, the easier it would be for Parker to be lenient.

Sunday the three of us went to early Communion at the National Cathedral, were back by the phone by the time the jury was due to resume deliberations. It was Father's Day. If the jurors had not finished by mid-afternoon, Judge Parker had granted permission for them to meet their families for dinner at a restaurant to be selected by the marshals, with the understanding that they were not to discuss the case. "All conversations will be monitored by Deputy U.S. Marshals," his ruling stated. "In the event that such a discussion occurs, the marshal shall terminate the conversation immediately and the family member shall be escorted from the gathering." A strained kind of Father's Day celebration, I thought. But surely before then they'd reach a verdict.

I wrote out a fourth and then fifth draft of the press statement. Jo Ann suggested I prepare a statement for a Not Guilty verdict, too, "just in case." I didn't, of course: Jo Ann, as usual, was closing her eyes to reality.

Mid-afternoon came: There would be no verdict Sunday. Scott had set up a business meeting in New York for Monday, assuming as we did that it would all be over by then. He wanted to cancel it and stay with us, but I insisted he go ahead.

Monday was a repeat of Saturday and Sunday: sitting in the apartment all day, dressed for the dash downtown, praying, reading the Bible, waiting for the phone call that never came. Late in the afternoon the jury published its future schedule, as it had each day: they would recess at 7:30 p.m., resume deliberations Tuesday morning at nine.

Jo Ann and I were sitting down to supper at 6:30 when Vince telephoned. *The verdict was in.*

The judge would wait for us 45 minutes.

I left some rubber on the road getting to the Metro garage. We entered the courthouse exactly three quarters of an hour after Vince's call. Cameramen and press people were arriving on the run from every direction, apparently caught as much by surprise as we had been. The courtroom was packed to the walls, the prosecuting and defense attorneys at their tables, Judge Parker already seated in his high-backed chair. The windowless room was in semishadow, the lights dimmed and funereal. John was led in, looking small as always ringed by marshals.

Then the jury filed in from the rear. Stony-faced and solemn, above all they looked exhausted. Once more, as I had not stopped doing for eight weeks, I attempted to read some sign of sympathy and compassion on any of the twelve faces, but their expressions were as impassive as before.

"This Honorable Court is again in session," intoned a clerk of court. The court clerk rose and repeated the formula that chilled my very soul, no matter how often I heard her say it:

"United States of America versus John W. Hinckley, Jr."

"Counsel," Judge Parker addressed the lawyers for both

sides, "the Court was advised that the jury had reached a verdict at 6:20 o'clock, p.m., this date."

"Will the foreman of the jury please rise," the clerk instructed.

A stolid-looking powerfully built young man in the front row of the jury box stood up, a large brown envelope in his hand. Twenty-two years old—youngest of the jurors and five years younger than John—he was the one of the twelve on whose face I had never detected a flicker of emotion.

The clerk turned to John. "Will the defendant please rise and face the jury."

"Mr. Foreman," the judge said, "would you please unseal the verdict?"

The tall young black opened the envelope and handed a sheaf of papers to the clerk who in turn passed it to Judge Parker.

"The Court will read the verdict as tendered by the jury foreman," Parker said. He bent his head over the document, turning rapidly from page to page without speaking. When he began to read aloud at last, the words came so fast I couldn't understand them:

"As to Count 1, Not Guilty by Reason of Insanity." That's what it *sounded* like. But it couldn't have been.

"As to Count 2, Not Guilty by Reason of Insanity.

"As to Count 3, Not Guilty by Reason of Insanity."

Was I the only one who was hearing this? There was no stir in the crowded courtroom.

Count 4, Not Guilty . . . Count 5, Not Guilty . . . Every one of the thirteen charges: "Not Guilty by Reason of Insanity."

I was dreaming, of course; my head felt light, detached. A cry from Jo Ann brought me back to the wooden bench where we sat. I grabbed her in my arms and she sobbed on my shoulder. The clerk was polling the jury. "Ladies and gentlemen of the jury, if your verdict is the same as that announced by the Court, please respond 'yes' when I call your name. Juror Number One?"

"Yes."

"Juror Number Two?"

"Yes."

All twelve of them, one by one. Yes, yes, yes!

Even the judge had apparently not taken in what had

happened. "The date of further proceedings in this matter, including sentencing," Parker announced, "will be set for July the twelfth at ten a.m." He shook his head as though in annoyance at himself. "The defendant shall be remanded immediately," he substituted.

The strange, stunned silence which had settled over the courtroom with the reading of the verdict erupted in a babble of voices. Reporters were rushing for the door. John was swaying slightly on his feet, head back, eyes closed. At a gesture from the judge, the marshals led him swiftly from the courtroom. The babble became an uproar and an outraged Parker spoke sharply to someone at the back of the room: "Mr. Marshal, if you can't keep order there, get someone else who can!"

He then addressed the jury. He sounded almost relieved, I thought, to have some routine procedure to fall back on, after an outcome that had clearly rocked him as much as the rest of us. He thanked the jurors for their weeks of patient attention, and reminded them that their names and addresses would now be furnished to the media. "You may, therefore, reasonably anticipate that you will be contacted by the press for an interview. Whether or not you grant an interview is, of course, solely within your discretion."

The clerk instructed the rest of us to remain seated as the judge rose. For the last time we watched that proud, gray-haired man make his labored way, step-by-step, from the bench. The entire session had lasted eight minutes.

With Parker's departure I expected pandemonium to break out, but that curious hush had returned to the room—a stillness of people trying, as I was, to believe what they had just heard. Adelman, Chapman and Tucker, faces taut with shock and disappointment, were shaking hands with our attorneys.

As the courtroom silently emptied behind us, Jo Ann and I pushed through the swinging gate and stepped for the first time to the defense table. I realized that I was crying. I wrapped Vince in a bear hug, hoping he wouldn't see the tears. His own face had the drawn look of a marathoner who's crossed the finish line with the last ounce of his strength. Greg, too, whose hard work and unshakable conviction had done so much. Lon and Judy who never failed. I embraced them one by one, too filled with gratitude to speak.

Afterward, marshals admitted us to the basement for a

five-minute visit with a stunned and white-faced John. For the last time in a prison cell the three of us held hands and bowed our heads. "Lord, we asked You for a miracle," I said. "I gave up believing in it long ago, but You granted it just the same. Thank You, dear Lord. Thank You."

67

JO ANN:

The garage door onto the street opened and the police car roared up the ramp from the courthouse basement. It was growing dark outside where the TV trucks and camera crews waited, but a number of cars took off after us. "We'll shake them," the driver said. Looking out the back window a few minutes later, though, I saw a motorcycle staying close behind.

It was Evergreen all over, a police car spiriting us away from reporters on that first trip to Washington fifteen endless months ago. *It was over.* Almost as great as my joy that John at last would be getting help was relief that it was all behind us. The police car drove right into the parking garage at the Metro terminus where we'd left our own car two hours before. It was hard to believe we would not be catching the subway as usual next morning.

The motorcycle was waiting at the exit and trailed us to The Irene. The police car, behind us, cut him off in the driveway, letting us get safely inside the building. "They know where we live now," I worried. But by tomorrow, Jack assured me, no one would care. This would be yesterday's news story.

We could hardly wait to get up to the apartment and switch on the TV. For the first time we were actually looking forward to the evening news program: At last the nation would know that John had not been responsible for his tragic conduct. The first news reports must already have gone out because the unlisted telephone number was ringing as we walked in. Steve and Diane calling from Dallas to rejoice with us. Jack's sister Avilla phoned, and Evergreen neighbors, and new friends from Washington. My folks from Oklahoma City, Charles and Betty Blair, Scott from New York, many others.

Between calls we watched the news. It was on every channel. We flipped from one to another: We couldn't hear it enough. How many times would we listen to the words Not Guilty before we believed them?

But over every channel something else was communicated too . . . Not only disbelief, which we certainly shared, but . . . disapproval. Even anger. I felt my throat constrict. One commentator after another spoke as though he were reporting some monstrous miscarriage of justice.

The apartment intercom buzzed. It was Glenn and Betty Knecht, the pastor and his wife from the Wallace Presbyterian Church, phoning from downstairs. "Tell them we're not reporters, will you?" Glenn said. Sound trucks, TV vans and camera crews were all over the place outside The Irene, he told us, and the doorman was admitting no one. Jack got on the intercom, and the Knechts came up.

With Glenn and Betty we gave thanks to God for the American judicial system, for the jury that Jack and I, with our limited vision had been so pessimistic about, for working out His will in our weakness.

The ten p.m. news programs were even more negative than the earlier ones. People interviewed on the street expressed shock and indignation. Several lawmakers were calling for abolition of the insanity defense. It was as though, instead of a full and fair trial, the country had witnessed an evasion of the law.

But the country *didn't* witness the trial, Glenn pointed out, only what was reported of it. At the trial itself, for those who sat through the 42 long days in the courtroom, the facts emerged unmistakably. How could people who didn't have all those facts feel anything but distress?

"It's the *phrasing*," Jack believed. "*Not Guilty* . . . that's what makes people so angry." Everyone knew John was guilty of shooting those four people; they'd seen him do it with their own eyes. If the legal term were anything else—*Not*

Responsible by Reason of Insanity, as Vince had mentioned once—we wondered if there would be such an outcry.

Tuesday, Attorney General William French Smith and Treasury Secretary Donald Regan both appeared on morning talk shows to express "outrage" at the verdict. We sat stunned and dismayed in front of the TV set as other public figures followed throughout the day, most prefacing their comments by admitting they had not followed the testimony "all that closely," then going on to condemn the decision.

Mrs. Rucker, The Irene's manager, phoned to say the press was camped out in the street and watching all exits to the building. Again it was like that first week in Evergreen. Jack and I moved about our apartment-prison in a kind of daze. Just when we believed it was all over, a fresh storm had broken over our heads. Even two of the jurors backed away from their position, saying *they* had believed John was sane but had been worn down by the persistence of the majority, and dislike of being sequestered.

I surely sympathized with that—I knew what it felt like to have a policeman standing outside your door. Nor did I suppose there'd ever been a difficult trial where at least a couple of jury members hadn't had second thoughts afterward. But these two ladies were interviewed, photographed, quoted and requoted, day after day, while those who remained convinced about their decision were hardly heard of.

About noon Tuesday Vince issued a statement on behalf of Williams & Connolly.

The jury's verdict in *U.S. versus John W. Hinckley, Jr.* is a just verdict. All of the psychiatric experts who testified in this case agree that John W. Hinckley, Jr. was suffering from a mental disease on March 30, 1981. The government's burden of proving Mr. Hinckley's legal responsibility beyond a reasonable doubt on March 30 was a heavy burden. In our view, the jury properly concluded that the government failed to carry that burden.

A repeated theme in the post-trial coverage was that John was about to be "turned loose" on society. Some predicted immediately, others on August 9 when Judge Parker had scheduled a hearing to determine whether John was "entitled to release from custody." This was a routine review mandated fifty days after any defendant was hospitalized by court order, but the announcement of it gave rise to fear-filled speculation.

To try to set such fears at rest, Vince's statement continued,

> After consulting with John W. Hinckley, Jr. this morning, we wish to report that Mr. Hinckley will not be making any effort to seek release after the expiration of the statutory 50-day period as the law permits. This law firm will not represent John W. Hinckley, Jr. in any efforts to secure release until we are satisfied that he meets the criteria for release and that Mr. Hinckley is no longer a danger to himself or society.

Vince's statement reminded us of our own press release, written when Jack was so sure the verdict would be Guilty. We sat down at the rented dining room table and hastily amended it:

> Obviously we are very pleased by the verdict of Not Guilty by Reason of Insanity for our troubled son, John, whom we love very much.

It seemed impossible that we should still have to argue a case that had been won, but because no other voice had been raised in praise of the verdict we added,

> We wish to express our deep respect and gratitude to the members of the jury who worked long and diligently at their difficult task. After listening intently to many weeks of testimony, the jury responsibly considered the evidence. It then arrived at the correct decision of Not Guilty by Reason of Insanity. We firmly believe that John's longstanding mental disorders were the cause of the tragic events of last year, and that he could not have committed such acts unless he were terribly ill.
>
> John will now be confined at St. Elizabeth's Mental Hospital in Washington, D.C., where he can receive proper therapy. We will make no effort whatsoever to have him released until he has recovered to the point that he is judged to be harmless and responsible.
>
> We are greatly relieved that the trial is finally over. Our prayers and sincere concern continue for the victims and

their families. Our heartfelt thanks go out to the many kind people who helped, encouraged and supported us. Most of all we praise our loving God who sustained us throughout this entire ordeal and answered our prayers so faithfully.

Mr. & Mrs. John Hinckley, Sr. and Family

Jack phoned the statement to Williams & Connolly to release on our behalf, but it got little play in the papers or on TV. The country was in an uproar, with no emotional room, apparently, for hearing the other side. ABC's "Nightline" announced the result of a poll they had conducted among 505 people, showing that 76% believed "justice had not been done." More ominous still, this same three out of four believed the insanity defense itself should be done away with.

Was this to be the most lasting result of the effort we and our lawyers had made—the denial of this fundamental principle of civilized law to other troubled people in the future? I thought of our hope that this public ordeal might make people more aware of mental illness. Was it, instead, to have the very opposite effect?

68

JACK:

Around noon on Wednesday we were allowed a ten minute phone conversation with John, our first at St. Elizabeth's. For the first time in fifteen months, he told us wonderingly, he could close a door and be alone. For the the first time in a year and a quarter, he'd gone to sleep without someone watching him. His room was very small, he said, just a bed, a chair and a metal locker, but the feature he kept coming back to was the marvel of a door he could close.

We told him we'd be permitted to see him the following morning. The hospital, however, did not encourage visits during the initial adjustment period. So the day after that, Friday, we'd head for home.

Newspaper and television coverage was continuing to attack the acquittal, the laws on which it was based, even Jo Ann and me, intimating that we had "bought" the verdict. If that were possible, the government, of course, would win every time. They'd spent far more to prosecute John than we had to defend him: One of their psychiatrists alone had cost more than all three of ours. But every program, every article, spoke of "John Hinckley's wealthy parents," as though that somehow explained the unexpected outcome.

Vince was jumped on too, largely for an offhand remark he'd made in the emotional moments following the verdict. I understood so well how it must have happened. Exhausted from weeks of working almost around the clock, Vince had found himself suddenly and startlingly the hero-of-the-hour. Courthouse personnel crowded around to shake his hand, while reporters called out to know how the victory felt. A committed team worker, shunning the limelight, Vince hastened to shrug off any personal credit: "Another day, another dollar."

The words were no sooner out of his mouth than he must have heard how they sounded. He *meant*, I was sure, that he'd done nothing exceptional. It was all in a day's work—he'd done nothing for this case that he didn't do for every case. But the idiom he chanced to use made it *sound* like: I'll defend any case—so long as I'm paid for it. Ridiculous to anyone who knew Vince, but the media pounced on it and rode him mercilessly.

The visit to St. Elizabeth's helped put it all in perspective.

In the bright summer sun it looked different from that rainy autumn day when we'd first driven through, trying to decide whether confinement in this outdated federal facility was even worth the struggle. I'd forgotten how immense the place was. The wide lawns and towering trees were more beautiful than I remembered, the buildings older and dingier.

The John Howard Pavilion was more isolated than I recalled, too, off by itself in the southeastern corner of the huge complex, next to that forlorn hospital graveyard with its rows of small white headstones. In the lobby Jo Ann and I registered with an officer behind a glassed and barred window and read the *Rules for Visitors* posted on the wall:

> Do not give anything to patient, or receive anything.
> At the end of visiting, remain seated.
> All pocketbooks (bags) must be locked up.
> All coats (outer) must be left in lobby.
> When patient's name is called, please form orderly line by the electric gates.

Beyond the security screen a turnstile and two electronically-controlled locked doors led into the hospital proper. In an office on the ground floor Director Joseph Henneberry and a staff doctor outlined the program John would follow. We were amazed at the detailed course of therapy they'd worked out. "So quickly!" I marveled.

"Oh," Mr. Henneberry said in a lilting Irish brogue, "we've been expecting John for some time now."

"*You* knew he belonged in a hospital," I acknowledged. "But how could you be so sure the jury would know?"

"Juries go by the evidence," the director said.

John was in a ward on the fourth floor. Taking out an enormous ring of keys, the doctor took us up in the key-operated elevator and led us through a labyrinth of locked doors. We would not be allowed into the ward itself, but would meet John in a chapel on that floor.

The chapel was three times as big as the one at Fort Meade, brightened by murals and banners, but the setup was unnervingly similar. A ward orderly brought John in, remaining in the chapel, as the marshals had, throughout the visit. John is a *patient*, I had to keep reminding myself, not a prisoner.

John had had his second night of privacy and his eyes were less sunken. As welcome as the door he could close to his bedroom, he said, were the doors to the toilet stalls. That was what he had hated most, the last fifteen months, eyes that never looked away, no matter where. . . .

In addition to the communal shower room, he told us, his

290

ward had a small cafeteria and a dayroom with a Ping-Pong table, magazines, games and a TV set. Within this closed society, Mr. Henneberry had explained, patients were encouraged to relate to each other as well as to their therapists—to make friendships, to cooperate on housekeeping chores. Indeed, Mr. Henneberry had told us, this would be a major element in John's therapy: for the first time in eight or nine years to form actual relationships with the people around him.

My mind went back to John's first year at Texas Tech and the succession of roommates in the freshman dorm with whom he failed to get along. Now he would have to relate, with no choice in the matter, to two dozen men with whom he would spend every waking hour of every day. From the patient population I'd seen, most would be black, and all, of course, would have mental and emotional problems as serious as, or worse than, his own.

Saying goodbye to John in that fourth-floor chapel, with the orderly looking on, was hard. Not for just days this time, but weeks or months, depending on how swiftly he adapted to hospital routine. Downstairs Mr. Henneberry was waiting for us. Hospital guards had phoned: Somehow word that we were visiting St. Elizabeth's had gotten out; a camera crew was at the entrance. Guards escorted us to a locked rear gate, but a TV cameraman was stationed here, too, machine grinding. Outside The Irene still other cameramen were waiting. Up in the apartment we threw ourselves into packing, as though our lives hinged on the speed with which we could close suitcases. We were going home!

We'd emptied cupboards and the refrigerator over the last few days, so at supper time we went out. Once more we were followed. We sprinted into a restaurant, came out 45 minutes later into a blaze of floodlights and whirring cameras. Media people pursued us right up to the doors of the apartment garage and were waiting there at eight the next morning when, car loaded to the roof, we left The Irene for the last time.

A TV van and a motorcycle trailed us right onto the Interstate. At the city limit I glanced in the rear-view mirror. They were continuing on around the Beltway, returning to town. As our roads diverged the camera crew leaned from the window, good-naturedly waving us away from Washington.

291

69

JO ANN:

Evergreen.

Our quiet street, our own home at last. Here we would stay, out of sight of the world, until the world lost interest.

But . . . when would it happen?

The outcry over the verdict, instead of dying down, grew louder, fueled in part by John himself. There was a telephone on his ward, which he was supposed to use only to call us or his lawyers. A week after his arrival he instead telephoned the *Washington Post*, and read aloud parts of the speech he had prepared to deliver in the courtroom after the Guilty verdict he, like everyone else, expected. Jack came home from his first day back at the office, with the Denver papers under his arm, a heartsick expression on his face.

"On March 30, 1981," the papers quoted John, "I was asking to be loved. I was asking my family to take me back and I was asking Jodie Foster to hold me in her heart. My assassination attempt was an act of love."

Of course a fresh outpouring of angry comment followed. The hospital from then on dialed John's calls for him, but by longstanding policy did not censor patients' mail. So John wrote. . . .

It got to be like the first week after the shooting—dreading to pick up a paper or switch on the TV for fear of some frightful news break. A four-page letter from John to the *New York Times* was picked up by papers across the country. Most of the letter John had copied from his "conviction speech."

The shooting outside the Washington Hilton hotel was the greatest love offering in the history of the world. I sacrificed myself and committed the ultimate crime in hopes of winning the heart of a girl. It was an unprecedented demonstration of love. But does the American public appreciate what I've done? Does Jodie Foster appreciate what I've done? . . .

At one time Miss Foster was a star and I was the insignificant fan. Now everything is changed. I am Napoleon and she is Josephine. I am Romeo and she is Juliet. I am John Hinckley, Jr. and she is Jodie Foster. I may be in prison and she may be making a movie in Paris or Hollywood but Jodie and I will always be together, in life and in death.

Waves of pity and grief swept over me as I read: The months already spent behind bars, the years that still stretched ahead, had apparently not touched his pathetic delusion in any way. Jodie . . . Jodie . . . always Jodie. How an already angry public would react, I could only wait in dread to learn.

Inevitably, more backlash: The jury was mercilessly attacked—though every fresh communication from John seemed to me to prove their judgment right. Lawmakers across the country stepped up the clamor for changes in state and federal laws governing the insanity defense. That continued to distress Jack and me more than anything—the harm to countless others, ill and defenseless, that could be the long-term result of John's case.

The most often-expressed fear was that John was going to "walk out" of St. Elizabeth's sometime soon. He appeared to believe this himself. If doctors at St. Elizabeth's found him sane at the end of the fifty-day evaluation period now in progress, he told the *Washington Post,* "I'm going to walk out the door whether the public likes it or not."

Slowly it dawned on us that he was pinning hope on that mandatory hearing scheduled by Judge Parker for August 9. He wanted to appear in court in person, to demonstrate how normal he was. Vince and his team, of course, convinced that John was anything but, refused to represent him. As August approached, John grew more insistent. Once more we went through the pattern of John's firing the lawyers, Jack trying to patch things up between them. If no one would "speak out" for him, John warned, he would enlist a public defender to plead his case before Judge Parker.

Six days before the August 9 hearing, Vince and Greg at last talked John into waiving his court appearance. Jack and I breathed our first sigh of relief since the uproar over the verdict exploded six weeks before. Without John in the courtroom, with no challenge raised to his commitment—surely the routine legal procedure would rate no headlines.

The hospital felt that it was too early still for us to come east to visit John. So we confined ourselves to those labored one-sided phone conversations, making no mention of the hearing at which St. Elizabeth's evaluation would be submitted and which John would not attend.

But as it turned out, John did appear on Monday, August 9, in courtroom eleven of the U.S. Court House. Though John, Vince and Greg had all signed a statement waiving his right to contest the commitment, Judge Parker insisted that John be present—perhaps, Vince thought, to prevent any future contention that some legal finepoint had been overlooked. I felt so sorry for Judge Parker, as I did for everyone connected with this case. He'd done a meticulous and conscientious job and, like the jury, received nothing but abuse since the trial's end.

Judge Parker called John before his bench to make sure he was "knowingly and voluntarily" giving up the opportunity to challenge the hospital's evaluation. Then, stating that there was "clear and convincing evidence" that John suffered from "a severe, chronic mental disorder" and that he remained "a danger to himself as well as a danger to others," the judge committed him to St. Elizabeth's for an indefinite period.

Jack and I were miserable, having to follow the proceedings, like the rest of the country, on TV. There was a photograph of John leaving the courthouse, accompanied again by federal marshals. Beneath his open-necked white shirt I saw the collar of a bullet-proof vest.

At the close of the hearing, Judge Parker released the hospital's eighteen-page psychiatric evaluation to the public. Next day's papers carried excerpts. John had a Schizotypal Personality, St. Elizabeth's doctors had concluded, and recurrent Major Depression, but these diagnoses "did not adequately convey his autistic-like thinking and serious defects in reality testing. . . ."

It is our opinion that he is currently in need of inpatient hospitalization and that without such treatment Mr. Hinckley will in the reasonable future be likely to engage in self or other-directed destructive acts. . . .

Jodie Foster's presence dominates. . . . He could spend every minute of every interview speaking about her. . . . The sequence of murder and suicide is described as 'perfect love.' He removes them from a corrupt society and they can be happy in the hereafter.''

It was tragically clear even from these excerpts, that John's thinking remained as confused as ever. How could it be otherwise, I asked myself. Kept in a solitary cell for a year and a quarter, subjected to pressures that even a well person might crumble under . . . how could we have expected John to be better now than on that March day more than sixteen months ago?

70

JACK:

I moved through the days of that summer in a kind of weary numbness. Vanderbilt's problems occupied most of my time. Its stock price, along with other oil companies', was continuing to fall, almost to the vanishing point.

It wasn't money problems that defeated me though; I'd been through failures and hard times before. It was John's ongoing crisis. We were in a race that would never be over. Just as we reached the finish line, the ribbon was moved. The track stretched on forever, we could never stop running. My diary was full of puzzlement and despair:

Why won't this nightmare come to an end . . . ? Mental illness is the worst disease that can strike a human being and his family . . . I have no desire to go on. We've lost our son, our good name, our money, some friends. . . .

In August John mailed a poem to the *National Enquirer* which they printed, bringing on the greatest storm of protest yet. Titled "Bloody Love," it was a sick fantasy I could not imagine any paper publishing. Whenever I saw the *Enquirer* on a newsstand with John's picture on the front page, I'd turn the whole stack upside down.

In Washington, Attorney General William French Smith told a Senate committee that the insanity defense should be abolished. The committee even went so far as to summon a Hollywood actor to testify about a fictitious TV episode in which a criminal tries to escape justice by faking insanity; the actor, in consequence, opposed the insanity defense. I had half a mind to go before the committee myself—tell them about the scores of tragically sick real people behind the bars of the John Howard Pavilion.

Much as I grieved over the backlash to John's case, however, wild horses couldn't have dragged me back into the public eye again. At last the media seemed to be getting the message: Jo Ann and I weren't talking to them, and fewer requests to do so came each week.

In September we were permitted a face-to-face visit with John. We found him as bafflingly difficult to deal with as ever. Just then he was agitated because the hospital had stepped in to censor his outgoing mail. He got back on the theme of finding a public defender, this time to sue the hospital and Mr. Henneberry for depriving him of his right to free speech.

John's newfound passion for publicity was incomprehensible to Jo Ann and me. Doctors tried to explain that for many years the media—movies, television, books—had been reality to him, replacements for the flesh and blood contacts he failed to form. Seeing his name in print after the shooting, no matter how negatively, gave him the sense of real existence that his illness had robbed him of.

We tried to understand. But our own longing for privacy made it hard. Those visits in the fourth-floor chapel, always with an orderly present, were tense for us all. We were beginning to see the wisdom in the hospital's policy of asking families not to hover too close, at least at the outset.

Even over the telephone after we returned home, it was hard to leave my own emotions out of it. Some group wanted to do a docudrama on the shooting, John told us proudly one time. Or: *Penthouse* was interviewing him by mail. Or: He was writing the American Civil Liberties Union for help against hospital restrictions. I'd try to keep my angry reactions under control. *Hands off*, I would tell myself. *You can't do it. God can.* It was my constant refrain—half promise, half prayer—for so much in my life these days. . . .

In October Jo Ann and I attended a convention of the Independent Petroleum Association in Dallas. It was the first time we had ventured away from Evergreen in two and a half years using our own name. As we checked into the convention hotel I saw them—stacked on the lobby newsstand, a pile of tabloid papers with three-inch headlines: **HINCKLEY THREATENS FOSTER.**

It was some new outburst from John—I didn't bother to read the details. I walked over to the unattended stand, picked up the entire pile of papers and stuffed them—unpaid for—into my briefcase. When we got to our room I dumped the lot in the wastebasket.

Wherever we went that fall, some negative report about John seemed to precede us, almost as though to tell us, you can't escape this. What jarred me into speaking out at last, though, was an article in the October *Reader's Digest*. Titled "The Insanity Defense Is Insane" and written by no less an authority-figure than a United States senator, it capsulized the emotional reaction to John's acquittal.

"We've got to answer this," I told Jo Ann, "for the people who'll follow John."

"Won't it start reporters after us again?" she worried.

I didn't think so. Not if our message, too, appeared in the *Digest*, with its large circulation. "We can speak our piece there and not have to do it again."

But the *Digest*, when I wrote them, wasn't interested. Their letter was tactful, but the message was clear: I hardly had the stature to contradict a senator. I certainly agreed—I only wished someone of standing *would* speak out for the facts. But I wrote the article anyway, pleading with the American people not to jettison a fundamental standard. Perhaps, I wrote, an occasional "normal" criminal might attempt to misuse the defense, but it would be next-to-impossible to succeed. Quite unlike this theoretical trickster, in fact, patients in the John Howard Pavilion were always trying to convince people they were *more* rational than they actually were.

Jo Ann and I knew, I wrote, how exasperating John's current behavior was:

> Since the shooting, John has developed an unattractive obsession for notoriety. He likes to see himself in the news. He has elements of grandiosity and narcissism in his personality that are offensive to us all. But this, too, is consistent with his illness.

To us it seemed obvious, I said, that no one in his right mind would write the kind of things John had been mailing off from St. Elizabeth's. The underlying reason for the public rage, we concluded, was that all of us understood so little about mental illness. Though it filled more than a third of all hospital beds, though one in five adults suffered from some form of it, still to most people mental illness remained a forbidden subject.

"That *is* the problem, isn't it?" Jo Ann said as we finished the final rewrite of the article and mailed it off unsolicited. "People don't find out anything about mental problems until there's a tragedy close to home."

We knew this not only from experience but from our mail. Much of it nowadays was from parents, husbands, wives, children of the mentally ill, often echoing our own heartbreak. "We didn't understand what made her do those things." "If only we'd known in time."

The third week in November there was a phone call from New York: The *Digest* liked our article, thought it deserved to be read. It would appear in their March issue.

Five days later there was more good news. Scott and Christa Meyer, the young woman Scott had been dating since August, telephoned to tell us they were engaged. Of course Jo Ann was immediately full of plans for a party at our house to introduce Christa to our friends. "Show her off, you mean," I teased. Christa is a stunning brunette as well as a bright young lawyer. It was so good and so right that at 33 Scott should have something wonderful like this happen to him.

298

In December Jo Ann and I flew east to be with John again at Christmas time. He was silent and depressed during our visits in the fourth-floor chapel, perhaps because of the season, perhaps because of interior battles no one else could guess at. He had been at St. Elizabeth's six months and the hoped-for relationships with others on his ward had not formed. Doctors reported to Mr. Henneberry that Jodie Foster still occupied every waking thought. Until there was progress there, other changes would be few and slow.

Once again Jo Ann and I were the only people in our motel, a Howard Johnson's on the south side of town. Once more we wished one another Happy Anniversary far from home. The year 1983 would be a better one, we promised each other. John was getting help—no one ever told us improvement would come swiftly. James Brady's courageous struggle was producing results. Scott was engaged to someone who should make him as happy as Steve had made Diane. We'd find a buyer for the company. Next year we'd make more time for each other. We had a son who was sick and we'd stand by him with our whole hearts—but we could do that privately. When our article appeared in the March *Reader's Digest*, I figured our public life would be behind us.

71

JO ANN:

We chose Sunday, February 13, two weeks before their wedding, for Christa and Scott's party. I ordered thirty invitations printed in silver lettering and mailed them to the Evergreen friends and neighbors who'd been so supportive through the bad times. At last we could ask them to rejoice with us.

Every one of the enclosure cards came back marked "accept"—sixty people coming! I started cooking and freezing things weeks ahead. For days I worked on an elaborate liver pâté mold: The final step was slicing and inserting dozens of olives. Because it fell the weekend of Valentine's Day, we didn't tell John about the party. The date was one of those bleak anniversaries when our anxiety rose in spite of ourselves. Two years before, on Valentine's Day, he'd stood in the entryway to John Lennon's apartment in New York, meaning to shoot himself in an imagined death pact with Jodie Foster. The following year, by coincidence, it was the day Vince and Greg traveled to New Haven to talk with her. This year . . . surely by now the fantasy was at rest.

A few days before the party I got out both extra leaves for the dining room table and wiped off the dust. It had been a long time since we had a party around this table; it had become just a surface for sorting and answering mail.

I took the crystal prisms from the chandelier and washed them one by one. The last time I'd done this was for Christmas dinner, 1980, over two years before. I tried not to think of John's face at that meal, staring down at his untouched plate.

The flower arrangements I'd ordered arrived Saturday just as I finished vacuuming. Even the weather cooperated. Sunday dawned cold and cloudless, no snow in the forecast. Guests were invited for six o'clock. I cooked Jack a large breakfast. "You'll just have to snack at lunchtime," I told him, "I need the kitchen all day." I was putting away the breakfast dishes when the telephone rang. "Will you answer it?" I called to Jack. I hoped it wasn't someone calling to say they couldn't make it!

From the living room I heard Jack say, "Oh no. . . ."

I snatched up the kitchen phone. It was Mr. Henneberry at St. Elizabeth's. John had been found unconscious and barely breathing, on the floor of his bedroom. He was on a respirator at Greater Southeast Community Hospital where doctors could not yet say if he would live. Apparently he had hoarded medication, then overdosed sometime during the night.

Time stopped, then spun crazily backward. It was Butner and Ft. Meade all over again! Jack was frantically dialing the

300

hospital number that Mr. Henneberry had given us. A doctor on the Critical Care Unit told us John was alive, but would give no prognosis. Then Greg Craig called. He had gotten to the hospital as fast as the heavy snow in Washington would permit; he would remain there as long as necessary. Greg was convinced the hospital staff was doing everything possible. John's color had been blue when they brought him in, Greg said, his blood pressure 60/0. Greg called several times that morning: talking to him, knowing he was a few feet from John, made it seem somehow less hopelessly far away.

Between calls I dashed to the bedroom and packed our suitcases; I'd learned to do it in fifteen minutes. Once more there was that awful conflict—to head for the airport meant to leave the telephone, to be out of touch for hours on end. Federal marshals had been summoned and stationed outside the Critical Care Unit. Jack made a dozen or more calls, speaking to the head marshal, to nurses, to Mr. Henneberry again. John had apparently fallen from his bed in the night in a violent attack of nausea: his stomach had emptied itself of the pills while he was unconscious, which was the reason he was alive at this moment.

Greg said the media were besieging the hospital. He warned us that a press conference just held in the lobby, which the networks would release this afternoon, would sound extremely pessimistic. Neither the hospital staff nor St. Elizabeth's doctors had answered reporters' questions as to the medication involved, but it was believed to be an anti-depressant. Once again John must have planned this over many weeks, pretending day after day to swallow the single dose he was given.

Once again, we phoned Diane and Steve, and Mother and Daddy, to prepare them for the upcoming news report. We'd been on the phone with Scott and with Christa, of course, as soon as we ourselves knew.

And all the while a kind of anger was building in me. Partly at this savage sickness that could destroy a human being's will to live. Partly at the timing, on this day that was to have belonged to Scott. For two years every thought, prayer, effort of the whole family had been John, John, John. Scott had not only had to shoulder the day-to-day running of Vanderbilt, working nights, skipping vacations, but deal month after month with directors and media people who called the office every time his brother's name made headlines. At last he and Christa were to be the center of attention—and once more John's need pushed other priorities aside.

But what, at this moment, could we do for John's need? "What will it accomplish," Greg asked, "for you to come to Washington and sit in a hospital corridor?" St. Elizabeth's doctors didn't want us to come at all: "John needs to confront reality independent of his family."

We wavered back and forth, one minute checking Sunday flights to Washington, the next looking at the Monday morning schedules. If we were going to let our party guests come ahead we had to decide soon—food had to come out of the freezer.

When the hospital reported John's condition "stabilized" by mid-afternoon, we decided to hold the reception as planned. These were the neighbors who'd stood with us through so much already—why not this crisis, too. I was running water over the mold to loosen the liver pâté when a groan from Jack brought me running to the dining room window.

"Reporters," he said.

Up on the street men were focusing cameras from a car window. How, I wondered disgustedly, could photographs of anguished parents interest anyone at all?

Then I thought of the guests arriving in two hours. We didn't believe these men could possibly know about the party we'd planned, but. . . . radio and television were just now carrying the earlier press conference when the outlook was so negative. I could see tomorrow's headlines: *Hinckley's parents hold party as son lies dying.*

Jack telephoned Bill Sells, who went out and asked the men to leave. They refused. Jack called the sheriff, who sent a patrol car around with the same request. The deputy, too, was turned down. "It's a public street," he told us. "We can't prevent them from parking up there."

And *we* couldn't allow our lives to be regulated by what might be said about us in the media. With Sue Sells' help a telephone chain was organized to contact every couple on our invitation list, telling them we were going ahead with the reception in Scott and Christa's honor, but that the decision to come or not would have to be theirs. Reporters were watching the house, they could be photographed, approached for an interview.

When I got back to the kitchen at last, the liver pâté mold was a shapeless mass at the bottom of the sink.

I got into my dress, set out the food, lit the candles with my mind 2,000 miles away. It began to get dark early that February Sunday. Fifteen minutes before the first guests arrived the reporters drove away. Every single person came. I hoped Christa and Scott felt loved—I know I did. It turned out, in God's mysterious timing, to be the best possible way to live through that nightmare day, with these close friends literally holding us tight—joy and grief all mixed together, and no need to hide either one.

Later that night there was another optimistic report from the hospital. By Monday afternoon the toxic level in John's system was only 20% of what it had been when he arrived, and he was off the critical list.

Of all the things parents can be asked to do for a child, to do nothing is the hardest of all. We'd agreed to wait till Wednesday to go to Washington. Tuesday night John's psychiatrist from St. Elizabeth's phoned us. John was going through a major adjustment period at the present time, she said, one which required "space"—that was her word—between himself and us. She asked us, for the time being, to stay away.

She would never reveal John's confidences. The only explanation we ever had for what he had done was the bizarre one John himself wrote to a reporter: Jodie and he had been in contact by "brain waves." His death was to have been a Valentine's Day gift in which she was to join, to be united with him forever.

All through March we waited for the revived flurry of media attention to die down. Perhaps Jack was right that our *Digest* article would at one time have satisfied anyone interested in hearing from us. But the March issue had happened to reach the stands on Valentine's Day, along with headlines about the suicide attempt. Again, we were inundated with requests for interviews. We'd broken our silence with the *Digest* piece, the argument ran, so we could have no objection to appearing on such and such a talk show.

Perhaps the way to end the pressure *would* be to go on TV—say our say once and for all. I was terrified at the idea of deliberately standing up in front of the cameras we'd been running from for two years, but as long as it was only once. . . . We chose Barbara Walters, flew to New York on April 10 to meet her.

And after all, I didn't have to stand up in front of cameras. Jack and I sat on a sofa in a small hotel room, the only corner of it not crammed with cables and consoles and perspiring technicians. We were there six hours under the blinding brightness and stifling heat of floodlights, while the makeup lady darted in to freshen our powder and I gained a new respect for the stamina of television people. Miss Walters was so understanding, so genuinely concerned for the problems of the mentally ill, that I wondered why I had been afraid.

"But the best is—it's over," I said to Jack as we headed the next day from New York down to Washington and our first visit with John since the suicide attempt in February. "No more having to talk about it."

In fact, it was just beginning.

72

JACK:

In some mysterious way I have never grasped, that suicide attempt on Valentine's Day weekend was a turning point for John. He had plunged into the deepest valley of depression and delusion, from which the only way out was up.

We sensed a difference the minute the orderly with his jingling ring of keys brought John into the chapel. John was carrying his new guitar—an early present from us for his 28th birthday coming up next month. A therapist had bought it with the check we sent, and John wanted to thank us.

That was the first thing—he thanked us! At Christmas four months earlier there had been little acknowledgment of the gifts we'd brought from the family. That was one of the things that made this illness so excruciating for all involved—lack of awareness of other people's feelings, just as the schizophrenic failed to acknowledge his own.

John thanked us now, though, and then—wonder of wonders—perched on one of the chapel's wooden chairs, he strummed a chord for us. Then another, then several more in a pleasant, rippling pattern.

It was the first time we had seen our son play the guitar.

The moment passed and shyly he laid the instrument down. "Do you like the tone?" he asked. To me, it had sounded like a choir of angels—but that wasn't all. As he asked the question, instead of keeping his gaze fixed on the floor, he looked me straight in the eye.

It was the conversation we had with Mr. Henneberry later, however, in his office on the ground floor, that encouraged us most of all. John had dreaded the return to St. Elizabeth's after his overdose Mr. Henneberry told us in his rolling brogue. Apparently John was remembering the windowless cell where he had been placed following his hanging attempt at Fort Meade—the fold-down shelf with its thin mattress, the short-sleeved shirts in the November chill. These measures had been for his own protection, but John had interpreted them as punishment and expected the same treatment now.

At St. Elizabeth's, however, there'd been no shift in quarters, no change in his regimen. In mental hospitals attempted suicide was tragically familiar. The staff saw such events as manifestations of disease and responded no more reproachfully than they would to a fever. Patients, too, welcomed him back to his fourth-floor ward. "When he realized he was being given back his old room," Mr. Henneberry said, "he stood in the doorway and cried." John . . . crying? John who never showed emotion? Something had gotten through to him at that moment, Mr. Henneberry believed, some message deeper than words. People *cared* about him. Not the John of his fantasies—not a rock star or a twisted national hero. Just John—who swept the floors and stood in the cafeteria line with the others. John in his isolation and despair. That was the John they knew here. That was the John they liked and valued.

We returned to Evergreen, and to the mail which always built up while we were gone, most of it nowadays from relatives of the mentally ill. Many wrote to pass on advice—apparently believing that we had some say-so in John's treatment, which, of course, we did not. Since the word schizophrenia was first mentioned at the trial we'd received hundreds of diets—recalling his years on fast-foods and soft drinks, we could well believe that poor nutrition had aggravated John's condition. Others urged exorcism of "the demons which are known to cause this disease." We didn't discount this advice either—no reader of the Bible could—though some of the methods struck us as bizarre. One man wrote from India offering to mail us a special stone which would draw the evil spirits into itself. Hypoglycemia, allergies, vitamin and yeast deficiencies—each had its theorists.

A far greater number, however, wrote not offering help, but seeking it. "What can we do? Where can we find answers?" We didn't have any answers. We didn't know who did. Although mental illness was the nation's number one health problem, research into its causes and cures was pitifully inadequate. For every cancer patient, I discovered, $170 a year was spent on cancer research, $150 a year on heart research for every heart patient. For each mental patient the research figure was seven dollars.

Even where help was available, the people who needed it often could not find it. Silence and secrecy seemed to surround the whole world of the mentally disturbed. Someone ought to be doing something to combat the stigma—to raise public awareness of the prevalence of this problem. To publicize warning signals and expand research.

For two-and-a-half years it never occurred to me that the "someone" was me. Money was what was needed for education and research, lots and lots of money. But a successful fund raiser had to be a public figure, make himself as conspicuous as possible—the very opposite of Jo Ann's and my desires.

In late April, the Barbara Walters interviews were aired, and far from ending the matter, requests for appearances increased a hundredfold. We turned down all but one kind. Everywhere around the country, we learned, there were self-support groups—parents, children, spouses of patients in state hospitals or other institutions gathering together for mutual encouragement and guidance. These weren't public events, but get-togethers of people who knew as no others could, the fears and frustrations and heartbreak of living with this type of illness. In August, 1983, we accepted an invitation to speak to the annual meeting of the National Alliance for the Mentally Ill in St. Louis; from there we were invited to branches around the country.

We discovered similar problems wherever we went. These people felt painfully cut off from their communities—not so much by anything other people did, as by their own secretiveness. Understandably they felt protective of the son, wife or parent who was suffering the illness. They needed society's help and support for their own burden, but had been unwilling or unable to reveal their problem to the world at large.

Jo Ann and I might have felt that way too—only we never knew there was mental illness in our family until John's had exploded in a supremely public act. We'd had no chance to hide the problem even if we'd wanted to.

Would we have wanted to? I thought of the evasion and pretense that surrounded my mother's cancer in the 1940s. Today cancer is acknowledged for the objective battleground it is—with resultant progress. "Mental illness must come out of the closet too," we began to tell these groups, "and we who are closest to it are the ones who will have to start."

"Who's going to listen to us?" some objected. Again, the answer stared us in the face: everyone who'd been appalled and outraged by what happened on March 30, 1981. Left to myself, I wanted to put the shadow of that event as far behind me as possible. But of course I wasn't left to myself. I'd offered my life to God—and that's an offer, I was learning, that He doesn't refuse. His marching orders came in a letter from a stranger—one of a dozen similar ones that week. Except that this one was a little less gentle than the rest.

"Your name is mud, anyway, Hinckley," it pointed out. "What have you got to lose by going to bat for the mentally ill?" Our name . . . the name I'd been so proud of. That name was mud. . . .

And therefore, at last, God could use me. He doesn't use us all shiny, spotless and strong; He uses us soiled and broken.

Jo Ann and I started an organization devoted entirely to research and public education about mental illness. Where before we'd locked our doors against reporters, we now began asking for interviews—newspapers, radio, TV—anyway we could get out the message.

From November 1983 to May 1984 we rented our home in Evergreen and took an apartment outside Washington while we set up the headquarters for the American Mental Health Fund. That winter the sale of Vanderbilt finally went through on terms advantageous to everyone, letting Jo Ann and me pay off the debts we'd incurred and give full time to this work. The new owners of the company retained Scott as president.

There were many reasons for choosing Washington as the Fund's base; the personal one of course was that we could be near John. By the fall of '83, two and a half years after the shooting, doctors felt that John was ready for a new phase of treatment: family therapy. This breakthrough technique looks at people's behavior not in isolation but as part of an interacting group. The problem at St. Elizabeth's was finding families to work with. A tragic percentage of the patients there either had no family ties at all, or had been dropped by their relatives at the time they were committed.

We were apparently one of very few families available for this type of therapy, and the staff was as ready for our participation now as they'd been insistent during John's adjustment period that we allow him "breathing room."

We drove across the city to St. Elizabeth's every Tuesday afternoon, passed through the metal detector, stood on the little platform for the manual check, then were admitted through the locked doors to an office on the ground floor adjoining Mr. Henneberry's. Like the rest of the building, it was strictly utilitarian with a metal desk and chairs. Dr. Patterson is a tall, distinguished-looking black man with a compassionate manner and an ever-present smile—both of which we needed as the six-month experiment unfolded. John was brought down from the fourth floor by a ward attendant with the usual huge ring of keys, the only times we met outside the fourth-floor chapel. Dr. Patterson would pull his chair out from behind his desk to form a circle with ours, seeing to it that we switched positions from week to week—Jo Ann next to me one time, John between us another—the relationships always changing. That came to me to symbolize the dynamics of those meetings: the breaking up of ancient patterns, most often unconscious, in the ways we related to each other.

Many times I dreaded the approach of Tuesday. Our once-silent, docile John was finding his voice, and most of what he had to say was directed at me. Years ago, when Jo Ann and I used to tell each other wonderingly that our youngest child was too good to be true, we were closer to the fact than we knew. Of course he had angers, resentments, jealousies like anyone else: like water too long backed up by a dam, they came spilling out all at once leaving a more confident, more socially adept person behind.

John told us one day he'd been elected president of his ward that month, with responsibility for moderating the weekly meeting between doctors, ward personnel and patients. A staff psychologist who attended one session kept speaking up without waiting to be recognized. "I had to tell him," John said, "that he was out of order."

Jo Ann and I made progress, too. I had to learn that not all problems will yield to logic, that there can be many "right" solutions. Jo Ann had to discover that peace is not always the answer; she had to allow John and me to confront each other without stepping in to short-circuit healthy arguments.

We returned to Evergreen in the summer of 1984, hoping someday to resume these sessions. Our home on Brookline Road is on the market now, as we look for a place near the Fund's headquarters, near our son. The move will be hard on Jo Ann especially, leaving friends and the community that has been so supportive. "But I don't think I'll crawl into a shell," she told me the other day. I don't think she will either. Jo Ann's got something better than a shell. She has a solid place to stand, no matter what changes around her. She used to want me to provide that place—used to call me her "rock." She knows now that home, husband, friends are only tokens of the real thing. Ask Jo Ann what her favorite Bible verse is and she'll tell you, *God only is my rock. . . .*

As for John—what the future holds we can't even guess. The tormenting obsession with Jodie Foster, at least, is over, that sick fantasy finally laid to rest. John is making new friends now, learning to care for others—to know what *real* love is all about. He has the legal right to petition the courts every six months for a hearing to determine whether he still constitutes a danger to himself or others. The decision, after hearing psychiatric testimony, rests with the judge.

I don't have to know how everything will turn out. I know the job God has given Jo Ann and me to do, the rest of our lives. That's all I need to know. For a man who always had to be in control, that's a step in the right direction.

Epilogue

JACK:

As time passes, I've come to understand how expert opinion can legitmately differ in matters as complex as the human mind and mental illness. It would be surprising if it didn't: I saw experts disagree every day in the business world. One geologist is convinced there is oil in a certain spot, another is sure there isn't. One broker believes a stock is about to go up and buys, another feels the opposite and sells. Architects and engineers can be found defending the design and construction of a building, while others condemn them. Why then should we expect all psychiatric experts to agree in an insanity defense trial?

What I still do *not* understand is the logic of those who wish to abolish or cripple the insanity defense. NOBODY benefits when a severely mentally ill felon is sent to prison rather than to a maximum security mental hospital. If hospitalized, he can receive therapy and medication, and be confined until he is judged to be no longer a threat to society or himself. If sent to prison, however, he will likely receive no treatment for his sickness, yet be paroled in a few years in a worse condition than ever. Society and the ill felon are both losers.

The insanity defense is *not* a major problem in our system of justice. It is used in only about *two* percent of all criminal trials and is *rarely* successful. Yet it is the only means we have of making the important distinction between illness and evil. Allegations of widespread abuse cannot be substantiated by the facts. It is a popular and easy political target because most mentally ill persons don't vote. What *is* needed, in my view, are uniform sentencing laws so that *no one* judged to be not guilty by reason of insanity is set free, but is committed to a secure mental institution until found to be no longer dangerous.

By making it virtually impossible to achieve acquittal by reason of insanity, we simply will be punishing many innocent persons for becoming mentally ill. And that is revenge, not justice.

A NOTE TO PARENTS

Tragic statistics tell us that many readers of *Breaking Points* have been following our story with concern for one of their own loved ones.

To such families we extend not only our hearts but our hands. In 1983 we founded the American Mental Health Fund, a non-profit foundation financed in part by royalties from this book, in the hope that it can become a link between need and supply.

If you want more information about mental illness, fill out the coupon below and mail it to:

American Mental Health Fund
P.O. Box 17389
Washington, D.C. 20041

— — — — — — — — — —

Name _____
Street Address _____
City/state/zip code _____
Telephone # _____

SOME FACTS ABOUT MENTAL ILLNESS

A recent government study shows that approximately 29 million adults—one in five—suffer from some form of mental or emotional illness in any six month period. An additional 50 million suffer the anxiety of relating to a family member with the disability.

It is estimated that about two million Americans will experience schizophrenia sometime during their lives, most likely between the ages of 15 and 30. And schizophrenia is only one of several mental illnesses. Other common forms include phobias, depression, suicidal tendencies, acute anxiety and personality disorders. In fact, more hospital beds are occupied by the mentally ill than by patients suffering from cancer, lung and heart diseases *combined*.

Some $30 billion is spent each year on behalf of patients afflicted with mental illness. It's time to bring mental illness out of the closet, remove the stigma, expand research, find causes and cures.

WARNING SIGNALS

But first a warning about the warning! In itself, none of these conditions constitutes a symptom of mental illness. *Most* young people will have some of these experiences some of the time.

> *Sadness,* for example—it's part of the growing up process.

> *Withdrawal* is another of life's basic rhythms. Perfectly healthy individuals vary greatly in the amount of solitude they require. Every family will have more and less gregarious members.

And so on . . . over-anxious parents can inadvertently create an *unhealthy* emotional environment by scrutinizing their children for signs of abnormality. Characteristics noted below merit a closer look only when they are:

> Pronounced

> Persistent or recurrent over a period of time

> Progressive—tending to become more, rather than less, extreme

With this caution in mind, we offer the following thumbnail descriptions of behavior that *may* be a call for help.

*Confused or disordered thinking
  ● Loss of touch with reality
    —Delusions: persistence of erroneous convictions in the face of contrary evidence
    —Hallucinations
  ● Nonsequiturs, disconnected speech

*Obsessions: absorption with a subject or idea to the exclusion of others
*Compulsions
*Uncontrollable urges

*Inability to cope
  ● With minor problems
  ● With daily routine

*Difficulty in making/keeping friends
  ● poor social skills
  ● isolation, withdrawal from society
  ● ''loner'' life-style

*A *pattern* of failure across-the-board:
  ● at school
  ● at work
  ● in sports
  ● in personal relationships

*Prolonged or severe depression
  ● Suicide threats/attempts

*Immaturity
  ● Infantile behavior (such as bed-wetting)
  ● Over-dependence on the mother
    —excessive clinging (as a child)
    —continuing dependence (in teens and twenties)
  ● Failure to keep pace with peer-group

*A series of physical ailments which do not run a typical course, and/or fail to respond to treatment

| *Neglect of personal hygiene, disheveled and unsanitary surroundings | *or* | *Exaggerated concern for order and for cleanliness |

*Difficulty adjusting to new people and places

*Undue anxiety and worry
- Phobias
- Feelings of being persecuted

*Too much or too little sleep

*Excessive self-centeredness
- Indifference to other people's feelings, doings, ideas
- Lack of sympathy with another's pain or need

*Substantial rapid weight-gain or loss

*Muted, "flat" emotions   *or*   *Inappropriate emotions
- Absence of angry/ delighted/sorrowing reactions to stimuli

- Sharp, inexplicable mood swings

- Silliness at serious moments, unpredictable tears

*Negative self-image and outlook
- "Inferiority" complex
- Feelings of worthlessness

*Frequent random changes of plans
- Inability to stick with a job, a school program, a living arrangement
- Failure to keep appointments, abide by decisions

*Extreme aggressiveness   *or*   *Exaggerated docility
- Combativeness, hostility
- Violence, rage

- Lack of normal competitiveness and self-assertion
- Refusal to confront, avoidance of argument

*Risk-taking

*Lack of zest and enthusiasm
- listlessness, sadness, mood habitually "down"
- limited or missing sense of humor

DISPELLING THE MYTHS

Unfortunately, many myths exist about the nature of mental disorders. For example, did you know that:

- Mentally ill persons are frequently intelligent and lucid. They may look and act very normal much of the time.

- Although severe mental illness and mental retardation are both devastating afflictions, they are not the same and should not be confused with each other.

- Most mentally ill persons are not dangerous or violent. They need to be loved and respected as human beings, rather than feared.

- Many mental patients achieve full recovery, while most others are able to lead productive lives with proper medication and support.

- Mental illness is not self-inflicted. Its victims are no more to blame for their conditions than those who contract the flu.

The possible causes of severe mental illness are numerous—genetic, biologic, chemical imbalance, environmental conditions all contribute. However, it is *not* caused by normal parental behavior.

WHERE TO TURN FOR HELP

If you suspect a problem, what then? How do you get an accurate diagnosis, settle on the proper treatment, find the right doctor? As of now, there are no universally satisfactory answers. There's no central clearing-house where lay people can go for guidance. We suggest you start by contacting:

A. *Advocacy groups,* composed of relatives and supporters of the mentally ill, who have personal experience of local facilities and therapists. The two largest organizations are:

The National Alliance for the Mentally Ill
1901 N. Fort Myer Drive, Suite 500
Arlington, Virginia 22209   Telephone: (703) 524-760(

The National Mental Health Association
1021 Prince Street
Alexandria, VA 22314-2932   Telephone: (703) 684-7722

B. A *Community Mental Health Center* in your area.

C. The nearest *teaching hospital*.

Ask to see the head of the child psychiatry department. (Department heads are elected by their peers, the best professional vote-of-confidence.) Describe the symptoms that concern you, ask for referrals.

Also, talk to the nurses in the psychiatric wing (they observe doctors and programs day-in, day-out). Ask, "If it were *your* child exhibiting these symptoms, what would you do?"

D. *Other resources* include:
  1. Your family physician (for referral suggestions).
  2. State mental hospitals.
  3. Private psychiatric clinics, psychiatric units of private hospitals.
  4. The yellow pages of your phone book under mental health services, psychiatrists and psychologists.
  5. Family Service Association of America (branches in every large town).

In An Emergency

Dial 0 or 911.

Call the police or an ambulance service; get to a hospital.

Call your local mental health hotline or suicide prevention center. (Find out now whether these round-the-clock services are available in your area, keep the numbers handy.)

And while your child is in treatment, a few . . .

Do's and Don't's

Do	*Don't*
. . . cultivate openness and matter-of-factness about the disease.	. . . be ashamed. No one is immune to mental illness; no one is at fault. It strikes 1 in 5 adults, 1 in 3 families.

Do	*Don't*
. . . change doctors if you're not satisfied.	. . . feel obligated to continue an unproductive course of therapy on account of the money, time, or personal relationship already invested in it. Nor should you assume that you must stay with private doctors and hospitals until your assets are gone. Many government-sponsored hospitals and therapists are exceptionally good.
Shop around: since relationship plays such a large role in healing of mental illness, the right mesh of doctor and patient is critical.	
. . . let your child know that *you* know he's hurting. Mental illness is not self-inflicted. However much you disapprove of his conduct, you can be sure his self-opinion is even more condemning.	. . . whatever the provocation, don't throw the ill person out of the home. Telling him, "you're on your own" only increases pressures the sick has already found too much to handle. Do all you can do to *reduce stress*.
. . . respect the confidentiality of the patient-therapist relationship. If you need information to aid in home support efforts . . .	. . . If the home situation becomes too destructive (or dangerous) to others in the family, a substitute might be:
	● a concerned relative's or friend's home
● get the patient's permission before talking to the doctor.	● a halfway house

Do	*Don't*

- do so only in his presence.

● a public or private psychiatric facility.

- use another therapist for your own needs.

. . be aware of situations that may increase stress:

- a change in the status quo: a move, new school, birth or death in the family, death of an idol or hero.

- birthdays or other anniversaries (whether the milestone is positive or negative).

- special seasons: Christmas, Thanksgiving, other holidays which evoke the hope and closeness sought by the schizophrenic.

. . . deny the anger and frustration *you* may be feeling. Faced with the child's serious illness, family members are apt to play down their own distress as unimportant by comparison.

. . recognize the strain which mental illness places on the rest of the family

Do	*Don't*

- Join a support group to share both problems and ways of coping.

  You're a human being too; you'll be a better resource for your loved ones by respecting your own needs.

- Seek professional counseling for parents and siblings as well as the child in crisis.

- Remember that mental illness is *not* a ''do it yourself'' project.

AFTERWORD

Many readers have written us since the hardcover edition of *BREAKING POINTS* was published to tell us how closely they relate to our experiences with mental illness. They've had many of the same frustrations and problems that we went through. In some cases, the similarities were uncanny. We realize now more than ever that we are not alone—that families everywhere are trying to deal (as best they can) with this secret sickness called mental illness.

We're so pleased to know that our book is doing what we had hoped—helping other families with similar problems. We've also heard from parents who've said they recognize the symptoms in their own child more clearly, and who reluctantly admit that they can ignore those symptoms no longer. Most importantly, we've been encouraged and sustained by the love and support of caring persons everywhere.

We're pleased to report that we've made excellent progress in raising public awareness of mental illness, erasing the stigma attached to it and expanding research. Recently, the influential Advertising Council accepted the American Mental Health Fund's request for assistance in a nationwide educational campaign. For the first time in history, this means that millions of persons will now learn about mental illness through public service ads on TV and radio and in newspapers and magazines. The messages will be released through some 20,000 media outlets across the country. We must raise about $500,000 per year to keep this crucial campaign going. You can help by contributing to the American Mental Health Fund, P.O. Box 17389, Washington, D.C. 20041-2999. In return, about *$25 million* worth of advertising time and space will be *donated* as a public service by the media, Ad Council and others. We fervently hope that, before long, the facts and warning signals of mental illness will become as familiar to families everywhere as those of cancer or other physical disorders are now.

We've moved to the East to be nearer to our work and to our son, John. We see him every two weeks in family therapy sessions with Dr. Patterson. John has made considerable progress in the three and a half years he has been at St. Elizabeths Hospital on the outskirts of Washington, D.C. He has grown in his ability to form relationships with others, something we encourage and support. Although it has not been easy, it certainly has been worth the effort. We are very thankful that he has a dedicated treatment team and a God and friends who care about him.

—Jack and Jo Ann Hinckley